NOVA SCOTIA

A COLOUR GUIDEBOOK

Stephen Poole and Al Kingsbury
Photographs by Keith Vaughan

FORMAC PUBLISHING COMPANY LIMITED
HALIFAX

CONTENTS

Formac Publishing Company Limited achknowledges the support of the Cultural Affairs Section, Nova Scotia Department of Tourism and Culture. We acknowledge the financial support of the Government of Canada through the Book Publishing Industry Development Program (BPIDP) for our publishing activities.

For publisher information and photo credits, please see page 208.

CONTENTS

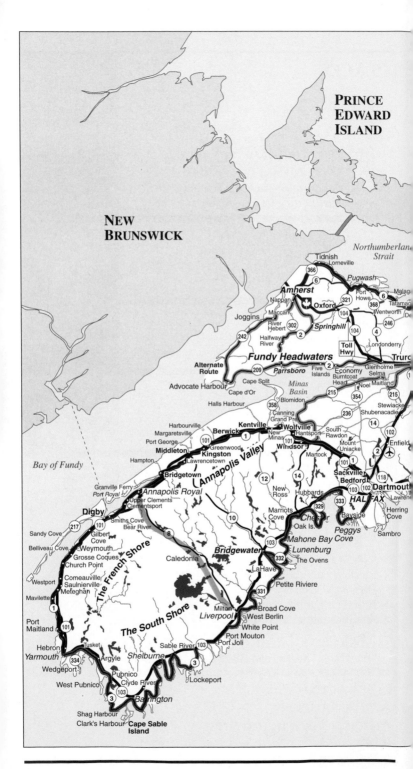

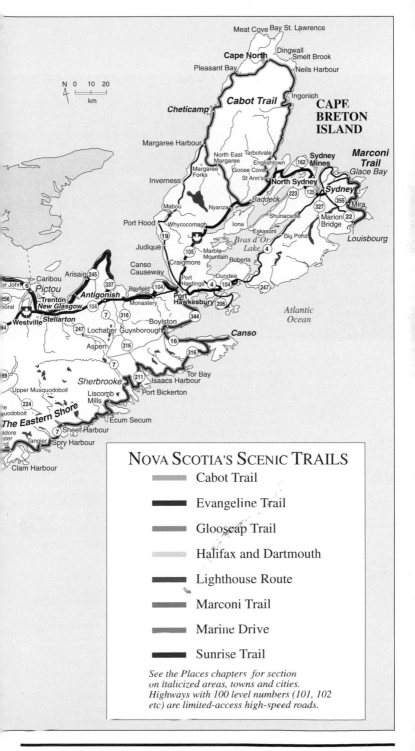

NOVA SCOTIA'S SCENIC TRAILS

Cabot Trail

Evangeline Trail

Glooscap Trail

Halifax and Dartmouth

Lighthouse Route

Marconi Trail

Marine Drive

Sunrise Trail

See the Places chapters for section on italicized areas, towns and cities. Highways with 100 level numbers (101, 102 etc) are limited-access high-speed roads.

GETTING AROUND

Though Nova Scotia is one of Canada's smallest provinces, its land mass is equal to the combined area of Massachusetts, New Hampshire, and Vermont, so a visitor can easily fill a day or two in one location, or spend weeks exploring the countryside, and enjoying its many attractions.

Shaped somewhat like a lobster found off its coast, Nova Scotia stretches 730 kilometres (450 mi) from Yarmouth to Sydney. You can drive this in under eight hours along new highways, but plan to take the older, more scenic routes, for a relaxing drive, with plenty of opportunities for sightseeing, and for visiting interesting local museums and shops. For those with limited time, however, the 100-series highway routes, which extend to all areas of the province, are an excellent way to reach particular destinations in a hurry. While they bypass the picturesque villages, many of them offer panoramic vistas not seen on older routes.

AMHERST ENTRY POINT

Most motoring visitors enter the province at Amherst, at the border point with New Brunswick. A trip through the Wentworth Valley via the Cobequid Pass toll highway is the usual route to the central point of Truro, or take the lower route, winding around Folly Lake. Then the visitor can follow the TransCanada Highway to scenic Cape Breton Island, or branch off to the metropolitan area of Halifax-Dartmouth. If time is limited, a couple of days can be enjoyed taking in the sights of the cities and their museums, but be sure to include a drive to spectacular Peggys Cove. Day trips can be planned to the South Shore or Annapolis Valley, but it's better to plan two or three days to make the loop along one route to Yarmouth, following the shoreline one way, and driving through the province's agricultural heartland on the other.

If Cape Breton is your destination, and time is limited, follow the TransCanada to Baddeck, where you can make a stop at the Alexander Graham Bell Museum, and then head for the Cabot Trail, taking the counter-clockwise route from Ingonish to Cheticamp. If additional days can be scheduled, be sure to include a visit to Fortress Louisbourg and the Glace Bay Miners' Museum, on the east side of the island.

THE FERRY ARRIVING IN YARMOUTH HARBOUR

YARMOUTH ENTRY POINT

Arriving at Yarmouth by ferry from Maine, the visitor is faced with the choice of following the Lighthouse Route (see p. 95) along the province's scenic South Shore, or taking the Evangeline Trail (see p. 114) along the French Shore and through the pastoral Annapolis Valley. If a decision is difficult, enjoy the best of both worlds by taking either route about half way, then cutting across country to enjoy contrasting scenery. Depending on your schedule, you might plan one to three days to enjoy charming villages and historic sites. Both routes have a wealth of history to exhibit, opportunities for recreation, and spectacular scenery to enjoy.

HALIFAX ENTRY POINT

Halifax-Dartmouth metro area (see p. 76) demands at least a day for sightseeing, but two or three days would be better, especially if you didn't include a side trip to Peggys Cove on the way from Yarmouth. You will want to visit Halifax Citadel National Historic Site, stroll along the waterfront, and do some shopping at Historic Properties. Evening entertainment might include taking in a play at Neptune Theatre, or experiencing Shakespeare By The Sea in Point Pleasant Park. A water excursion on Halifax Harbour and the Northwest Arm adds a different perspective to your visit.

Plan a day or two for the drive to Cape Breton, taking in some sights along the way, like historic Sherbrooke Village on Marine Drive (see p. 140). After crossing the Canso Causeway, follow Route 4 through St. Peters and along the Bras d'Or Lakes. Perhaps you will have time for tea at Rita's Tea Room in Big Pond.

A couple of days in Cape Breton will leave you wanting to stay longer, but from Sydney you can visit Fortress Louisbourg (see p. 161), and take in the Miners' Museum in Glace Bay (see p. 167) in one day. The Cabot Trail (see p. 145) can be done in a day, but you will want to make a list of things to do, and places to stop, on your next trip. An overnight stay at Baddeck, or perhaps Cheticamp or Margaree, will let you enjoy a taste of the Celtic or Acadian culture of those areas.

If you have to head for home, take another day to make your way to Amherst, enjoying the byways of the Sunrise Trail (see p. 134) or the Glooscap Trail (see p. 129).

Visitors beginning their Nova Scotia tour at Halifax have the opportunity to adjust their schedule by planning two to three days exploring the Annapolis Valley and South Shore. A day could be enjoyed along Marine Drive, and if more time is available, a visit to Cape Breton should be planned.

LAND AND SEA

BY ROBERT J. MCCALLA AND AL KINGSBURY

Spectacular scenery, a rich blend of history and culture in seaside villages and vibrant metropolitan areas, and a full calendar of festivals and events combine to offer the visitor to Nova Scotia an unforgettable experience.

Located on Canada's east coast, within a day's drive of the United States border, and just hours from major airports of Boston and New York, Nova Scotia prides itself as being "Canada's Ocean Playground," with its 7450 kilometres (4625 mi.) of beaches, coves, salt marshes, headlands and cliffs. Its geology, climate, plants and animals — as well as its peoples — all have been shaped by the sea.

Nova Scotia is part of the Appalachian Region, which extends from the southeastern United States to Newfoundland in the northeast. Along the Atlantic coast, rugged beauty, like the mass of granite rising from the sea at Peggys Cove, draws thousands of visitors each year. By contrast, Cape Breton Island and the northern mainland, along the Northumberland Strait, boast some fine beaches.

The world's highest tides have worn spectacular sea cliffs along the shores of the Bay of Fundy. Its effects are most dramatic at

PEGGYS COVE GRANITE RESISTS THE SEA

8

Advocate Bay, along Cape Chignecto (see p. 131) and in the area of Cape Split which divides the Minas Channel from the Minas Basin.

Millions of years ago, this area was swamp land, where deposits of organic matter later became coal, to be mined at Joggins, Springhill, and in communities in Pictou, Inverness and Cape Breton counties. You can tour underground coal seams at the Springhill Miners' Museum (see p. 131) and the Miners' Museum at Glace Bay (see p. 167). Embedded within the

ROCKHOUNDNG NEAR PARRSBORO

sedimentary rocks is an excellent record of past plant and animal life. The areas around Joggins and near Parrsboro are famous for fossils (see p. 131-132).

The province's land surface has been scarred by glaciers at least four times during the last 100,000 years, leaving behind deposits of drumlins (egg-shaped hills) and erratics (large boulders).

The melting of the glaciers caused a rise in sea level which flooded the shoreline, creating deep bays and sheltered harbours along the Atlantic coast. Halifax Harbour, one of the world's finest, owes its existence to both glacial erosion and a rise in sea level.

TIDES

Coastal Nova Scotia is influenced by the twice-daily ebb and flow of the tides. These effects are most spectacular in the upper reaches of the Bay of Fundy where the tidal range has exceeded 16 metres (53 ft.), and huge mud flats are exposed at low tide. Several companies take advantage of the upriver surge of tidal waters by providing white-water rafting excursions on the Shubenacadie River

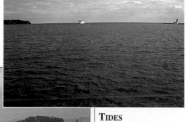

TIDES DRAMATICALLY CHANGE THE BAY OF FUNDY SEASCAPE

(see p. 130). This phenomenon, known as tidal bore, can be seen along many of the rivers that flow into Cobequid Bay and the Cumberland Basin.

SCENIC TRAILS

A series of tourist trails has been developed over various sections of the province to lead visitors to scenic points of interest and attractions.

The Lighthouse Route (see p. 95) guides the visitor through picturesque towns and villages along the South Shore and the Evangeline Trail (see p. 114) highlights the province's Acadian heritage and agricultural heartland. A drive along the Glooscap Trail (see p. 129) reveals the wonder of the world's highest tides and the Sunrise Trail (see p. 134) leads to beaches where waters are warmed by the gulf stream. The Eastern Shore is home to Marine Drive (see p. 140), where 18th-century life is recreated at Sherbrooke Village, and history comes alive at Louisbourg, where the Fleur-de-lis and Marconi trails (see p. 161) meet on Cape Breton Island.

The Cabot Trail (see p. 145) continues its reign as the province's premiere tourist attraction, and the island also boasts the Ceilidh Trail, (see p. 159) where Gaelic culture abounds.

CLIMATE

Nova Scotia has a modified continental climate. Once again, the sea exerts its influence, making winters warmer and summers cooler than in the Canadian interior. The same effect takes place within the province; temperatures become more continental as you move away from the coast. And while you can blame the ocean for Nova Scotia's cold, damp springs (the sea is slow to warm), it is also responsible for our fine autumns (it takes just as long to cool).

Precipitation is plentiful and evenly distributed throughout the year. On average, Halifax records precipitation on 153 days of the year. The Cape Breton Highlands and southwestern mainland receive more moisture than the northern mainland and the Annapolis Valley, mainly because of onshore winds.

FLORA

The forests of Nova Scotia are mixed, typical of the Acadia Forest found throughout the Maritime provinces. Softwood — mostly balsam fir, red, white and black spruce, and white pine — are generally found in poorly drained areas, while the hardwoods — mainly red maple, yellow birch,

sugar maple, and white birch — prefer drier ground. During autumn, many Nova Scotian hillsides blaze with colour as hardwood leaves turn from soft greens to vivid yellows, oranges, and reds. The most dramatic display of fall colour is along Cape Breton's Cabot Trail.

The natural open spaces in Nova Scotia — the salt marshes, bogs, coastal dunes, shallow lakes and ponds, stream banks, and barrens — have their own distinctive plant communities. In the salt marshes, for example, angiosperms, algae, and grasses trap sediment and help in the transition of the marsh from a saltwater environment to a freshwater one. You'll find many of these marshes in the Minas Basin and Chignecto Bay, although large areas, like Grand Pré, have been converted to dykeland.

BIRDS AND MAMMALS

With its diverse landscape and strategic position along the Atlantic flyway, Nova Scotia hosts a wide variety of birds. Some, like jays, grouses, and sparrows, are typical of boreal forest regions. Others create more of a stir. Bald eagles and osprey can be found close to marine and freshwater feeding areas, particularly in the more remote areas of the northern mainland, and on Cape Breton Island. Eagle tours are provided in Cape Breton's Bras d'Or Lakes region (see p. 159).

NOVA SCOTIA IS HOME TO A WIDE VARIETY OF BIRDS AND ANIMALS: OWL (LEFT), GULL (TOP), BALD EAGLE (ABOVE), WHITE-TAILED DEER (BELOW)

In August, huge flocks of shorebirds (sandpipers, plovers, and phalaropes) gather in the upper reaches of the Bay of Fundy to feed on the nutrient-rich mudflats before resuming their southward migration (Evangeline Beach, near Grand Pré, is a crowded stopover). They can also be found at Brier Island, where they take advantage of nutrient upwelling, and along the Atlantic coast in sheltered harbours with exposed mudflats and salt marshes.

The best place to observe seabirds — razorbills, guillemots, kittiwakes, cormorants, and puffins — is at Hertford and Ciboux, tiny islands off the coast of Cape Dauphin in Cape Breton. The "Bird Islands" are protected sanctuaries and can only be reached by boat tours that leave from Big Bras d'Or.

Nova Scotia's land mammals range in size from the mole to the moose. Moose and deer are found throughout the province. Other species (skunks, for example) that are found on mainland Nova Scotia are not present on Cape Breton Island. A relatively recent arrival, the coyote is the most vilified of Nova Scotia's mammals, given its penchant for killing sheep.

Marine mammals, including seals,

11

PILOT WHALES NEAR
CHETICAMP

whales, porpoises, and dolphins, are among the province's most popular attractions. Numerous species of whales visit Nova Scotia's coastal waters. The Bay of Fundy, near Brier Island, is a good place to see fin and humpback whales (see p. 61); pilot and minke whales are often sighted in the Gulf of St. Lawrence, especially along the west coast of Cape Breton Island (see p. 62).

SETTLEMENT

The prehistoric evidence of native settlement is sparse. At the time of European contact an estimated 3000-3500 Mi'kmaq were living in the area that is now Nova Scotia, New Brunswick, and Prince Edward Island. In Nova Scotia the largest concentration was probably on Cape Breton Island.

European exploration of Nova Scotia may have included the Norse, but there is no hard evidence to show this. Certainly, the English and Portuguese had explored the coast by the beginning of the 16th century.

The story of European settlement starts with the French at Port Royal in 1604 and includes the Acadian population (see p. 19) which numbered 13,000 at the time of their deportation in 1755. The story of subsequent immigration (and the return of the Acadians) is told in the following chapters.

Today, more than 900,000 people live in Nova Scotia. Although close to 350,000 live in Halifax Regional Municipality, Nova Scotia is mainly a rural and small-town area. Even the urban communities are small. Truro has fewer than 12,000 people; Yarmouth, in southwest Nova Scotia, has a population of only 7500; Amherst, at the border with New Brunswick, has fewer than 10,000; Lunenburg's population is under 3000; and 115,000 reside in Cape Breton Regional Municipality.

There are more than 70 cultural groups in the province

(identified by mother tongue), but the vast majority of people trace their roots to the British Isles. Nova Scotia's telephone books are full of Scots surnames, especially on Cape Breton Island and along the Northumberland Shore. Still, other peoples — the Mi'kmaq and Acadians are most visible — have retained strong cultural identities that will certainly enrich your visit to Nova Scotia.

PEOPLES

THE MI'KMAQ

TRADITIONAL MI'KMAQ COSTUMES

Until recently, the story of the Mi'kmaq has been told in the margins of Nova Scotia's historical accounts. So little is known of pre-contact Mi'kmaq society that this chapter has often been treated as a passing mention of noble savages living in a state of nature. The arrival of the Europeans, so the story goes, overawed the Mi'kmaq and led to the immediate and utter destruction of their society. In descriptions of the Old World's struggle for control over the New World, the Mi'kmaq have been assigned two roles — intractable savages where the English were concerned, and unwitting allies for the French. The coming of thousands of settlers to Nova Scotia in the last four decades of the 18th century gave ample excuse in those chronicles to simply ignore them.

Lately, the history of the Mi'kmaq in Nova Scotia has been reexamined, as part of the growing recognition of minority rights and cultures in Canada. Now a different story can be told.

It is not known when the Mi'kmaq arrived in this area, or whether their culture emerged from a mixing of more than one linguistic group, but it is probable that their ancestors have been living here since about 2000 B.C.

The Mi'kmaq were hunters and fishers. They spent much of the year on the coast where shellfish, fish, and sea birds were an abundant source of food. For a few weeks in the late spring and fall, large groups of Mi'kmaq would gather at traditional sites along rivers and streams to catch salmon and eel in their weirs. These times of plenty were the occasion for socializing and celebration. Although not political entities, these gatherings brought together people who shared resources as well as ties of family and friendship.

Seasonal change and its effect on the food supply made it necessary for the Mi'kmaq to disperse at other times of the year. For example, the hunt for moose and caribou during the fall mating season lent itself to small groupings of one or

MI'KMAQ ARTS AND CRAFTS ARE FLOURISHING

two families. After the freeze-up, diffuse settlement allowed the Mi'kmaq to make the most of the meagre resources afforded by harsh winters. Winter usually meant another move inland, as fresh food was difficult to come by along the coast.

There is a temptation, given the limited material record, to offer idyllic accounts of early Mi'kmaq society. No doubt Mi'kmaq did have a special relationship with nature, but nature could be cruel as well as kind. Subsistence living left the people vulnerable to the natural cycles that brought food shortages and severe winters.

LaHave River

February was known by some as the month of snow-blinding, or sore eyes. In addition, the Mi'kmaq frequently skirmished with other native peoples. Both the Inuit and the Iroquois were traditional enemies. But these enemies could not inflict the suffering that came with European contact.

In the 16th century, the fishery and fur trade drew more and more Europeans to the New World. By the end of that century, the beaver hat was all the rage in Europe. Native expertise was required to meet the demand for fur. In exchange for pelts, the Mi'kmaq received copper kettles and metal knives, which made traditional tasks much easier. The Mi'kmaq were willing participants in this trade — not the passive victims they have so often been made out to be.

But the trade had effects the Mi'kmaq could not have foreseen. They, like other native people, had little or no resistance to imported diseases such as smallpox and influenza. Their population was ravaged. Some have estimated that as many as 35,000 Mi'kmaq once lived in what are now the Maritime Provinces. By 1600, only about 3500 remained.

There were more subtle consequences as well. As the Mi'kmaq spent more and more time at the fur trade, other elements of their traditional hunt were neglected. They grew increasingly dependent on Europeans for food. The intense commerce of the fur trade brought irrevocable change.

Still, Mi'kmaq society was far from total disarray. When Sieur de Monts and Samuel de Champlain established their colony at Port Royal in 1604, the Mi'kmaq dealt with the French from strength. The French needed Mi'kmaq help to survive the harsh winter.

The baptism of Chief Membertou and many of his followers at Port Royal in 1610 did not indicate, as is often supposed, that the Mi'kmaq were now at the beck and call of the French. They wished to continue the fur trade, and if the French wanted them to become Christians, so be it; Christianity was not anathema to the broad spiritualism of the Mi'kmaq. In short, it was not Mi'kmaq docility that enabled the French to remain at Port Royal.

During the next century, as France and England engaged in a tug of war over Acadie (the name given by the French to the Mi'kmaq territory), French colonists depended on the Mi'kmaq for companionship and advice.

The English, however, showed little interest in colonization. In fact, there was considerable pressure from New England to discourage permanent settlement for fear that it would obstruct the harbours that had become so crucial to the New England fishery.

In 1713, the Treaty of Utrecht gave what is now mainland Nova Scotia over to the British, while the French strengthened their hold over present-day Cape Breton, then known as Ile-Royale. But the Mi'kmaq had not been involved in any negotiations; they did not recognize any rights the English claimed to have over Mi'kmaq lands.

So, they fought the British. In 1720 the Mi'kmaq destroyed a British ship at anchor in the Minas Basin. When, in 1731, the British commander decided to build a fortification at Minas, the Mi'kmaq chief in the area reminded him that although King George may have conquered Annapolis Royal, British sovereignty did not extend beyond the garrison. The Mi'kmaq acknowledged the British military presence at Annapolis and Canso, but elsewhere they continued to control their own lands.

Nova Scotia's growing strategic importance in Britain's empire made settlement more of a priority. As a consequence, the Mi'kmaq, with French encouragement, intensified their attacks on the British in what historians describe as the "Anglo-Mi'kmaq War." Most Mi'kmaq raiding took place along the coast, at such places as Canso and Lunenburg, although there was a successful attack on a

small British detachment at Dartmouth. There was, however, never any hope or attempt to defeat the British garrison at Halifax, which had been founded in 1749.

The British and Mi'kmaq attempted to reconcile the problems of British settlement in Mi'kmaq territory. In 1752, the British signed a treaty of peace with Jean-Baptiste Cope, chief of a Mi'kmaq band on the Eastern Shore.

Hostilities, however, continued until the French defeat in 1760, when the Mi'kmaq signed "treaties of peace and friendship" with the British. In 1763, the Crown issued a Royal Proclamation that included clauses reserving lands for Native peoples in North America, and affirming the rights of Mi'kmaq and other Indian nations.

But the colonial authorities had neither the will nor the wherewithal to keep these promises, and the Mi'kmaq could no longer back up demands with a viable military threat. By this time, they needed French support, and the French had been defeated.

**TREATY DAY
FLAG-RAISING**

To make matters worse, that defeat, together with the Deportation of the Acadians in 1755, had removed important obstacles to further colonization. Thousands of settlers came to Nova Scotia from New England in the 1760s. Thousands more came from the Thirteen Colonies during and after the American Revolution. In eastern Nova Scotia and Cape Breton (by this time a British colony as well), hundreds of Scots were settling vast tracts of land. The new settlers were given "tickets of location" to occupy Mi'kmaq territory; reserved lands were shrinking.

Like the commerce of the fur trade, the pressures of settlement changed Mi'kmaq society profoundly. With migratory routes cut off, and many of the best hunting and fishing grounds occupied, the Mi'kmaq sought other ways to eke out a living. Some turned to subsistence farming, but the reserved lands were usually poor and incapable of serving as the sole means of support. Fish were caught and sold in neighbouring settlements. Baskets, axe handles, and decorative handiwork were also made for sale. Despite these efforts, survival was the goal for many Mi'kmaq during much of the 19th century.

When Nova Scotia entered Confederation in 1867, the Department of Indian Affairs took over the administration of reserve lands. Soon after, a decision was made to copy the system of fixed reserves that existed elsewhere in Canada. But reserve lands in Nova Scotia were scattered thinly among small groups of Mi'kmaq, and coveted by no one. The policy was a failure.

**NEGEMOW
BASKET SHOP,
WHYCOCOMAGH**

Things did not improve much at the start of the 20th century. Mi'kmaq heroes were conspicuous during the First World War, but there was no improvement in circumstances at home. In fact, the economic hardship that confronted the Maritimes in the 1920s and everywhere else in the 1930s hit the Mi'kmaq particularly hard.

During the 1940s, the federal government decided to consolidate the reserve system in an effort to reduce social service costs. Where meagre incentives failed, the government sometimes resorted to coercion to get people to move from the smaller reserves. Those who were persuaded found little to do in their new home. Subsistence farming was no longer an option on the larger reserves, as housing covered much of the arable land. Once the resources allocated for the construction of new housing were exhausted, many Mi'kmaq sought work

17

in other places. It is estimated that as many as 30 percent of Mi'kmaq men in Nova Scotia left for New England during the 1940s and '50s. Many of those who did not emigrate or return

MI'KMAQ VETERANS MARCH ON TREATY DAY

to the smaller reserves went on welfare.

In 1969 the federal government's White Paper on Indian Policy advocated a movement towards integration. The Union of Nova Scotia Indians joined Canada's native communities in resisting the government's efforts at assimilation.

In 1972 the National Indian Brotherhood, in a policy paper of its own, advocated Indian control of Indian education. Despite a move towards band-controlled institutions — a most powerful weapon against cultural assimilation — native groups still encountered considerable resistance in advancing other claims.

Further problems were revealed during the much-publicized inquiry into the wrongful murder conviction of Donald Marshall Jr. In 1971, Marshall, a member of the Membertou Reserve in Sydney, and the son of the Grand Chief of the Mi'kmaq Nation, was sent to jail for a murder he did not commit. He spent 11 years in prison. The inquiry found that racism in the Nova Scotia justice system was partly to blame for the tragedy.

Marshall was in the courts again in1999, arguing natives have the right to fish commercially under an old treaty. The Supreme Court agreed. Government, non-native and native fishermen are still sussing out who gets to fish the depleted stocks.

Despite these problems, and despite continuing poverty and high unemployment among Nova Scotia Mi'kmaq, things have improved. Federal money is being made available for Mi'kmaq-run enterprises. Band councils are exercising increased control over Mi'kmaq affairs. Perhaps the most encouraging development is that Mi'kmaq pride in their culture and heritage is being shared by more and more members of the general public through events such as traditional powwows held in June through October, and Mi'kmaq Treaty Day, October 1.

Visitors to Nova Scotia should take time to admire the material culture of the Mi'kmaq. Handcrafts, including fine examples of quill work and basketry, are available at outlets

throughout the province. In Halifax, the Micmac Heritage Gallery on Barrington Street maintains a beautiful collection of paintings and sculpture by native artists.

It is ironic that the Mi'kmaq have found, through bitter experience, that the best way of overcoming prejudice is by asserting their distinctiveness. We are all beneficiaries.

THE ACADIANS

The Acadian people were French farmers who settled in the beautiful and fertile Annapolis Valley. With well-established communities by the middle of the 18th century, these were Nova Scotia's earliest European settlers. They lived close to the land, in tightly knit communities. Like the Arcadians of ancient Greece (after whom Acadia was named), they seemed to be the embodiment of innocence living in a land of rural paradise. Of course, their lives were more complex than this. The Acadians became caught in the French-British struggle for supremacy in the New World, and their story took a tragic turn.

Soon after they arrived, the Acadian farmers saw the potential of the Bay of Fundy's salt meadows — marshlands that were occasionally reached by the bay's highest tides. They built dykes to hold back the sea, and they planted fields of grain on the reclaimed marshlands.

Wheat thrived on the rich Fundy sediment. But dykeland farming meant more than good crops. Villages were no longer built around a town square or church as they had been in France. Houses were strung along the edge of the uplands overlooking the salt meadows. The building and maintenance of dykes required a cooperative effort, with each farmstead looking after its own stretch of marsh.

The Acadians struggled to remain neutral as the French and British

ORDER OF GOOD CHEER, PORT ROYAL

DYKELANDS NEAR WOLFVILLE

19

PORT ROYAL NATIONAL HISTORIC SITE

advanced competing claims against Mi'kmaq territory. After 1713, when the Treaty of Utrecht gave mainland Nova Scotia over to the British, the Acadians demanded that their oath of loyalty to the Crown be conditional upon not having to bear arms against the French. They also petitioned the French leader at Louisbourg, beseeching him not to drag them into hostilities with the British.

In June of 1755, volunteers from Massachusetts together with a few British soldiers attacked Fort Beauséjour, near the New Brunswick border. The fort was taken and 300 Acadians were found inside — apparently pressed into service by the French commander. Following this, the Acadians were asked to take an unconditional oath of allegiance to the British Crown, which they refused to do. The protection of their stated neutrality was wearing thin. The Acadians' worst fears were about to be realized.

As British officials in Halifax struggled to increase their control and to defend against French attacks, they concluded that the 10,000 Acadians would have to be deported. On July 28, 1755, Governor Charles Lawrence and his Council at Halifax made the fateful decision. In August, Acadians around Beauséjour were imprisoned. On September 5, the male inhabitants of Grand Pré and the surrounding area were gathered in the church at Saint-Charles-des-Mines and told that their land, houses, and livestock would be confiscated, and that they would be deported.

Thus began a period of exile and despair. People, who for close to a century had considered themselves Acadians, not French colonists, were forced from their homeland. Anglophones call it the Expulsion; the Acadians, *le Grand Dérangement* (Great Upheaval). Acadians were shipped all along the New England coast, as far south as Georgia. Often they were not wanted. Virginia refused to accept its allotment. Instead, the refugees were sent to England as prisoners of war and then on to France. When Louisbourg fell in 1758, the process began anew. Acadians from Ile-Royale (Cape Breton) and Île Saint-Jean (Prince Edward

ACADIAN FLAGS ALONG THE FRENCH SHORE

Island) were repatriated to France. Many of the Acadians who landed in New England made their way to South Louisiana, where they became known as "Cajuns."

Following the end of the war and the Treaty of Paris in 1763, the French

GRAND PRÉ NATIONAL HISTORIC SITE

invited those Acadians who had spent the war years in English ports back to France. The Acadians were French and Catholic; it was assumed they would be delighted to return to their motherland. Not so. The Acadians found the tradition of the *corvée*, with its restrictions on travel and work, oppressive. Breton courts were full of Acadians who tried to combine several jobs — farming, fishing, and carpentry. They were exiles in France, as they had been in Britain.

And those who had managed to escape deportation were exiles in Nova Scotia. They withdrew to the forests or fled to remote corners of the province. Many died during that first winter. Others were caught and imprisoned at Halifax, Windsor, or Annapolis Royal. Still, a group of Acadians in Nova Scotia somehow persisted.

In 1764 the British authorities relented. But the Acadians would not return to their farmlands; these were now occupied by New Englanders. Instead, they settled in remote parts of the province — at Clare, between Yarmouth and Digby, in an area now known as the French Shore; in Argyle, to the south of Yarmouth; at Cheticamp and Isle Madame on Cape Breton Island; in Minudie, Nappan, and Maccan, near Amherst; at Pomquet, Tracadie, and Havre-Boucher on the North Shore; and a few at Chezzetcook, near Halifax. The Acadians were isolated and out of the way.

DEPORTATION CROSS MARKING EXPULSION SITE

This isolation spawned a very different Acadian culture. Farmers became woodsmen, shipbuilders, and fishermen. There developed a divergence of speech habits and accents — even between Clare and Argyle, which lie just to the north and south of Yarmouth. Ironically, the deliberate policy of isolating the Acadians sometimes contributed to the preservation of their culture — in places like Cheticamp, Arichat, and Isle Madame. In communities such as Minudie, Nappan, Maccan, and Chezzetcook, the French language was suffocated by the pressure to assimilate.

In those villages where Acadian culture continues to flourish, the

L'ÉGLISE SAINT BERNARD ON THE FRENCH SHORE

Catholic Church has a highly visible presence. In Pointe de L'Église (Church Point) on the French Shore, a beautiful wooden steeple soars above Université Sainte-Anne, founded by Eudist priests as Nova Scotia's only francophone university. Just minutes away, in the community of St. Bernard, is a magnificent 1,000-seat Gothic church, which now, the guide laments, is filled only on Easter Sunday and Christmas Day! Cheticamp has its own exquisite church.

During the last half of the 19th century, the Church played an important role in what has been described as the Acadian Renaissance. At Acadian conventions in 1881, 1884, and 1890, church leaders and others championed the cause of Acadian nationalism in the face of pressure from both Quebec and English Canada to assimilate. St-Jean-Baptiste Day (a Quebec holiday) was rejected in favour of the Assumption of the Madonna. The Acadian flag expressed a filial attachment to France with the adoption of the tricolour; but the yellow Stella Maris, the Marian star of the sea, symbolized Acadian nationalism. From the pulpit and within the community, some Catholic priests have been fierce defenders of Acadian culture and language.

The Société Nationale l'Assomption, founded in the 1880s, spearheaded a campaign to raise funds among Acadians throughout North America for a memorial church at Grand Pré that would commemorate the Deportation. In 1922 the cornerstone was blessed by Bishop Edouard Leblanc, the first Acadian bishop in the Maritimes.

Today, visitors to Grand Pré National Historic Site, near Wolfville, can tour this commemorative site. The church houses exhibits on the Deportation, and a stained glass window by Halifax artist T. E. Smith-Lamothe depicts the event. A bronze statue of Evangeline surveys the park.

RUG HOOKING DEMONSTRATION AT THE COOPERATIVE ARTISANALE, CHETICAMP

Visitors are also welcome at the many Acadian festivals held throughout the province. Two of the largest are the Festival Acadien de Clare, which takes place on the French Shore in early July, and the Festival de l'Escaouette at Cheticamp later in the month. Cheticamp has also become a centre for Acadian handcrafts (see p.150).

In recent years, the Acadians have

benefited from the growing recognition of minority language rights. In 1981, Nova Scotia's Bill 65 provided for Acadian schools, with French being the primary language of instruction for the first six grades. Such initiatives, while well meaning, are received with some ambivalence in Acadian communities. Many Acadian parents are torn. They want to prescrve their culture and language but many view English as the language of opportunity in Nova Scotia.

Still, it may be foolhardy to lose too much sleep over the future of the Acadian communities in this province. A people put so completely asunder in 1755 knows something of survival. That Acadian communities could take root in Nova Scotia following such a great upheaval was in itself remarkable. But the Acadians have done more than survive. They have endured the hard times with humour, pride, and a spirited resourcefulness.

ACADIAN DAYS AT GRAND PRÉ

THE NEW ENGLAND PLANTERS

BY BRIAN CUTHBERTSON

The identity of a group of 8000 New Englanders who came to this land between 1759 and 1768 was forged at a conference in Wolfville in 1987. Before the conference, these colonists were known variously as "neutral Yankees," "pre-Loyalists," and "planters" (an old English word for colonists). They were treated by mainstream historians as the unimportant antecedents of a much larger and more significant colonial American immigration to Nova Scotia — hence the name "pre-Loyalist." But the "planters" emerged

ACADIA UNIVERSITY, WOLFVILLE

from the conference as Planters, some attendees claiming that they had witnessed the birth of a new ethnic group. A zeal for ethnicity and heritage had produced another offspring.

The Planters came to Nova Scotia by formal invitation. Three years after Nova Scotia's Acadians were deported, the French Fortress of Louisbourg, the "Dunkirk of America," was taken by the British. With the French gone and the Acadian lands vacant, Halifax officials looked to New England for immigrants who would be loyal to the Crown.

Governor Charles Lawrence issued a proclamation on October 12, 1758, and a second in early 1759, inviting proposals for the settlement of Acadian lands or any other lands the New Englanders might covet. Lawrence had been involved in an ongoing struggle with Halifax's New England merchant elite over the establishment of an elective assembly. The Lords of Trade in London ordered Lawrence to hold elections. Ten days before the October 12 proclamation was issued, Nova Scotia's first Legislative Assembly met. The opportunity to settle the soil with British stock could not be missed.

Responses poured in. It was all very civilized. Grantees

sent agents to Halifax to discuss terms and to get the lay of the land. Surveys were carried out at government expense. Sites for Planter townships were identified. Persistent Mi'kmaq raids postponed settlement, but it was a postponement of the inevitable. At no other time in Nova Scotia's history was such enthusiasm shared by both colonizers and colonists.

THE PLANTERS' BARRACKS COUNTRY INN AT STARRS POINT DATES BACK TO 1760

For the colonists, it was an enthusiasm stoked by the market opportunities they saw in Nova Scotia. In southwestern New England — coastal Connecticut, Rhode Island, and eastern Massachusetts — settlement had flourished to the point where the land had become overburdened. Nova Scotia offered up to 405 hectares (1,000 acres) per person on the most favourable terms. And the New Englanders could continue their traditional pursuits of fishing, farming, and logging with a good deal more breathing space.

So, they came. Those who wanted to farm settled on former Acadian lands in the Annapolis Valley and the Minas Basin, at townships like Horton, Cornwallis, Annapolis, and Falmouth. Some occupied the Acadian farmlands on the Isthmus of Chignecto. Fishers, long familiar with the best anchorages of the South Shore, settled Liverpool, Barrington, and Yarmouth. Everywhere, farmers, fishers, and loggers found farms, fish, and logs in abundance. It seemed as though life in New England could continue in Nova Scotia.

Indeed, in many ways, Nova Scotia appeared to be a "greater New England" (as some historians have described it). There were inextricable commercial links. Nova Scotia now had its Legislative Assembly, and every township of at least 50 families could elect two members to it. At townships like Annapolis, the earliest settlers met to appoint lot layers and other officials, continuing the tradition of the New England town meeting. The courts were similar to New England's. And the government declared its tolerance of the Planters' dissenting religion; Congregationalist meeting houses soon appeared in the new townships.

But the transition was not seamless. For example, the Liverpool Planters soon learned that their view of autonomy differed slightly from the Nova Scotia government's. When some grantees failed to arrive in the township, the Council at Halifax appointed a committee to distribute the forfeited lands. Several residents of Liverpool were rebuffed in an attempt to form their own committee for the purpose. The velvety language of Lawrence's proclamations and the township grants belied the government's centralist will.

That was not all. The Acadians and Mi'kmaq had not

MANY PLANTER FAMILIES SETTLED IN THE ANNAPOLIS VALLEY

been completely expunged, as advertised. Planter settlement was affected by their continued presence (to say nothing of the profound effect the Planters had on them). Acadians worked as wage labourers repairing damaged dykes on Planter land, but they must have done so grudgingly. Although the Mi'kmaq had signed treaties of peace and friendship in 1761, this did not make the settlement of Nova Scotia by non-natives any more palatable to them. The Mi'kmaq sought to secure lands so that they could continue their traditional lifestyle.

The Planters did not flock to the cause during the American Revolutionary War. This is not to say that they were without sympathy. In 1776, Jonathan Eddy led a group of Planters in a failed rebellion against the British forces at Fort Cumberland. Others, from western Nova Scotia, returned to New England to support the Revolution. But there was also an enthusiastic Planter militia that was loyal to the Crown.

There was another response to the Revolution. Many people in the Planter communities wanted nothing to do with either side. Why? There are many theories: that a strong British naval and commercial presence in Halifax held the rest of Nova Scotia in check; that the rigours of life in a frontier colony precluded a developed political sensibility; that the Planters had missed out on a key decade of foment in New England; and that their revolutionary zeal was redirected into the evangelical movement led by charismatic New Light preacher (and Planter) Henry Alline.

Whatever the reason, one thing is certain: by the end of the Revolution, more than the Gulf of Maine separated the Planters from their American cousins.

Then, for the most part, we lose track of them. The Planters go missing in the flurry of Loyalist arrivals that followed the American Revolution. Only recently has the search begun in Nova Scotia for a Planter legacy that survived this Loyalist influx.

The Old Kings Courthouse Museum, on Cornwallis Street in Kentville, has been designated a centre for Planter Studies. The museum houses a Parks Canada exhibit, which includes a short film on Planter settlement in the area. For those visitors with Planter roots, the museum's archives include Kings County genealogical records.

The Province has chosen some high-profile buildings to tell the Planter story. The Barrington Meeting House, part of the Nova Scotia Museum Complex, was built in the 1760s by Planters who had recently arrived from Massachusetts. In the New England tradition, it was the site of religious services, town meetings, and elections for more than 100 years. The Planters were practical when it came to both worldly and otherworldly matters, and the Barrington Meeting House reflects this; it is more function than artifice.

The Simeon Perkins House, built in 1766 as the home of one of Liverpool's wealthier residents, is also a part of the Nova Scotia Museum Complex (see p. 107). An 18th-century officers' barracks (now an elegant country inn) still stands at Starrs Point, just north of Wolfville. Its style is distinctly New England, and the interior of the barracks remains fairly true to the original.

Several other houses scattered throughout the Planter areas of Nova Scotia, especially in Kings County, appear to have predated the Revolution. Publications of the Planter Studies Centre, Acadia University in Wolfville, are assisting in the discovery of these heritage properties. One of the distinctive features of Planter homes is the gambrel roof; it has two slopes, the lower one having a steeper pitch. Recent archaeological evidence also suggests that some Planter houses were built on Acadian foundations.

There are other less tangible examples of Nova Scotia's Planter legacy. The Baptist Church in western and southwestern Nova Scotia owes much of its vitality to a Planter-inspired religious revival (often called Nova Scotia's "Great Awakening") led by Henry Alline, of Falmouth. While many Congregationalist clergy returned to New England to support the Revolution, Alline crisscrossed Nova Scotia, selling his own brand of evangelism, with its emphasis on personal religious experience. The Congregationalist churches were seriously undermined. The Baptist polity that emerged early in the 19th century was, in many ways, an attempt to lend some structure and orthodoxy to the intense religious expression that had found its most eloquent voice in the sermons and hymns of Henry Alline.

THE OLD MEETING HOUSE, BARRINGTON

As the Baptist Church grew, there was a need to instruct people in the new orthodoxy. Also, a schism in Halifax's St. Paul's Anglican Church had led to the formation of a new Baptist congregation with influential and well-educated members. The Baptists saw that education might be used as a tool for loosening the grip that the Halifax establishment had on the province. In 1838 Queen's College (later Acadia College, then Acadia University) was founded at Wolfville. Ironically, Acadia owes a good deal to Alline, whose preaching revealed a considerable suspicion of education.

There is another legacy in the old Planter townships. Wolfville's pace is quickened slightly by the university; but the town, like most other towns in the Annapolis Valley, still moves to the steady rhythm of the harvest. On the South Shore, fortunes remain tied to the fishery — fortunes that now reflect its dismal state. Of course, there has been change, but more than anywhere else in Nova Scotia, the Planter settlements convey a sense of timelessness.

THE ENGLISH

ST. GEORGE'S
CHURCH, HALIFAX

Few people in this province consider themselves English. Yet, when pressed by the 1991 Census of Canada, just under half of those Nova Scotians claiming a single ethnic origin said they had English roots.

How can we understand this contradiction? For one thing, ethnic identity in Canada is most strongly associated with people who are not Anglo-Saxon. Also, many of those with English ancestry in the province are descendants of New England Planters or Loyalists. The "Yankee" heritage of the Planters has always been stressed, and recent accounts of the Loyalists suggest that they, too, were much more American than British in their outlook. Finally, there was little effort made to colonize Nova Scotia with English settlers.

The explanation lies in British policy in colonial Nova Scotia. Like Newfoundland, Nova Scotia's chief value was seen to lie in its cod fishery. When the Treaty of Utrecht handed peninsular Nova Scotia over to the British in 1713, a number of British adventurers sought land in the new colony so that they could bring out settlers. New England merchants were opposed. They already exercised dominion from the sea; a land-based population in the new colony would interfere.

London agreed. No effort was made to colonize. The War of the Austrian Succession changed British attitudes toward Nova Scotia. At the behest of Massachusetts Governor William Shirley, Louisbourg was taken by New England militia in 1745. The fortress was restored to the French by the Treaty of Aix-la-Chapelle, but the British had awakened to the strategic importance of Nova Scotia. It could protect New

England from any French designs on the territory. The angry shouts of New Englanders, outraged by the decision to give up Louisbourg, ensured that British attention would remain focused on Nova Scotia.

The colonization and fortification of Nova Scotia became part of British policy. In May of 1749, Colonel Cornwallis and 2500 settlers sailed for the colony. At Chebucto Harbour, they established the town of Halifax.

THE PUBLIC GARDENS, HALIFAX

But Cornwallis was not enamoured with those early Haligonians whom he found to be lazy and untrustworthy. This, in contrast to a group of Swiss and German settlers whose diligence he admired. So he urged the authorities in London to look to these "Foreign Protestants" as a source of potential colonists.

They did, and a substantial number of German, Swiss, and French Protestants arrived in Nova Scotia between 1750 and 1752. But the French and the Mi'kmaq did what they could to discourage settlement, and the outbreak of the Seven Years War made further colonization impossible.

With the French threat gone and the Acadians driven from their lands, the 1760s were a time of mass immigration to Nova Scotia. These new arrivals came in search of cheap yet rich land to cultivate, which was no longer available in New England, and to locate closer to the fishing banks. After the American Revolution, thousands of Loyalists, most from the former middle and southern American colonies, came to Nova Scotia. They rapidly rose to prominence in government and the judiciary, reinforcing loyalty to the Crown and things English.

English settlers did arrive — artisans and disbanded soldiers — but they did so without fanfare. Rising rents in Yorkshire caused groups of farmers, many with the means to purchase partially developed farms from New England Planters, to emigrate to Cumberland County. British policy discouraged such emigration of experienced farmers, but well over 1000 Yorkshire people arrived between 1772 and 1775.

During the late 18th and early 19th centuries, when economic pressures and religious persecution brought waves of Scottish and Irish immigrants to Nova Scotia, relatively few English were among them. Those who did arrive quickly blended into the existing population.

ST. PAUL'S ANGLICAN CHURCH, HALIFAX

It is foolhardy to attempt a description of the English legacy in this province. The best that can be said is that once you identify everything else, what's left over is English. However, if you seek the most striking examples of Nova Scotia's English heritage, then look no further than Halifax — for a century, the seat of the colonial government. The reconstructed fortifications of Citadel Hill bring back the days when Halifax was a British garrison town. And St. Paul's Anglican Church was Britain's first overseas cathedral — the "Westminster Abbey of the New World."

THE LOYALISTS

Each summer, Shelburne celebrates its Loyalist heritage
during Founders' Days. Among the events is a Loyalist Tea
— a function reminiscent of the civility and refinement that
the Loyalists brought to their new home — or so we imagine.

Nova Scotian mythology has created a Loyalist
persona. He is a white, British, Anglican, Tory merchant or
office-holder from a good New England family. His virtue
is untarnished by the levelling principles of American
republicanism. During the American Revolutionary War, he
suffered grievously and sacrificed all for Britain's
Constitution and Empire. To his new home, he brought a
sense of purpose out of which was eventually born a new
country — Canada. If you pass through Saint John, New
Brunswick, on your way to Nova Scotia, you can see him
during the Loyalist Days celebration there: his name is
Squire John.

In truth, the 20,000 or so Loyalists who came to Nova
Scotia in the wake of the American Revolution were
surprisingly diverse. The war had caused elemental
divisions within the Thirteen Colonies. It had split families
and communities. Loyalties crossed lines of gender,
ethnicity, religion, and class so that the composition of
either side was broadly representative of colonial society.
Sure, Nova Scotia received its share of "Squire Johns," but
there was also a significant number of Black Loyalists, for
example, among the many others who came.

With such a diverse group, it is hardly surprising that

not all Loyalists had been moved by a steadfast faith in Britain and things British. Some were. Others, once in Nova Scotia, claimed to have been, in the hope that these testimonials would be rewarded by the British authorities. Back home, these people had been more interested in maintaining position and wealth within the existing system than in that system itself. Others, like the Catholic Scottish Highlanders of North Carolina, sided with the British out of preference for the devil they knew over the one they didn't. For them, as for the Black Loyalists, British rule was the lesser of two evils. All of these people had suffered in varying degrees because they had ended up on the losing side of a civil war; relatively few had suffered for love of Britain.

LOYALIST TEA PARTY, SHELBURNE

The Loyalists hoped for much better in Nova Scotia. Initially, the security that British rule could offer must have given comfort. Gone was the threat to person and property — a threat not much reduced by the signing of the Treaty of Paris, in 1783. But security was little recompense for their privations.

The wealthy and powerful among their number had high hopes for Nova Scotia, but they encountered immediate obstacles — the chief of which was the government in Halifax. The Loyalist elite took a rather pious view of their Halifax counterparts, many of whom had profited from the war. Although the existing administrative structure precluded Halifax officialdom from dealing efficiently with the spate of Loyalist demands for land, the Loyalists saw the influence of moral turpitude as well.

Following a winter of intense lobbying by powerful members of the Loyalist elite in Nova Scotia and London, two new provinces, New Brunswick and Cape Breton, were created in the summer of 1784. From the beginning, Cape Breton failed to fulfill its Loyalist promise (about 500 Loyalists settled there; original plans called for 3,000), though 15,000 found their way to New Brunswick.

Reality fell short of expectation for other Nova Scotia Loyalists. For those who settled Shelburne, the hope was that it would soon become a port to rival Halifax. Barely a year old, Shelburne's population had ballooned to near 10,000 by 1784, making it the largest town in British North America. In addition to taverns, sawmills, shipyards, churches, and schools, Shelburne also boasted three newspapers, a jeweller, a hairdresser, and a dance instructor!

But Shelburne did not live up to its promise. It could not. The harbour was fine, but it was too far removed from prime fishing grounds. The soil was poor. Once government stopped supplying the new settlers with provisions, it became painfully clear that Shelburne could not support so many people.

LOYALIST GARDEN PARTY, SHELBURNE

Some left the town to settle other parts of Nova Scotia, but many would return to the United States. And Shelburne was not the only Loyalist town to experience significant outmigration. Some historians estimate that as many as two-thirds of Nova Scotia's Loyalist immigrants eventually returned to the States. For these people, at least, economic hardship was more reviled than republicanism.

Even the more modest expectations of other Loyalists were often not met. The Black Loyalist experience at Shelburne and neighbouring Birchtown provides a good example. In the Thirteen Colonies, many Blacks had opposed the Revolutionary forces in exchange for their freedom. Under British rule, they expected to be treated like other Loyalists. In this, they would be bitterly disappointed.

AT THE ROSS-THOMSON HOUSE, SHELBURNE

SHELBURNE LOYALIST FABRIC
SHELBURNE
NOVA SCOTIA

Few of the 1,500 Black Loyalists who lived in the Shelburne area received land. Those who did, got the dregs. Black wage labourers worked for a pittance. Their willingness to work for less led a group of disbanded soldiers to riot against them in the summer of 1784. The violence lasted 10 days; 20 Black Loyalist homes were destroyed. In 1789 many Birchtown residents were selling clothing and blankets for food. By 1792 they had had enough. Blacks from Shelburne and Birchtown were among the 1,200 Black Loyalists who left Nova Scotia for West Africa, where they founded Freetown in Sierra Leone. Few regretted leaving; had they been able, many more would have gone.

Of course, many Loyalists did not leave, and did not want to leave, Nova Scotia. Once it became apparent that local economies could not sustain artificially high populations, as in Shelburne, people began migrating to other parts of the province. Smaller, more stable communities resulted — at Shelburne; Digby and Annapolis; Halifax, Windsor, and Truro; Guysborough and Chedabucto Bay; Cumberland County; Antigonish and Pictou; and around Sydney, in Cape Breton. Loyalist immigration strengthened many of these communities. For example, significant numbers of Scots and Irish, many of them disbanded soldiers, joined their countrymen in Nova Scotia.

Loyalists changed their new home in less obvious ways. Standards of education had declined in Nova Scotia during the upheaval of the Revolution. The departure of well-educated dissenting clergy who left for New England in support of the Revolution was partly to blame; so were the leaders of a religious revival who scoffed at education. But those members of the Loyalist elite who valued the cultural and educational institutions they had left behind sought to reestablish them in Nova Scotia. Reading societies emerged. King's College was founded at Windsor (it relocated to Halifax in 1923). Theatrical productions were staged at Halifax. A higher value was placed on literature. All of these pursuits came to be seen as necessary elements of a cultured society.

Today, the most tangible evidence of Nova Scotia's Loyalist legacy is in Shelburne. The Shelburne County Museum has an exhibit on the town's Loyalist origins, and its resource centre contains extensive genealogical material, including the muster book of the Free Black settlement at Birchtown. Several Loyalist-era buildings are on or near the harbourfront.

As for some of the more pervasive contributions attributed to the Loyalists — that they brought to Nova Scotia and Canada an enduring element of conservatism and a reverence for things British; that their influence helps to explain why Nova Scotians and Canadians tolerate a more interventionist state than do Americans; and that they are, in large part, responsible for any anti-American sentiment in Nova Scotia and Canada — there is far less evidence for these claims.

What is certain is that the Loyalist myth remains a powerful force in the Maritime Provinces and that, rightly or wrongly, a large part of who we are is thought to have come from who they were.

THE BLACKS

The politics of today help to shape the way history is told. As Nova Scotia's Blacks engage in a community-based struggle for collective rights, historians have begun searching for the seeds of a Black collective identity in the early institutions of Black Nova Scotia. This is in marked contrast to the 1960s, when concerns over discrimination and segregation drove the political discourse. Then, the history of Blacks in Nova Scotia was seen, in large part, as the history of what was done to them by Whites.

Most of Nova Scotia's earliest Blacks were slaves (there were exceptions: Barbara Cuffy, a free Black, was among the founders of Liverpool). In 1751 ten Halifax Blacks were auctioned in Boston — advertised as carpenters, caulkers, sail makers, and rope makers. Blacks were also bought and sold in Halifax. There were slaves and servants attached to the households of the New England Planters who came to Nova Scotia in the 1760s.

Slaves were also among the Black Loyalists who came to Nova Scotia in the wake of the American Revolution, but the majority were free. In an effort to lure away support from the revolutionary cause and, to a lesser extent, to enlist extra fighting men, British officials in the Thirteen Colonies promised freedom to any slave who would side with their cause. Obviously, by the end of the war, the only way the British could keep their promise was by transporting the Black Loyalists to a British colony. The names of those who were free to go were recorded in the Book of Negroes by the British Commander in Chief.

Thirty-five hundred free Black Loyalists came to Nova Scotia and what is now New Brunswick — two-thirds from the South, the remainder from the middle colonies. As free people, they could hope to be treated like other Loyalists.

They were not. The Nova Scotia government was swamped by petitions for land. They had enough trouble satisfying the claims of wealthy Loyalists; the Blacks were placed at the bottom of the list. Each head of a household should have received 100 acres (40.5 hectares) plus 50 additional acres for each household member. Most received an acre or two. At communities throughout the province — Clements, Granville, Birchtown, Brindley Town, Preston, Annapolis, Halifax, Chedabucto, Tracadie, and Liverpool — the experience was the same. If the government could find some poor land adjacent to the White settlements, then they might get around to giving some of it to the Blacks.

Conditions were awful. Under the leadership of David George, a revivalist preacher in the Allinite tradition (see p. 26), the Black Baptist Church provided a flicker of hope. But the departure of almost 1200 Black Loyalists for Sierra Leone in 1792 — church leaders, including George, were among those who left — weakened the remaining community.

Just a few years later there was a second wave of Black migration to Nova Scotia — this time the Maroons of Jamaica. In Jamaica, the Maroons had waged a successful 140-year battle to remain free from colonial rule. The government could not enslave them, so in 1796 they deported 550 Maroons from Trelawney Town, claiming that they had violated terms of a ceasefire.

The Maroons ended up in Halifax, where they presented the governor and the military commander with a source of cheap labour, subsidized by the Jamaican government. They were settled at Preston, where several worked at the estate of Governor Wentworth; others strengthened the fortifications at Citadel Hill. But they did not become servile. In 1800 almost every Maroon left for Sierra Leone. By their refusal to submit to authority, the Maroons have become a powerful symbol for Nova Scotia Blacks.

About 2000 "Black refugees" came to Nova Scotia from the United States between 1813 and 1816. Like the Black Loyalists, they had been promised freedom under British rule in exchange for supporting the British in the War of 1812 against America. Unlike the Loyalists, the refugees were not confronted by inadequate government planning. This time, there was no plan.

Things went badly. Indifference and a few grants of "poor relief" were the most the government would offer; it was more interested in preventing further Black immigration, claiming that it discouraged "better-quality" White settlers from coming. Everyone suffered from the economic slump that came with peace. The years 1816 ("the year with no summer") and 1817 ("the year of the mice") were particularly devastating.

In 1854, under the inspired leadership of Richard Preston, 12 Black Baptist congregations formed the African (later United) Baptist Association. Vitalized by the

THE AFRICVILLE REUNION IS HELD EACH JULY AT SEAVIEW PARK, WHERE AFRICVILLE HOMES USED TO STAND

Association, the churches helped to sustain and inspire their communities. The Association sought to raise the standard of education for Blacks, and it became an important vehicle in the struggle for collective rights — the contribution most cherished by today's Black Nova Scotians.

The story of Africville helps to explain why. By the 1960s, this community, strung along the shores of the Bedford Basin in Halifax, had become an eyesore and an embarrassment. As a symbol of the evils of segregation, it suffered from neglect; it had few of the services enjoyed by the rest of Halifax. As a further insult, an infectious diseases hospital, a tar factory, a fertilizer plant, slaughter houses, and the Halifax city dump were all located nearby.

City planners advocated demolition of the community to "improve" the housing conditions. Africville's residents objected, proposing that the City upgrade services instead. The City ignored these pleas, and pushed its plan forward. In 1964 the City of Halifax began relocating people. Africville was razed and its residents moved into subsidized housing. The move received widespread acclaim — even from some Black leaders outside the community — though not from the people of Africville.

Now, Africville is mourned. A viable community was destroyed; Africville residents had not wanted to move. Outsiders had seen poverty amidst industrial sprawl. What they did not look for, and therefore could not see, was the sense of community that existed in spite of it all.

The lessons learned from Africville permeate contemporary Black culture in Nova Scotia. The Africville Genealogy Society was established in order to "preserve the past, care for the present, and prepare for the future."

At the Black Cultural Centre in Cherrybrook, near Dartmouth, visitors can get a sense of the important role that the struggle for a collective identity has played for the Blacks of this province. This year-round educational facility is dedicated to the preservation and promotion of Black heritage and culture. Achievements in music, education, sports, business, religion, and the military are honoured in a series of films and exhibits. An hour-and-a-half-long guided tour of the centre is offered, and a brochure entitled *Nova Scotia's Black Heritage Trail*, also available at the centre, will guide you to other sites of Black cultural activity.

THE SCOTS

At the outset, an apology. In Nova Scotia, it's the Highlanders who get all the attention, though there were probably just as many Lowland Scots who came here. However, the Lowlanders did not usually arrive in groups. They were more likely to be skilled tradesmen and artisans who moved into existing settlements. They spoke Scots, a dialect of English, and soon were indistinguishable from the general population. Little account has been given of them other than passing mentions of their arrival. Unfortunately, what follows continues in that tradition. Hopefully, it is better to draw the ire of the Lowlanders than to incur the wrath of the Highlanders.

Acadia did not become Nova Scotia (New Scotland) amid a rush of Scottish immigration. It became Nova Scotia when William Alexander was granted the territory by Royal Charter in 1621. Efforts to make Nova Scotia Scottish were quite modest. An attempt to establish a settlement at Baleine Cove in present-day Cape Breton lost steam after only a few weeks. Things went a little better at present-day Annapolis Royal, where Alexander's son and namesake managed to build a fort. But in 1632, after three years, the younger Alexander was defeated by the latest peace with France. He was obliged to return the site to the French.

That was it for nearly 150 years. During that time English, German, Irish, and New England settlers joined the Mi'kmaq and French on these shores, while future Nova Scotians continued to skirmish in the western highlands and islands of Scotland.

In 1746 the English dealt the Highlands a crushing blow at Culloden. The English could now work in earnest at pacifying a land that they had long viewed as wildly uncivilized.

At first, Scottish emigration was most often voluntary. Peace and the introduction of inoculation to the Highlands

SCOTS WERE PROMISED CLEARED LANDS; MOST HAD TO DO IT THEMSELVES

contributed to overpopulation, straining the land. Soldiers who had fought on New World soil told friends and neighbours of its abundance. Propagandists for New World ventures that would profit by immigration described a land of plenty. Soon Highland lairds raised a hue and cry — not because they were losing their most impoverished and least productive tenants, but because those who were well accommodated were seeking their fortune in the New World.

This is not to say that the 189 Scots who arrived at Pictou in 1773 aboard the *Hector* had travelled first class. Eighteen had been taken by smallpox and dysentery. Many of those spared were ill; all were weary. Still, with the exception of William "Piper" Fraser who was allowed to remain on board at the behest of his fellow passengers, those who came had been able to afford their passage. These were not the passive victims of capricious landlords; they wanted to see what the New World had to offer.

To their dismay, and to the dismay of the tens of thousands who came later, Nova Scotia offered more forest than anything else. The Philadelphia Company, which backed the *Hector* venture, had promised land. There was land in abundance, but the company had failed to mention that it was covered with massive spruce and pine trees. For immigrants from the barren western highlands and islands, these might just as well have been cast in iron.

RE-ENACTMENT OF THE LANDING OF THE *HECTOR*, PICTOU

THE *HECTOR*
RECONSTRUCTION,
PICTOU

Trees were an obsession for early Scottish settlers. Bard
MacLean came to Barney's River (Pictou County) in 1819.
His Gaelic verses lose something in the translation, but his
views on trees come across loud and clear: "Before I make a
clearing and raise crops and tear the tyrannous forest up
from its roots by the strength of my
arms, I'll be worn out, and almost spent
before my children have grown up."

Once the new arrivals got the hang
of it, they set to working on the trees
with a vengeance. In Pictou County,
considerable land was cleared but was
never cultivated.

The land those early Scots left
behind had undergone intense
subdivision. Here, land seemed

MCCULLOCH
HOUSE, PICTOU

unlimited and the settlers were extravagant in their
purchases. They also defended property rights with a zeal
noted by contemporaries. There was no such thing as
enough land. The earliest settlers took hold of the choicest
tracts, usually those abutting the shores of ocean, lake, or
stream. Latecomers moved inland, to the "rear." And they
were soon looking further afield.

In their search for land, some settlers moved eastward
from Pictou County towards Antigonish County and on to
Cape Breton. There were exceptions. The MacNeils, for
example, knew exactly where they were going when they
left the Hebridean island of Barra. Three clansmen had
fought the French at Louisbourg in 1758 and had
recognized the promise of Iona, in the Bras d'Or Lakes, on
one of their excursions. They took word back to Scotland,
and the MacNeils arrived in number. Still, it seems most
Cape Breton pioneers arrived there because the more fertile
soil to the west was already occupied.

This pattern of settlement has had a marked effect on
the character of northeastern Nova Scotia. The earliest
settlers were better off than many who came after. Among
their number were skilled tradesmen and families who
came to realize ambitions that had long been held in check
by shrinking property lines. These Pictou County Scots
were also, for the most part, Presbyterian.

Naturally, the changes that Culloden left in its wake took
time to reach the more remote regions of the Scottish
Highlands, as did John Knox's Presbyterianism. Neither was

If you possess the fighting spirit of your forefathers
JOIN THE
236ᵀᴴ KILTIES BATTALION

All the officers have already been in the trenches and are going back •

THEY KNOW THE BOYS NEED THEM - AYE - AND NEED YOU, TOO

Don the **MACLEAN TARTAN** and do your bit -

THE KILTIES WILL GO QUICKLY - AND AS A UNIT -

God Save the King

Lt. Col. **PERCY A. GUTHRIE** O. C.
(Formerly 10ᵗʰ Battalion White Ghurkas)

Go to the nearest recruiting office and insist on joining the Kilties.

THE **236 MACLEAN KILTIES BATTALION.**

FIRST WORLD WAR RECRUITING POSTER

welcomed. Some Highlanders left for Nova Scotia in the face of the kind of modernization that the Highland Improvement Program of 1803 tried to impose; they were unwilling to give up traditional pastoral ways for the life of a villager. Others wanted nothing to do with the Protestant Dissenters. Many of those who chose to stay behind were eventually made to leave. These are the people who settled the more remote regions of eastern Nova Scotia and Cape Breton, reproducing the settlement pattern of their homeland. Their ambition was of a different kind than their Pictou County neighbours. They sought to preserve the old ways in the New World. In this, they were aided by their isolation.

Theology as well as geography set Catholics apart from Protestants. Presbyterianism extols the virtues of hard work and success, and success can be won through education. John Knox looked forward to the day when there would be a kirk in every community, a schoolhouse nearby, and an institute of higher learning for those who truly wished to advance themselves.

In Pictou County, Thomas McCulloch, a secessionist minister, took up Knox's ideal. He founded Pictou Academy in 1816, an institution where education and religion have been closely allied. Hundreds of Nova Scotia's early professionals — lawyers, doctors, and clergy — got their start at the Academy. McCulloch became the first principal of Dalhousie College (later University), at Halifax, in 1838.

Of course, Catholic Scots also valued higher education — they founded Saint Francis Xavier University in Antigonish — but for them education did not have the same redemptive power as it did for their Presbyterian neighbours.

In those areas of Nova Scotia where Catholic Scots settled, greater attention was given to leisure. A tradition of subsistence farming, supplemented by fishing and logging, left time for play.

This tradition survives in parts of Cape Breton. The stretch of shoreline running south from Mabou in Inverness County is still predominantly Catholic. Mabou is home to the recently disbanded Rankin Family, whose musical success is deeply rooted in the past. Farther down the shore

are the native homes of Ashley MacIsaac and Natalie MacMaster, two of Cape Breton's most talented young fiddlers.

For reasons of both temperament and geography, people in the remote areas of Cape Breton retained much of their Highland character. Music is one means by which this Celtic heritage was preserved; the Gaelic language was another. Well into this century,

Gaelic was spoken in the homes of many Cape Breton communities.

Now Gaelic is spoken only by a small number of Nova Scotians, though renewed interest has been sparked in part by the success of Gaelic-influenced music. The coal boom that began late last century drew many folks from the shore and the farm to Sydney and other industrial towns. At first, only those who had not flourished by land and sea came. Eventually, even those who fished successfully and tilled the rich soil of the intervales (a local name for choice lands bordering on water) were drawn to town and city. The houses and farms left behind soon fell to neglect. So did the Gaelic.

Industrial Cape Breton was by no means the only attraction. Many Pictou and Antigonish County Scots went to Stellarton and New Glasgow to work at heavy industry there. Halifax drew professionals. Boston was a Mecca for many. Others went off to prairie wheat farms or Alberta oil fields. The picture of Maritimers goin' down the road to find their fortune in the "Boston States" and then later to Toronto is cliché, but it happened. The Gaelic was left behind.

Today there is a strong current of romanticism running through Nova Scotia's Scottishness. In large part, this is the result of one man's vision. Angus L. Macdonald was premier of Nova Scotia for 16 of the 21 years between 1933 and 1954. While in office, he successfully combined his highly romanticized — albeit sincere and passionate — view of Nova Scotia's highland past with his keen interest in tourism. He set out to make Nova Scotia Scottish. He established Keltic Lodge at Ingonish. He supported Reverend A. W. R. MacKenzie in his efforts to locate a Gaelic College at South Gut St. Anns. He saw the Appalachian region of Cape Breton become the "Cape Breton Highlands." And, by 1951, "Angus L." had installed a piper at the Nova Scotia–New Brunswick border.

Still, much of Nova Scotia's Scottish culture remains vital and real. Gaelic tradition, as embodied in events like the Antigonish Highland Games, has been marketed by the tourism industry, but the young piper with the serious face is not there to entertain tourists. She has come to compete.

HEAVY EVENTS AT THE ANTIGONISH HIGHLAND GAMES

Likewise, the Nova Scotia government has responded to a growing interest in genealogy. But that interest is real. In villages where clan members meet at every corner, genealogy remains a matter of consequence. Cape Bretoners are forever asking, "What's your father's name?" Organizations like the Beaton Institute in Sydney and Highland Roots in Iona welcome queries with enthusiasm.

But the most powerful expression of Scottish culture in Nova Scotia is musical. The Barra MacNeils and Rita MacNeil lead the way; there are many who follow. Cape Breton fiddlers can make your hair stand on end. In their music you will hear something essentially Scottish and genuinely Nova Scotian.

THE GERMANS

In 1713 the Treaty of Utrecht made mainland Nova Scotia a colony of Britain, but it did not make the colony British. Far from it. When the British founded Halifax in 1749, Nova Scotia's principal inhabitants were still the Mi'kmaq and the Acadians. This was seen by the authorities as a situation that needed fixing.

Although Britain seemed the obvious source of colonists, official policy discouraged emigration because it was

OXEN AT THE SOUTH SHORE EXHIBITION, BRIDGEWATER

believed that England was not overpopulated and needed to retain all her farmers and industrial workers. To top it off, Governor Edward Cornwallis found the English settlers he brought out to settle Halifax, many of whom were disbanded soldiers and seamen, were lazy and untrustworthy.

Among those first Halifax settlers were also a number of Swiss and Germans. These people impressed Cornwallis. He wrote to the Lords Commissioners for Trade and Plantation in London, urging them to send some more of the "Foreign Protestants" to Nova Scotia. Cornwallis's request fit neatly with British policy. John Dick, a minor British agent at Rotterdam, was hired to recruit settlers. He and his sub-agent in Frankfurt-on-Main went to work.

In many respects, their job was quite simple. France's Louis XIV made war with a singular zeal, and much of what is now Germany and Switzerland was in disarray. Some people experienced economic hardship, and the war-weary feared impressment. Others were eager to take advantage of land grants. John Dick found many potential recruits among farmers and labourers. The will to emigrate was there; Germans had been settling Pennsylvania for years. Dick's task was to divert some of those who were Pennsylvania-bound to Nova Scotia.

LUNENBURG COUNTY

John Dick was successful in his mission. In the summer of 1750, three shiploads of around 700 "Foreign Protestants" arrived at Halifax aboard the *Ann*. Like most early Nova Scotia settlers, they were disappointed. They were promised cleared land. Instead, they were housed in a garrison. To pay for their passage, they were put to work building roads and strengthening fortifications. And the forts were needed. The French had not given up on Nova Scotia, and the Mi'kmaq were hostile towards the British at Halifax. For nearly three years the settlers were confined to the safety of the garrison, until the Mi'kmaq threat subsided and a suitable area for settlement was found.

Despite these problems, "Foreign Protestants" continued to arrive at Halifax. About 1,000 settlers came in the spring of 1751, and a like number the following year. Today, most Nova Scotians of German or Swiss descent can trace their beginnings in this province to those three years in the middle of the 18th century.

In early June 1753, a small flotilla of boats left Halifax Harbour bound for Merliguesh Bay, the site chosen by the governor for settlement by the German-speaking immigrants. The town was named Lunenburg in honour of King George I (he was the German Elector of Brunswick-Lunëburg). The new settlers, described by their contemporaries as industrious and thrifty, began clearing land immediately. At last they were doing what most had come here to do.

The comfort derived from familiar work was to be short-lived. An uneasy peace with the French and Mi'kmaq began to crumble shortly after the settlers arrived at Lunenburg. By 1755 hostilities were close to full blown. The British decision to expel the Acadians created new enemies for the settlers. Those Acadians who managed to escape deportation fled to the forest, and many allied themselves with the Mi'kmaq.

OLD TOWN, LUNENBURG

In 1756 came the formal declaration of war. In May of that year, Governor Lawrence reported that a party of Indians and Acadians had carried off and scalped some of the inhabitants of Lunenburg. French privateers made the seaward environs of Lunenburg inhospitable. Even after the fall of the French fortress at Louisbourg in 1758, Mi'kmaq raids on the town continued, finally petering out in 1760. In those

43

LITTLE DUTCH CHURCH, HALIFAX

difficult early years, many Lunenburgers must have looked upon the hardships of their homeland with fond nostalgia.

Not all of the new settlers had gone to Lunenburg in 1753. Some of the earlier arrivals who had found ways of making a living, and others who had little interest in farming, stayed on in Halifax. They settled in the north end of the city. Today, the "Little Dutch Church" (the Germans, or Deutsch, became known locally as "Dutch") still stands on Brunswick Street. The church started out as Lutheran and served a German congregation.

In 1761, a group of Germans petitioned for land on the western slope of the Halifax peninsula. Dutch Village Road still runs along what was once a boundary of this "Dutch" village.

Germans and those of German extraction continued to filter into Nova Scotia. Some came from Germany to escape the hardship brought on by the Seven Years War. Several hundred German Pennsylvanians were part of the substantial New England emigration to Nova Scotia in the 1760s. German mercenaries who had fought American independence were rewarded with land. And a number of Loyalist immigrants were also of German descent. Still, Lunenburg was the heart of Nova Scotia's German community.

When peace with the French and Mi'kmaq finally came, that community flourished. Settlement reached to the southwest, where the villages of East and West Berlin are found today. It moved northeast to Mahone Bay and on to the shores of St. Margarets Bay. And it followed the LaHave River inland to Bridgewater and New Germany.

The Lutheran Church was their anchor. In Lunenburg, a congregation was established in 1753, and the first Lutheran Church was completed in 1770. Two years later, the congregation's first minister arrived from Germany.

Today, Lunenburg's is the oldest continually worshipping Lutheran congregation in Canada.

The church drew people together, and services conducted in German helped to preserve the language. Out of the melange of settlers from Germany and the Swiss cantons grew a distinctive dialect, "Lunenburg Dutch."

As early as 1760, Lunenburg Lutherans procured a German schoolmaster. However, he found it impossible to live on his students' fees and accepted a government salary in return for teaching in English in the morning, and in the afternoon in German. Outside the church, assimilation met with little resistance. Still, German could be heard on Lunenburg streets during the Depression, and it lived on as a household language until the end of the Second World War.

Today, those looking for signs of German ethnicity in Lunenburg will find them in the Lutheran church, which remains vital in the town, and in traces of the "Lunenburg Dutch" dialect — the th sound is often pronounced t or d. Some claim that the architectural styles of Lunenburg's older homes, some dating back to the 18th century, reveal German influence, but there is also much of New England in them. Local restaurants serve potato soup, Lunenburg pudding, and sauerkraut — all dishes with German origins — alongside some of Nova Scotia's best seafood cuisine.

Today, clear signs of German ethnicity can be seen elsewhere in the province. Since 1950 a substantial number of German immigrants have come to Nova Scotia. The availability of land has been the main attraction. Along the Northumberland Strait the cost of land is negligible by European standards. Several German families operate successful businesses in this area — a golf course at Brule Point near Tatamagouche and a winery in nearby Malagash, to name a couple. Tatamagouche hosts an Oktoberfest in the last week of September.

Still, German roots run deepest in Lunenburg County. Many families — Eisenors, Publicovers and Whynots, to name a few — have been in Nova Scotia for nearly 250 years.

THE IRISH

THE UNIACKE ESTATE, MOUNT UNIACKE

ST. MARY'S UNIVERSITY, HALIFAX

There has been little to draw attention to the Irish in this province. In Cape Breton and eastern Nova Scotia, a significant Catholic Irish presence goes unnoticed amid the skirl of the pipes and the ubiquitous Scottish tartans. The Protestant Irish or "Ulster Scots" who came to the area along the Bay of Fundy's Minas Basin are often overlooked — this is where the Acadian tragedy was played out. And in the larger centres, especially Halifax and Sydney, a substantial Irish population has taken on the character of the population at large. The Irish are here, but you have to look to find them.

They were among the first arrivals to Nova Scotia. Irish stonemasons and soldiers were at the French Fortress of Louisbourg on Ile-Royale (Cape Breton Island). The Newfoundland fishery brought others. The merchants of southeastern Ireland got involved in a rich provisions trade to supply the Newfoundland fishery. With cargoes of salt beef and salt pork came scores of young Irishmen to work as seasonal labourers in the cod fishery. Some of these eventually made their way to Halifax; others came to the smaller settlements along the Eastern Shore and on Ile-Royale. As trade expanded in the Gulf of St. Lawrence region, more and more people came directly to Nova Scotia from southeastern Ireland. Like Newfoundland, most of Nova Scotia's Irish come from Waterford and its environs.

Most, but not all. A significant Protestant Irish community can be found

along the Minas Basin. Colonel Alexander MacNutt, an adventurer from Londonderry, New Hampshire, got wind of Governor Lawrence's proclamation inviting the resettlement of Acadian lands by subjects loyal to the Crown. In 1760 authorities promised the Colonel a large grant of land in exchange for settling Irish Protestants in Nova Scotia. He arranged for an advertisement to be placed in the *Belfast Newsletter* and, in 1761, about 300 Irish Protestants, mostly from Donegal and Derry, were sent over. The following year another 70 arrived. MacNutt's grand schemes were halted, but not before a sizeable community of Ulstermen had been established.

FROM A C.W. JEFFREYS DRAWING OF CONDITIONS ON SHIPS CARRYING IRISH IMMIGRANTS TO CANADA

These Protestant Irish who took up lands in Onslow, Londonderry, Truro, Windsor, and Horton (and, eventually, in Stewiacke and Economy) were joined by people with Ulster origins from New Hampshire.

There was little to distinguish them from their lowland Scottish neighbours, with whom they shared strong ties of kinship and the Presbyterian faith. Any lingering sense of Irishness was quickly lost.

To an extent, the same was true of the Halifax Irish. Many worked as servants or labourers, but there were Irish at all levels of Halifax society. By 1782, a hard-drinking Irish Protestant, John Parr (whose drunken swagger earned him the nickname "Cock-Robin") was governor. In 1783, Richard Uniacke, another Irish Protestant and long-time champion of Catholic emancipation, succeeded in pushing a bill through the Assembly that removed the disabilities imposed by the British authorities 15 years earlier.

Irish Protestants, including several powerful merchants, were in the ascendancy, and many saw fit to have their Catholic countrymen join them there. Uniacke founded the Charitable Irish Society in 1786 to promote charitable endeavours and to encourage fellowship among its members, both Catholic and Protestant.

UNIACKE HOUSE, MOUNT UNIACKE

Dissonance gradually intruded on this harmony. Loyalist settlers brought with them a profound distrust of Catholics; the papists had shown their true colours during the Revolutionary War. The Irish uprising in 1798 confirmed suspicions — as if confirmation was required. Still, the Catholic Irish of Halifax seemed quiescent enough, and their number certainly posed no threat.

This was about to change. Following the Napoleonic Wars, there was a surge in Irish immigration to Nova Scotia. Again, most of these new arrivals were from southeastern Ireland, many via Newfoundland. The vast majority were Catholic, and their principal destination was Halifax.

An emerging Irish Catholic community made strides that provoked unease in certain Protestant quarters. In 1802 St.

Mary's Seminary, which would become St. Mary's University, was founded in order to meet the increasing demand for priests. By 1829 Catholics were allowed to sit in the Legislature. The first Irish Catholic, Lawrence O'Connor Doyle, was called to the Nova Scotia Bar in the same year.

Lawrence Doyle led a vigorous Halifax faction which supported Daniel O'Connell and the Irish nationalist struggle against the 1801 Act of Union. He also embraced Joseph Howe's fight for Responsible Government in Nova Scotia. That made Howe uneasy; he was certainly no Repealer. The shaky alliance of Repealers and Reformers in Nova Scotia's Liberal Party achieved Responsible Government in 1848, but there were charges that the Catholic Church controlled Doyle (his supporters included many clergy) and directed Nova Scotia's affairs.

For one of the few times in its history, Nova Scotia's Irish community was conspicuous, and on its way to becoming notorious. In 1855 Howe attempted to recruit soldiers, including a number of American Irish, to fight in the Crimean War. This violated American neutrality, and some of the recruits who arrived in Halifax complained to William Condon, president of the Charitable Irish Society, that they had been deceived by Howe into thinking that they were coming to work on the railroad. Condon raised the alarm; Howe abandoned the enlistment. He also vented some considerable spleen at the Irish Catholics.

Two years later, weary of Howe's condemnation, several members crossed the floor of the Legislature and helped to defeat the government on a vote of non-confidence. Howe was furious. The 1859 election was fought largely along Protestant-Catholic lines. When Howe was returned to power, the Halifax *Morning Chronicle* proclaimed "Protestant Nova Scotia is Free."

That freedom seemed threatened again by the American Fenians during the 1860s. They wanted Britain out of Ireland and were prepared to attack British North America to show they were in earnest. The force they dispatched to take care of Nova Scotia consisted of three imaginary battleships bound for Halifax and a rowboat in Yarmouth Harbour, manned by some local men who fought off boredom with a few shots from a rusty cannon. The threat passed and suspicions of Nova Scotia's Irish gradually faded, along with their sense of Irishness.

Recently, interest in the Irish component of Nova Scotian society has been renewed. Halifax's St. Mary's University has established a chair in Irish Studies. Fears that the Charitable Irish Society, which celebrated its 200th anniversary in 1986, had become anachronistic and lacked authenticity led to the formation of the Irish Association of Nova Scotia (*An Cumann*) in 1990. Enthusiasts now scour Nova Scotia's history in search of Irishness.

ST. MARY'S BASILICA, HALIFAX

GENEALOGY

BY AL KINGSBURY AND TERRENCE M. PUNCH

Nova Scotia was home to Canada's first French settlement four centuries ago, and several waves of people — English, Blacks, Scots, Germans, Irish and Dutch — have followed, so it's not surprising that many descendants of those immigrants are being drawn to the province each year in search of their family roots. Residents, too, have developed a keen interest in genealogy, and have put extensive efforts into compiling, preserving and cataloguing data. As a result, there are many sources of research available to people trying to trace their roots that can be used both before and during a visit to the province.

Details critical to finding family links are name, place and date (within two to three years) of births, deaths and marriages. If a place within Nova Scotia is not known, religion or ethnicity might help to localize a family. *In Which County? Nova Scotia Surnames from Birth Registers; 1864 to 1877*, by Terrence M. Punch, gives the distribution of 5,000 surnames. And before you do too much work, you should check Allan E. Marble's *A Catalogue of Published Genealogies of Nova Scotia Families*. Perhaps your family has been done before, and you will need only to update the published information to your branch of the family tree.

In Nova Scotia, no government records of births and deaths were kept prior to 1864. In a few areas, township books help, and an incomplete set of marriage licences exists that goes back to 1763. Otherwise, church registers, newspaper notices or headstone data must be used. Government records prior to 1908 can be viewed at the Public Archives of Nova Scotia. Records after that date are available through the provincial Deputy Registrar-General, who should first be contacted regarding fees and other details.

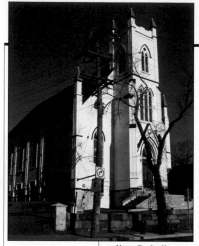

Church records can be an invaluable resource for genealogical research, and many of these are available in Nova Scotia. Members of the Church of Jesus Christ of Latter Day Saints (Mormon) microfilmed many church records, and these are accessible through their world-wide library system. The Nova Scotia Archives and Records Management (NSARM) has many pre-1908 church registers, especially Anglican, Methodist and Presbyterian ones, and other records are in church repositories or in local custody. Typically, registers open in the 1800s, although some start decades earlier. Catholic records of the French era (pre-1755) are best explored through the Centre d'Etudes Acadiennes at New Brunswick's Université de Moncton.

Many headstone inscriptions have been transcribed, and the results are often available at NSARM or with local historical or genealogical societies. Most surviving inscriptions date from after 1840, and these are particularly useful for deaths in the 1875-1950 period. Death and marriage notices in newspapers favoured anglophones, the prominent and the Protestant until about 1850, when coverage grew increasingly general. The NSARM has microfilm of most old newspapers, and data from the Halifax press (1769-1854) has been published by the Genealogical Association of Nova Scotia. Other information available at the archives includes census data, poll tax records, land grants and deeds, and probate records

Township books were kept in areas settled by New Englanders in western Nova Scotia. These generally covered births, marriages and deaths from the 1760s to the 1820s. They often recorded only those families having shares in the township, neglecting minorities, transient families and immigrants.

The major repository in the province is NSARM on University Avenue in Halifax. It is closed to the public on Sundays and public holidays, and Saturdays on holiday weekends, so Americans should note that three Canadian holidays differ from their own: Victoria Day (the first Monday before May 25); Canada Day (July 1); and Thanksgiving (the second Monday in October).

The provincial organization for family history is the Genealogical Association of Nova Scotia. It publishes *The Nova Scotia Genealogist*, an annual list of members' interests, readers' queries, book reviews, interesting short articles and other useful information.

Other active organizations that can be of help to anyone researching their family roots can be founding in the Listings section at the end of this book. Further particulars of existing records and where to find them can be obtained by consulting two standard works about the subject by Terrence M. Punch: *Genealogist's Handbook for Atlantic Canada Research* and *Genealogical Research in Nova Scotia*. They are available at the archives and at many local libraries.

FEATURES

THE 1917 EXPLOSION

BY ALAN RUFFMAN

THE EXPLOSION CLOUD

Down side streets, inside churches, in parts of Halifax and Dartmouth less travelled by visitors, lie pieces of the story of the 1917 Explosion. This horrendous event flattened the north ends of both cities towards the end of the First World War. Along the busy wharves, troops and supplies were sent off and welcomed home. The deep-water port received hundreds of vessels and held them in the security of the Bedford Basin until convoys could be formed to brave the Atlantic. It was with two such vessels in transit that things went so dreadfully wrong on that Thursday morning of December 6, 1917.

The *Mont Blanc*, a French vessel en route from New York to Bordeaux, was headed for the Basin to await a convoy. It was loaded with 2.924 kilotons of highly explosive gun cotton, picric acid, TNT, and benzol. The *Imo*, a Norwegian ship transporting Belgian relief supplies, was outbound from the Basin, in ballast, departing for New York to load a new cargo. The two vessels met in the Narrows of Halifax Harbour, where the channel constricts before opening up into the Basin. As you cross one of the two Halifax-Dartmouth bridges, look down at the area between them. This is where the ships collided, just before 8:45 on a cold, clear, winter's morning.

Later appeals to the Supreme Court of Canada and to the Privy Council in London, England, found both vessels equally to blame. The *Imo* was travelling too quickly and was far too close to the Dartmouth shore, leaving little room for the *Mont Blanc* to properly pass on the Dartmouth side of the channel. At the last moment, as the two vessels approached each other, the *Mont Blanc* turned towards the Halifax shore and cut across the bow of the *Imo*. The collision was inevitable.

As collisions go, it was not serious and would have gone unnoticed but for the fire that started on the *Mont Blanc*. It burned with increasing ferocity in the deck cargo — barrels of benzol. The abandoned vessel slowly drifted over to the Halifax shore. Moments after it nosed into the bank, right at the foot of Richmond Street, at 4 minutes and 35 seconds after 9:00 a.m., the *Mont Blanc* erupted ... and vanished. It was one of the greatest human-caused explosions the world had known — or would know — until the atomic bombs of the Second World War.

With supersonic speed, the shock front expanded and sheared the side hill of Fort Needham clean. More than 2,000 people — 5 percent of the urban population — died in an instant. Over ten square kilometres (2 sq. mi.) of Halifax was laid waste. An unchecked firestorm erupted in the ruins, and for a brief few minutes harbourfront wharves and streets on both sides of the Narrows were swept by an 18-metre (59-ft.) tsunami, or tidal wave, as the sea was thrown onto the land. Infrasound from the explosion was heard up to 400 kilometres (250 mi.) away, in northern Cape Breton Island, Yarmouth, Saint John, and the Miramichi area of New Brunswick.

Halifax and Dartmouth spent years recovering from the 1917 Explosion, and most signs of it are long since built over. An exploration of this event begins at the Maritime Museum of the Atlantic on Lower Water Street, on the Halifax waterfront. Here a permanent exhibit, "A Moment in Time," includes panoramic photographs of the devastation. Details published to assist in the identification of bodies evoke the personal dimension of the tragedy. Here is one example: "No. 456(a) -Male-about 50 years. – gray hair. Sandy moustache. Brown sweater. Gray woolen socks. New tan laced boots. One brown string tie." And the contents of mortuary bags give glimpses of people's lives at the instant of death.

In the North End, north of Young Street, are the pleasant boulevarded streets of the Hydrostone district. The Hydrostone development was the flagship reconstruction effort of the Halifax Relief Commission. It was a fortunate union of the talents of Thomas Adams, famous town planner of the Garden City Movement, and Montreal architect George Ross. Then at the forefront of urban design, The Hydrostone has stood the test of time and remains an attractive residential area.

WATERCOLOUR OF EXPLOSION VICTIMS BY ARTHUR LISMER

EXPLOSION DAMAGE

Nearby is Fort Needham, a large hill where the Halifax Explosion Memorial Bell Tower can be found. Turn down Needham Street (off Young) and enter the park on foot, heading north. If you turn hard left and climb the gentle grassy slope, you will find, hidden in a quiet part of the park, the Relief Commission's memorial cairn and plaque. Just to the north is the large angular Bell Tower, unveiled June 9, 1985. A brief memorial service is held each December 6, at the same moment the Explosion occurred.

A side trip to the head of the Northwest Arm will take you to another site that dramatically illustrates the force of the explosion. After circling around the Armdale Rotary, take the Herring Cove exit, then turn left at the traffic lights onto Purcells Cove Road. Then turn directly left onto Spinnaker Drive. At the end of the road, in a very dense development, is a small park by the shore. Here, mounted as if in flight, is the 517-kilogram (1,140-lb.) anchor shaft of the *Mont Blanc*. This missile flew some 3.8 kilometres (2.4 mi.), to bury itself deeply into the Edmonds Grounds.

ST. PAUL'S ANGLICAN CHURCH, WHERE A PIECE OF THE MONT BLANC STILL PIERCES THE WALL (TOP RIGHT OF PHOTO)

The 1917 Explosion also left its mark in scientific and literary spheres. It was to become a case study for physicist George Reynolds of the Manhattan Project in Los Alamos, as he calculated the theoretical Mach Stem Effect. These calculations helped the designers of the atomic bomb determine at what height the bomb should be detonated over Hiroshima to create the most damage. And for the ten-year-old Hugh MacLennan, the experience of the Explosion became a seed for his first published novel, *Barometer Rising*. This work established his career as one of Canada's most famous writers and continues to be recommended reading for anyone wanting to learn more about the impact of this disaster. Other readings include *Burden of Desire*, a steamy novel by ex-Haligonian Robert MacNeil, of PBS's *MacNeil Lehrer Report*. Michael Bird's popular historical account, *The Town That Died*, is quite readable, and Harry Chapman's *Dartmouth's Day of Anguish* was the first to focus on Dartmouth's experience. Janet Kitz's recent *Shattered City* and *Survivors* details the human side of the tragedy and should be available at local bookstores. On the 75th anniversary of the Explosion, St. Mary's University's Gorsebrook Institute for Atlantic Canada Studies sponsored a major multi-disciplinary conference on the 1917 Explosion, and the 30 papers in the proceedings, *Ground Zero*, add a whole new dimension to the event.

CULTURE

BY RON FOLEY MACDONALD

ART GALLERY OF NOVA SCOTIA, HALIFAX

Nova Scotians have long reconciled themselves to being on the margins of North America. It has come as something as a shock, however, to see the province creep into the limelight over the last few years. Most areas of the province's own indigenous arts scene are healthier than they've ever been. A boom in film and television has firmly established Nova Scotia as North America's fastest growing production centre. Halifax has surprised itself by becoming the anchor of an industry that has splashed the province across movie and television screens around the world in such shows as *Black Harbour*, *This Hour Has 22 Minutes*, *Theodore Tugboat*, *FoodEssence* and *Street Cents*. What's unexpected about this film and TV boom is the level of local production. Nova Scotian stories figure prominently, from Antigonish writer Sheldon Currie's earthy and surreal Cape Breton coal mining tales that formed the basis for *Margaret's Museum* to the deft semi-autobiographical family memoir of Thom Fitzgerald's award-winning *The Hanging Garden*. For a small province, Nova Scotia has grabbed an inordinately large slice of the Canadian film pie.

A FILM SHOOT IN HALIFAX

With just less than a million people, however, Nova Scotia can

PAINTING BY JOY
LAKING, BASS RIVER

offer culture on a human scale. A genuine folk culture still lingers, particularly in the Cape Breton fiddling tradition and the province-wide practice of colourful, slightly absurdist folk art. The attention and acclaim given to living artists and sculptors like the Naugler Brothers of Camperdown, just outside of Bridgewater, so justly celebrated at the Lunenburg County Folk Art Festival held every August, seems to offer something of a tempest in a teapot compared to the nation-wide tide that is sweeping the late Maud Lewis to folk art supremacy.

Lewis, with her bold, joyful, and bright pictures of oxen, kittens, and Digby County land-and-sea-scapes comes closer than any other artist to defining the elusive nature of Nova Scotia's soul.

If Maud Lewis's work captured Nova Scotia perfectly in a gentle mid-century rural mindset, the present and future are well represented by thriving galleries like Houston North in Lunenburg, Lyghtesome Gallery in Antigonish, and Studio 21 in Halifax. Many of the artists represented or on display are graduates of The Nova Scotia College of Art and Design, which distinguished itself in the '70's and '80's as an internationally recognized outpost of the *avant-garde*. Theatre has grown by leaps and bounds in Nova Scotia, reaping the benefit of a culture that still puts much value on the spoken word. At the top end is The Atlantic Theatre Festival (ATF) in Wolfville which has seen classic drama recreated in a 500-seat, marvelously converted hockey rink. The ATF serves up Shakespeare, Wilde, Chekov, Ibsen and the like from June to September.

Halifax's Neptune Theatre re-opened in the fall of 1997 with a new complex that includes a studio and an improved backstage. Theatre is also alive and well in smaller communities, as the performances of Ship's Company Theatre in Parrsboro, King's Theatre in Annapolis Royal, and Tantramar Theatre in Amherst all will attest. Other small companies like Dartmouth's Eastern Front Theatre, Guysborough County's Mulgrave Road Co-op Theatre, the Annapolis Valley's Two Planks and a Passion Theatre, and Windsor's modern puppet Mermaid Theatre regularly tour the province with social theatre that deals with many of the current issues affecting Nova

EASTERN FRONT
THEATRE

HALIFAX'S NEW
NEPTUNE THEATRE

Scotians. Other companies provide lighter, but still substantial, fare.

Halifax's Shakespeare By The Sea has blazed an extraordinary trail over the last few summer seasons, with open-air renditions of the Bard's works tailored specifically to the forts and ruins in Point Pleasant Park.

The close relationship among the sea, the land and the people of Nova Scotia provides a continuous context that constantly re-frames, reminds and subdues ambitions that run rampant elsewhere. Visually, the most obvious expression of this feeling can be seen in the tradition of realist painters like Alex Colville, Tom Forrestall, and Ken Tolmie. The starkness of their images indicates a quiet, but restless, accommodation with an all-pervasive sense of mystery.

That mystery has found another powerful outlet for expression in Nova Scotia's music. Two streams, one drawing from the ancient traditions of the province's early Scottish settlers, the other reflecting the cool, distant combination of slacker pop and ironic know-it-all-ism that is the hallmark of the alternative music scene, exist happily side by side. Occasionally some artists like ace fiddler Ashley MacIsaac or Gaelic singer Mary Jane Lamond will bridge the gap between the two solitudes, creating a sound that is utterly original and totally unforgettable.

SHAKESPEARE BY THE SEA

In literature, Nova Scotia boasts novelists such as Thomas Raddall, Ernest Buckler and Hugh MacLennan earlier this century. In non-fiction, Nova Scotia has produced one of the world's great folklorists in Helen Creighton. Her collections of folksongs, and folk tales have helped define the province's image of itself as a dreamy, pastoral, and mostly rural retreat that has resisted many of the encroachments of modern society. She has even inspired a reactive movement in the academic world: Ian McKay's *The Quest of the Folk* points to Creighton's role in the creation of Nova Scotia as a tourist destination by playing up the "simplicity" and "quaintness" of its people.

ASHLEY MACISAAC

It's a lively and vigorous debate that is mirrored in the vitality of Nova Scotia's contemporary literary scene. Led by extraordinary nature writers like Harold Horwood and Harry Thurston, Nova Scotia writers often match a mystic naturalism with a rigourous magic realism. Prose writers like Lesley Choyce and playwrights like Bryden MacDonald all deal heavily with non-realistic elements that approach a rural or small-town surrealism.

FESTIVAL ACADIEN, CLARE

On a more direct level, Nova Scotia has seen an explosion of small publications delving into local history and contemporary situations. Everything from hiking guides and pictorial catalogues of waterfalls to working-class oral histories are available, and these are just some of some of the many books emerging from across the province.

Festivals have become a great way to sample Nova Scotia culture in its own element. The Atlantic Film Festival in late September every year, the new Celtic Colours International Music Festival in Cape Breton held in October, the Bear River Music Festival, also in October, the Halifax-On-Music Alternative Music Festival in mid-fall, and The Annapolis Royal Arts Festival in early September all have developed prominent profiles. And with increased profile comes popularity; booking early has become a must.

Recent years have also seen a welcome of minority cultures. African Nova Scotians can boast of the only provincially dedicated Black Cultural Centre in Canada. With extraordinary young artists like poet and dramatist George Elliott Clarke, historian and filmmaker Sylvia Hamilton, poet Maxine Tynes, and musicians like the fluid and powerful vocal group Four The Moment, the African Nova Scotian community has raised its own powerful voice while renewing links to African-American and African cultures. Nova Scotia's Acadian culture has also experienced a surge of pride and activity, with musicians like Ron Bourgeois and documentarian Monique LeBlanc. There has also been a brighter spotlight of late on Mi'kmaq culture. The Mi'kmaq First Nation has always been distinguished by its gentleness, compassion, generosity, and family. Led by poet and elder Rita Joe, Mi'kmaq musicians, elders and spiritual leaders have become familiar sights at public functions and ceremonies.

The cultural sector has been recognized by the provincial government as a promising areas of growth. While cultural spending has fallen in most federal and provincial jurisdictions in the last few years, it has increased in Nova Scotia. A long time coming, perhaps, but this is a province that has finally come round to realizing its greatest strengths — the genuineness of its people and the strength of its traditions.

RECREATION

SALTWATER SWIMMING

In a province that has 7,000 kilometres (4,350 mi.) of coastline, you would expect to find beaches. And indeed, there are beautiful beaches throughout Nova Scotia. Along the eastern, southern, and Fundy shores long, sandy beaches invite a solitary stroll by the sea or a family afternoon of sand-castle building. But to suit most swimmers, these waters could use a little more Gulf Stream and a little less Labrador Current. At Lawrencetown Beach, just east of Dartmouth, waves are often large enough to attract local surfers, but most wear wetsuits.

Paradoxically, Nova Scotia's warmest water laps its northern shores. The Northumberland Strait is fairly sheltered, and at Caribou, Heather, Melmerby, and Pomquet you'll discover fine beaches perfect for family outings. In Cape Breton, the water at Inverness and Port Hood is also quite pleasant. At Ingonish, along the northern section of the Cabot Trail, is one of the province's most spectacular beaches. Keltic Lodge and  the opening and closing holes of the world-class Highlands Links Golf Course are perched on a dramatic bluff that overlooks the beach. You cannot get much farther north in Nova Scotia, yet the water here is surprisingly warm.

KAYAKING, CANOEING, AND RAFTING

Sea-kayaking has become very popular in recent years. Three publications by Scott Cunningham, *The South Shore/ The Bay of Fundy*, *The Eastern Shore* and *Cape Breton Island/The North Shore* describe coastal routes and include maps and chart references. The Eastern Shore, with its

rugged, undeveloped coastline is the choice of many kayakers. At Tangier, Cunningham runs Coastal Adventures, a reputable outfitter that offers rentals, clinics, and extended trips.

KEJIMKUJIK NATIONAL PARK

Nova Scotia's many inland waterways attract canoeists and kayakers. *Canoe Routes of Nova Scotia*, a joint publication of Canoe Nova Scotia and the Camping Association of Nova Scotia, describes 70 canoeing areas throughout the province. The Liscomb, St. Mary's, and Musquodoboit rivers, together with the Eastern Shore Lake System, make that part of the province a popular destination for inland as well as coastal paddlers. The Shubenacadie Canal and River System attracts many recreational canoeists, and the annual Canoe to the Sea race is held here each June.

Kejimkujik National Park is a 381-square-kilometre (147-sq.-mi.) wilderness area traversed by an extensive network of inland waterways. Some of these are ideal for an afternoon paddle with the family; others offer serious canoeists a challenge along back-country routes to primitive campsites. Look for white-tail deer, porcupine, loons, owls, and beaver on the way.

Four companies, Tidal Bore & Up-River Rafting, Shubenacadie River Runners, Tidal Bore Rafting and Adventure Quest Expeditions Inc., take advantage of the special effect produced by surging Fundy waters in the tidal section of the Shubenacadie River. Those interested in a wet and wild ride should plan to arrive at the peak of the monthly tidal cycle; at other times, the tidal bore is just a ripple. Numerous bald eagles nest in this area.

SURFER AT LAWRENCETOWN BEACH

FISHING

Several outfits in the province provide scheduled departures or private charters for those interested in saltwater sport fishing. A number of boats make daily trips from Cable Wharf in Halifax. Catches range from bottom fish to shark and other exotic species. Before booking your spot, find out what you will be likely to catch, and if possible, talk to someone who has been out on the boat you are considering.

Freshwater enthusiasts can exercise more independence. Brook trout can be caught in most Nova Scotian lakes and streams, and brown trout, introduced in 1923, are now found in several rivers. Perch, shad, and smallmouth bass are other popular catches. Licenses are required but are easily obtained from any office of the Department of

FISHING ST. MARYS
RIVER

Natural Resources or from many sporting goods and other retail stores. Some restrictions such as bag limits attach to these licenses, so be sure to make inquiries.

For purists, there is fly-fishing for salmon on one of Nova Scotia's scheduled rivers. Two of the best are the St. Marys on the Eastern Shore, and the Margaree in northeastern Cape Breton. If you choose the St. Marys, try a meal of planked salmon, a traditional Mi'kmaq delicacy and a specialty of the provincially run Liscombe Lodge. In Northeast Margaree, stop by the wonderful little museum operated by the Margaree Anglers Association.

BIRDS AND BEASTS

Nova Scotia is an important staging point along the Atlantic flyway for many species of migratory birds. Shorebirds — sandpipers, plovers, and willets — make stopovers along the nutrient-rich Minas shores during their southern migration. Each September, Evangeline Beach near Grand Pré hosts thousands. Migratory raptors gather at Brier Island (also a prime location for whale-watching) on the southern tip of Digby Neck.

More than 250 nesting pairs of bald eagles make their home in the province, and they are most visible during July and August. Eagles are commonly sighted along the banks of the Shubenacadie River and in northeastern Cape Breton.

The Van Schaiks — Joe, Mary, and Vince — have been operating Bird Island Boat Tours for over 20 years. The Bird Islands, Hertford and Ciboux, lie just off Cape Dauphin, near Big Bras d'Or, in Cape Breton. You may well spot bald eagles during the two-and-a-half-hour cruise, but the main attractions are the puffins, razorbills, guillemots, kittiwakes, and cormorants that nest in the sheer cliffs. All are visible during the summer months.

You'll also find some birding oddities in the province. In Wolfville and Middleton, chimney swifts gather at dusk for a startlingly acrobatic descent down chimneys. When the Harvey Veinot Causeway was built near Pictou, the pilings of the former causeway were left standing. Many visitors now do double takes as they drive into Pictou, for these pilings have become a rookery for great and double-breasted cormorants.

Some ocean tours afford wonderful opportunities to combine birding with whale-watching. Brier Island Whale and Seabird Cruises operates from Westport. It takes two short ferry trips to get there from Digby, but your troubles are usually rewarded. The mouth of the Fundy is a favourite feeding ground for several species of

A BREACHING
WHALE – AN
UNFORGETTABLE SITE

LOOKING FOR FOSSILS NEAR JOGGINS

whales. The late summer and fall are prime times for spotting harbour porpoises, whitesided dolphins, minkes, finbacks, and humpbacks, with less frequent sightings of right, pilot, beluga, and sperm whales. The whales usually cooperate, but not always the weather. Dense fog or high winds can cancel trips, although rainchecks are given for cancellations and for trips where no whales are spotted.

Several whale-watching cruises operate at the opposite end of the province. At Dingwall, just north of Cape Breton Highlands National Park, Nelson Morrison's Aspy Bay Tours offers a unique blend of whale-watching and storytelling. Morrison is a retired lobster fisherman whose father was a lighthouse keeper on St. Paul's Island, a notorious graveyard for shipping. The variety of whales — mostly minke and pilot — is not as great as in the Fundy, nor is the frequency of sightings, but few people seem to mind. Morrison keeps them entertained.

HIKING AND CYCLING

The province offers abundant opportunities for hiking. The Canadian Hostelling Association's *Hiking Trails of Nova Scotia* is a useful resource. Many of the 127 provincial parks have hiking trails, but the two national parks, Cape Breton Highlands and Kejimkujik, are the top attractions.

The 28 marked and serviced hiking trails in Cape Breton Highlands National Park are described in "Walking in the Highlands," a short guide put out by Parks Canada. Trails range from easy 20-minute walks to tough overnight treks. The scenery is spectacular. Kejimkujik is tamer than its Cape Breton counterpart. Most trails wind gently through thick forest. A network of lakes and rivers offers hikers the chance to combine walking with paddling. Serviced campgrounds are available in both national parks.

Another rewarding trail takes hikers to the end of Cape Split — the continuation of the Blomidon Peninsula that extends far out into the Minas Basin. The 13-kilometre (8-mi.) round-trip trail was originally cut by sheep that were left to graze on the peninsula. Along the way are spectacular cliffside views of the Fundy. Little Split, at the end of the cape, offers the only safe access to the shore.

More and more visitors are exploring Nova Scotia on bicycles. Throughout the summer months, tours are organized from Dartmouth and Halifax, and by a number of outfitters along the Cabot Trail. Bicycle Nova Scotia's Touring Committee has published a short guide, *Bicycle Tours in Nova Scotia*, to 20 of the province's most popular routes. Cyclists should be aware that the terrain can be difficult — especially along the Cabot Trail — and that the weather is highly changeable.

GOLF

There are a number of fine golf courses in the province. Between Digby and Falmouth in the Annapolis Valley are six 18-hole and three 9-hole courses. These are well maintained — a job made easier by the sunny Valley summers. The Pines Golf Club in Digby, one of two courses designed by Canadian architect Stanley Thompson, is the best course in the Valley region and plays through fragrant stands of pine and spruce. Green fees are reasonable and the Digby Pines Resort provides luxury accommodation.

Nova Scotia's North Shore is also favoured with warm, sunny summers. The Northumberland Sea Shore Golf Links at Pugwash, the Abercrombie Country Club near New Glasgow, and the Antigonish Golf Club are good bets. The Pugwash course is slightly more challenging and usually less crowded than the other two. Nine-hole courses at Pictou and Brule offer a fun round of golf with pretty views of the Northumberland Strait.

The 18-hole Osprey course at Bridgewater is one of eight golf clubs in the area. The only other one with 18 holes is the one at Chester, with its short, tight fairways. The 9-hole Bluenose Golf & Country Club in Lunenburg is worth playing for the view alone. The course rises steeply from the harbour across from Lunenburg, and the view of the town from the fairways will make you forget about golf.

NORTHUMBERLAND SEA SHORE GOLF LINKS, NEAR PUGWASH (BOTTOM)

The Halifax metropolitan area is well served. Still, several courses have restrictions on green-fee play and are often crowded, especially on weekends. Many metro area residents prefer to golf in the Annapolis Valley where the courses are less crowded and less "clubby."

Stanley Thompson's other course, and Nova Scotia's best, is the Highlands Links in Cape Breton Highlands National Park. Beginning on the spectacular Middle Head Peninsula, the course moves inland to the Highlands, providing a links experience that *Pocket Pro*, the Canadian Tour's guide, describes as "the closest thing to Scottish golf in the New World." The views are spectacular — especially from the 5th and 16th greens. Like George Knudson, one of Canada's most successful golfers, you might want to leave the clubs behind and just walk the course — it's that beautiful. The Ingonish area offers a wide range of accommodation, including the gracious Keltic Lodge Resort.

FESTIVALS AND EVENTS

ANTIGONISH HIGHLAND GAMES

SCOTTISH FESTIVALS

It has been said that parts of Cape Breton Island are more Scottish than Scotland itself. Of course, what is meant by Scottish is the Scotland that began to fade with the defeat of Bonnie Prince Charlie at Culloden in 1746 — a land of bagpipes, clan gatherings, and Gaelic.

Each August, the Gaelic College at South Gut St. Anns in Cape Breton holds a Gaelic Mod, a weekend of Gaelic language and song.

Halifax also holds a Scottish festival, and New Glasgow hosts the Festival of the Tartans, but the Antigonish Highland Games, held each July, are the best bet. These are the oldest Highland games still being held in North America. Modern track and field events are interspersed with the traditional heavy events like the caber toss. There is serious competition between young pipers and dancers. The games are not just a pageant for tourists.

Music is the most vital expression of Scottish culture in Nova Scotia. Each July, a week-long festival is held at Big Pond, home of Cape Breton singer Rita MacNeil. But the real hotbed of music in Cape Breton is Inverness County, along the southwestern shore. The Rankin Family is from here. So is John Allan Cameron. The area produces a steady stream of talented fiddlers, much in evidence at events like Judique-on-the-Floor Days or the Mabou Ceilidh, both held in July. During the summer, you could drop in on a number of concerts in the Mabou-Inverness area.

Finally, for those of Scottish descent, many Nova Scotia communities hold clan gatherings during the summer months. A Nova Scotia Visitor Information Centre can help you find out if your family is represented.

ACADIAN FESTIVALS

Several communities, including Halifax, Wedgeport and Tusket (near Yarmouth), the Municipality of Clare, Grand Pré, and Cheticamp, hold Acadian festivals during the summer months. With the exception of Cheticamp (situated along the Cabot Trail), most Acadian settlements lie outside the tourist loop. As a result, Acadian festivals tend to be community celebrations rather than tourist attractions. The Festival Acadien de Clare, for example, includes card games, dances, an ox-haul, a fishing tournament, and a smorgasbord of other community-based activities. This festival, held in early July, and the Festival de l'Escaouette held in Cheticamp later in the summer, are the most interesting of the Acadian celebrations. If you are in either area, visit the beautiful churches that anchor these communities.

ACADIAN DAYS AT GRAND PRÉ

OTHER COMMUNITY-BASED FESTIVALS

Many local festivals are celebrations of traditional activities like farming, logging, and fishing.

The Annapolis Valley's Apple Blossom Festival is held in late May, and the Bear River Cherry Carnival in July. Agricultural exhibitions take place throughout the summer months. Three of the largest are at Bridgewater (late July or early August), Truro (late August), and Windsor (mid-September).

APPLE BLOSSOMS

In an area renowned for its seafaring tradition, the agricultural South Shore Exhibition in Bridgewater seems an oddity. It is not. The Germans who settled the area in the 1750s were farmers before they became fishermen. The ox pulls are the main attraction at the "Big Ex." Teams of oxen pull three times their weight.

At Canso, the musical legacy of one of Canada's legendary folksinger/songwriters is celebrated in July at the Stan Rogers Folk Festival.

The fishery is the focus for many other community events across the province. The Pictou Lobster Carnival is held in early July. Digby Scallop Days follow in August.

Later that month, Lunenburg hosts the Nova Scotia Fisheries Exhibition and Fishermen's Reunion. A number of fishermen's competitions take place at these festivals, including net mending, wire splicing, fish filleting, and scallop shucking.

SEASIDE FESTIVALS

Lunenburg holds its Folk Harbour Festival each August, featuring North America's top folk performers. Held here around the same time is the Nova Scotia Folk Art Festival.

Each August, Chester Race Week is the excuse for Haligonian yachtsmen to hobnob with their American counterparts. At nearby Mahone Bay, a flourishing craft community takes advantage of the influx of visitors during the annual Wooden Boat Festival (late July/early August). The boats themselves are far from rough hewn; they are floating works of art. Mahone Bay is one of Nova Scotia's prettiest harbours, and the Sunday afternoon sail-past and salute is the highlight of the festival.

Baddeck is Cape Breton's answer to Chester and Mahone Bay. Many Americans spend their summers sailing Bras d'Or Lake, a picturesque inland sea. The area attracts prominent artists as well. Baddeck hosts a handcraft festival in mid-September. In recent years, the village has become a market town for Cape Breton folk artists. The annual regatta (early August) is fast approaching its centenary.

At the other end of the province, Annapolis Royal holds regattas on the July and August long weekends to go along with a host of other outstanding attractions.

SUMMER THEATRE

Many of these same seaside communities also stage live performances during the summer months. In Lunenburg, the magnificent 1907 Opera House has undergone restoration and is being revived as a venue for live theatre.

At the Chester Playhouse, the Chester Theatre Festival runs from early July to late August. Drama, dance, music, and visual arts are featured in the program. At Annapolis Royal, the King's Summer Theatre Festival offers live performances throughout July and August.

Inaugurated in 1995, the Atlantic Theatre Festival in Wolfville offers classic performances in a beautiful, 500-seat, thrust-stage theatre.

Several other communities put on summer theatre. Festival Antigonish stages performances at the Bauer Theatre and the university auditorium on the St. Francis Xavier campus. The annual festival includes several productions for children. The Ship's Company Theatre in Parrsboro performs aboard the old MV *Kipawo* ferry. Yarmouth holds a Summer Stage Theatre Festival as well. And the Mulgrave Road Co-op Theatre, which also does a fair amount of touring, offers a week-long summer festival in late July at Guysborough, on the Eastern Shore.

SPINNAKER ON THE NORTHWEST ARM, HALIFAX

FESTIVALS IN HALIFAX

It is a rare summer day in the Halifax area when there is no special event or festival taking place. One of the major attractions is the Nova Scotia International Tattoo, a musical extravaganza with a military flavour which runs for a week in July at the Metro Centre. There are festivals for other musical tastes as well. The Atlantic Jazz Festival (late July) and Dartmouth's Maritime Fiddle Festival and Jamboree (mid-July) are both top-notch musical events with little else in common. The International Buskerfest features street performers who gather from around the continent for this 10-day festival in early August. The buskers are a favourite with children.

INTERNATIONAL BUSKERFEST,

The Nova Scotia International Air Show is held in late August at Shearwater.

The Greek Festival (early June) and the Africville Reunion (late July) are two popular events with a multicultural theme. In late June, a Multicultural Festival is held along the Dartmouth waterfront. Ethnic food and music are the principal attractions.

The Atlantic Fringe Festival (early Sept.) offers alternative theatre while the Atlantic Film Festival (late Sept.) showcases independent films.

Finding the right festival can be a challenge — there are so many to choose from — but that same variety gives assurance that at least some of these events will enhance your stay in Nova Scotia.

FOOD

BY ELAINE ELLIOT

With a legacy of century-old dishes and an abundant supply of fresh fruit, produce, and seafood, Nova Scotian chefs are waiting to treat you to some great dining experiences.

Seventy percent of our visitors order seafood, and the menus around the province offer a generous selection. Although fish stocks on the Grand Banks are in decline, some species such as the world-renowned Digby scallops, North Atlantic lobster, haddock, halibut, and swordfish are plentiful and make excellent entrée options. A successful salmon-farming industry allows you to enjoy fresh or smoked Atlantic salmon year-round. Planked salmon cooked in the open air, smoked salmon, or baked, broiled, or poached salmon dishes are regional specialities.

Mussel farming is also thriving. Cultivated mussels are large and tender, and are served in the shell or in chowders. Gently steamed in a wine broth and topped with a sauce such as curry, tomato, or basil cream, mussels make an excellent appetizer or luncheon choice.

Halifax and Dartmouth offer the most diversified food experiences in the province. In addition to excellent Canadian cuisine, you will find many ethnic restaurants featuring Indian,

HADDON HALL, CHESTER

Oriental, northern Italian, Hungarian, Korean, and Greek fare.

In addition, several restaurants offer fashionable lighter dishes, such as vegetarian, pasta, and stir fry combinations. Intimate restaurants tucked in 18th-century buildings compete with upscale dining rooms, and most are a short walk from downtown hotels.

Travel the South Shore and sample the region's specialities. In Chester, Mahone Bay, or Shelburne try old-fashioned codfish cakes with rhubarb relish, solomon gundy (marinated herring and onion), or perhaps finnan haddie (smoked haddock baked in a light cream sauce and topped with "sweated" onions). Be sure to try one of the countless variations of chowder that appear on almost every menu — creamy broths with chunks of fresh haddock or halibut, tomato-based cioppinos laden with shellfish, shrimp and lobster bisques, or oyster stews.

Visit Lunenburg, a town with strong German heritage, and sample schnitzel, Lunenburg pudding, and sauerkraut. Take Route 1 through the Annapolis Valley. Interspersed with the bustling towns of Windsor, Wolfville, Kentville, Annapolis Royal, and Digby, orchards and farms provide the Valley's many inns and restaurants with the freshest of fruits and produce. Seasonal dishes use vine-ripened berries and melons, peaches, pears, cherries, and apples.

No holiday to Nova Scotia is complete without a visit to Cape Breton Island, and you should plan on spending at least three or four days enjoying the magnificent scenery and sampling the distinctively Scottish fare. Look for porridge or bannock breads, surprisingly tasteful presentations of root vegetables, and local lamb. Careful attention to the addition of herbs and spices contributes to the succulence of such dishes as gingered leg of lamb, lamb skewers with herbed butters, and lamb glazed with red currant jelly. And in addition to great dining, a few inns feature Gaelic ceilidhs — evenings of traditional music, dancing, and storytelling.

Advance planning is suggested before you begin a foray into the countryside. Many inns are seasonal, operating from early May through October; others are open year-round. A few offer limited public dining and others have just one seating per evening. Ask the innkeeper to recommend regional dining specialities. Reservations for peak travel times, such as July and at the height of fall foliage viewing, are strongly suggested.

BOATS AND LIGHTHOUSES

BY DAVID STEPHENS AND SUSAN RANDLES

BLUENOSE II

When Europeans first dropped anchor off Nova Scotia, they found the Mi'kmaq, with their sleek-birch-bark canoes, were accomplished seafarers. Over the centuries, almost every coastal hamlet had one or more ship under construction, using the ample supply of local timber and the knowledge and skill of master builders and seamen.

On the shores of Maitland, W. D. Lawrence built what is believed to be the largest wooden sailing ship in Canada. His home is now a museum dedicated to the man and the ship.

The undefeated champion of the Grand Banks fishing schooner fleet was the *Bluenose*. (A distinctive feature of a schooner is that the sails are attached to spars on the two masts rather than hanging from yardarms.) Built entirely of local materials (except for the masts) this sleek vessel was constructed in Lunenburg and launched on March 26, 1921. While the original tragically sank off Haiti in 1946, her memory lives on in the form of *Bluenose II*, a replica that sails each summer out of Halifax and Lunenburg. The Canadian dime bears a likeness of this winner of the International Fishermen's Trophy.

Long associated with fishing schooners, the sturdy dory still remains a nostalgic symbol of the fishing industry. At The Dory Shop Museum in Shelburne the almost forgotten art of dory-making is still practiced.

The development of the Cape Islander, a unique fishing boat with a high bow, wide mid-section, and

forward wheelhouse, resulted in a design that even today is still duplicated, although in various modified forms. The Archelaus Smith Museum on Cape Sable Island is a testament to this sturdy workhorse of the inshore fishery.

One of the finest collections of boats and models can be viewed at the Maritime Museum of the Atlantic in Halifax, while the Yarmouth County Museum is reputed to have Canada's largest collection of ship portraits. To experience first-hand the ongoing construction of a wooden ship, visit the Heritage Quay in Pictou where the *Hector* is being reconstructed using traditional materials and methods.

CAPE ISLANDER (TOP) AND NEWLY MADE DORIES

LIGHTHOUSES

Without these "signposts of the sea," mariners would be lost in fog, darkness and stormy seas. The honour of being the first lighthouse in Canada belongs to the circular stone tower built by the French between 1731 and 1734 at Louisbourg. Twice replaced, the present octagon tower is now part of the Fortress of Louisbourg National Historic Site.

Originally lit by oil, then kerosene, and finally electricity, several hundred lighthouses have guided ships past the dangers of the sea off Nova Scotia. Many were isolated and the keepers and their families were often the only inhabitants of the lonely islands. Totally automated today, many of the remaining 145 lighthouses and range lights (a pair of towers used to direct vessels into port) are being replaced with modern towers of fibreglass or metal. Others have been replaced by buoys, self-guiding harbour sector lights, or skeleton masts, as modern vessels rely increasingly on satellite navigational systems.

About 80 lights are accessible (with varying degrees of difficulty) on the mainland. Considering that they were erected as aids to navigation and not as attractions for visitors, it is surprising that so many can be easily visited.

A few lights have been incorporated into public or historic parks by local community groups and are open seasonally. One of the most photographed lighthouses in North America is the tall tapering tower at Peggys Cove. First erected in 1868 at the entrance to St. Margarets Bay, the original light was replaced with the present octagonal tower in 1915.

At Burncoat Head on the Bay of Fundy a lovely little park incorporates a replica of the keeper's house surmounted by the lantern. A similar light is located on the Eastern Shore at Port Bickerton, where the community has restored the 1901 home and roof-mounted lantern. Open

CAPE FORCHU

seasonally to the public and situated beside a modern operational light tower, the lighthouse allows visitors to appreciate the dedicated work of the light keeper. Another roof-mounted light at Gilbert Cove near Digby has also been restored by a local group.

One of the most common designs for lighthouses along our shores is the wooden tapered square or pyramid style commonly referred to as a "pepper shaker." The non-operational light at Walton Harbour is open to the public. This restored light is situated in a quiet little park with commanding views of the Bay of Fundy. A similar light graces the waterfront in Annapolis Royal. Moved several times due to constant shoreline erosion, the small Five Islands lighthouse can be seen in a local campground. Another tapered-design light is part of a public park at Abbotts Harbour, near West Pubnico. The little light tower overlooking the Bay of Fundy at Spencers Island is now a heritage property. Famous as the home of the ghost ship *Mary Celeste*, this tiny village is nestled along a gravel beach. At Margaretsville, a viewing platform surrounds the base of its lighthouse. The beauty of Neils Harbour, with its colourful fishing boats and the wharf below its lighthouse, is of the subject of many a photograph.

The unique "apple core" tower at Cape Forchu, near Yarmouth, is perhaps out-photographed only by the rock-mounted light at Peggys Cove. Although the Forchu light isn't open to the public, the keeper's house displays artifacts

PEGGYS COVE
SUNSET

of a bygone era. A replica of the Seal Island light is open seasonally in Barrington, while the lovely setting of the uniquely designed lighthouse at Fort Point in Liverpool makes it a popular attraction. Cape d'Or light near Advocate Harbour isn't unusual, but its location is dramatic, hugging the edge of a steep cliff. The tower at Cape George north of Antigonish is similar in design to the one at Peggys Cove and offers a sweeping view of the Canso Strait.

Its maritime heritage is a strong component of Nova Scotia's culture, and the lighthouses of the province offer visitors and residents alike many rewarding glimpses into the seafaring life of yesterday and today.

CRAFTS IN NOVA SCOTIA

CHRIS TYLER

Because Nova Scotia was one of the first places in North America to be settled by Europeans, the manufacture and repair of household tools, utensils, and farm implements were essential skills. Although the Mi'kmaq inhabitants already had a well-developed material culture that relied on locally available resources and some materials they acquired from fishermen, French and English settlers were dependent on home handcrafts for their needs. This early self-reliance may be one of the reasons that today the handcrafts of Nova Scotia are the strongest and most diverse in Canada.

JENNIFER'S CRAFT SHOPS CARRY GENUINE HAND-MADE, LOCAL PRODUCTS

The 19th century was a time of prosperity in the region and a time of expansiveness. Awareness of international trends and the Arts and Crafts Movement in England aroused interest in design and a new aesthetic. Many homes still continued the decorative but practical domestic crafts necessary to maintain a certain standard of living, and hooked mats, quilts, weaved goods, knitting, furniture and basketry were common handmade items of this era. All the Nova Scotia Museum sites around the province, and many local museums also, contain fine examples of traditional crafts from the 18th, 19th and early 20th centuries.

During the 1920s and '30s, craft activity grew as a leisure pursuit. A 1941 conference at St. Francis Xavier University in Antigonish laid the basis for the crafts' acceptance as a serious part of the resources of both the

ROSS FARM, NEW ROSS

educated individual and a well-balanced society. In 1942, Mary Black, a weaver and occupational therapist, was hired to create a craft program for the provincial government. A renaissance in many of the traditional crafts brought about by her work laid the groundwork for the craft industry in Nova Scotia today. The best single place to find crafts of superb quality is at the Mary E. Black Gallery at the Nova Scotia Centre for Craft and Design on Barrington St. in Halifax. Exhibits of the work of craftspeople and designers from around the province are on display year-round. The Centre also provides information on where to find crafts people in their studios.

The Nova Scotia College of Art and Design has also had an impact on the crafts through its avant garde thinking, and it continues to enliven the production of handmade artifacts around the province. Summer and fall craft markets have been spearheaded by the Nova Scotia Designer Crafts Council and by local entrepreneurs in different communities. The only wholesale craft trade show in Canada, the Atlantic Craft Trade Show, takes place in Halifax. It leads the way in the development of quality commercial crafts.

Handcrafts in Nova Scotia reflect the province's varied cultures and contribute about $150 million to the economy annually. Nova Scotian crafts are highly regarded nationally and, when the "One of a Kind" craft show opened in a new facility in Exhibition Park in Toronto in 1997, the Province of Nova Scotia was the first to be invited to promote the presence of Nova Scotia exhibitors. The quality and variety of traditional, commercial, and contemporary works make the earthenware, weaving, hooked rugs, quilts, woodwork, ironwork, and other exotic combinations of materials a cornucopia of both practical and decorative items.

You can find both the studios of artists and craftspeople and retail shops by using a copy of the annual *Buyers' Guide to Art and Crafts in Nova Scotia*, a comprehensive guide to producers, retail shops, artists, and galleries that can be found at any tourism information centre. Another excellent source of information is the *Studio Rally Map*, a resource that lists the studios of selected artists and crafts people in a convenient and attractive way that allows the visitor to tour around to see them. Using these two publications together will allow travellers to choose the kind of crafts they like in the areas they plan to visit.

ECONO MUSEUM, MAHONE BAY

PLACES

HALIFAX

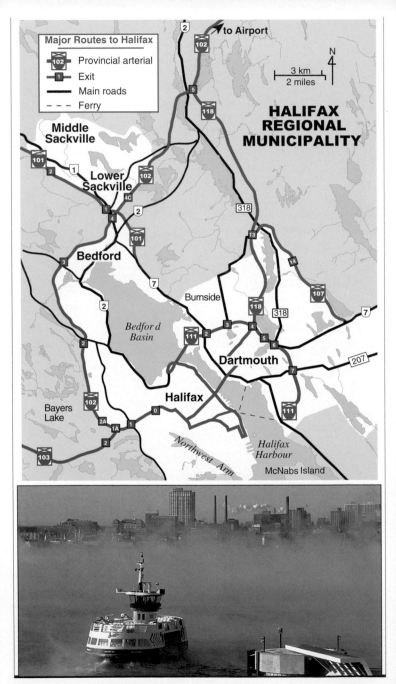

Major Routes to Halifax

- 102 Provincial arterial
- 1 Exit
- Main roads
- - - - Ferry

to Airport

N

3 km
2 miles

HALIFAX REGIONAL MUNICIPALITY

Middle Sackville

Lower Sackville

Bedford

Burnside

Bedford Basin

Bayers Lake

Dartmouth

Halifax

Northwest Arm

Halifax Harbour

McNabs Island

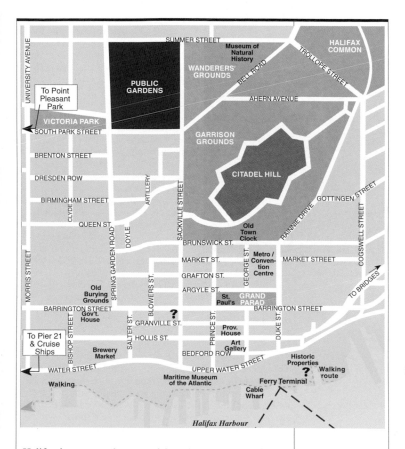

Halifax has emerged as one of Canada's most attractive cities to visit. It's a relatively small city, in an appealing setting, offering a variety of attractions. Halifax is at its best in summer and fall — and fall lasts longer than in the rest of Canada, with many beautiful days in October and even into November. Spring, on the other hand, often comes late, and there are even years when it doesn't seem to come at all.

The waterfront area has become the most popular place to spend time in the summer. The combination of a long boardwalk along the harbour, many attractive cafés, bars and restaurants, street entertainment, attractions like the Maritime Museum and the Historic Properties area, and the added thrill of occasional container ships or navy vessels passing by appeal to residents and visitors alike. Almost every visitor makes the trip up to the Citadel, which offers historical appeal together with wonderful views of the harbour. The Spring Garden Road area rivals the waterfront for friendly, low-key street life, and a variety of shops, bars, and restaurants.

The city's best bargain, and one kids love, is the ferry trip across the harbour. And within 40 minutes of downtown there are beautiful ocean beaches at Crystal

TOWN CRIER

77

MACDONALD BRIDGE, HALIFAX

Crescent and Lawrencetown, fine for warm summer afternoons when small children (and hardy adults) don't mind the relatively cool temperatures of the Atlantic shore. In the evenings, Halifax offers a surprisingly wide range of entertainment options, and that is one of the reasons why most visitors to Nova Scotia make a point of including the city on their itinerary. One caution: in the last couple of years summer and fall tourism has been on the increase, but accommodation hasn't expanded as quickly as demand. Don't count on being able to find a downtown hotel in summer or fall unless you've booked well in advance. If you don't have time to book much in advance, don't be surprised if you're offered rooms in the old-fashioned motel strip along the Bedford Highway, some distance from the downtown. Depending on your preferences, that may not be as appealing as being downtown, but the motels have their own 1950s charm.

SITE AND CLIMATE

Halifax sits atop a great slab of slate that rises from the harbour. There is precious little topsoil; it was the harbour that attracted Mi'kmaq for centuries and the British in 1749. The harbour extends inland about 16 kilometres (10 mi.) from its seaward approaches, through The Narrows spanned by the two bridges connecting Halifax and Dartmouth, and into the Bedford Basin. Except for an occasional freakish episode, it remains ice-free — a point long stressed by those interested in steering winter traffic the way of Halifax.

Recreational sailors happily coexist with shipping in the harbour. During the summer months, the Bedford Basin is flecked with hundreds of colourful sailboats. The Northwest Arm, on the southwest side of the Halifax peninsula, is also a yachting haven.

Summers in Halifax tend to be mild, with sunny days made fresh by sea breezes. Winters are cool and snowy.

SAILBOATS ON THE NORTHWEST ARM

INTERNATIONAL VISITORS' CENTRE, BARRINGTON STREET

Although there are days in January that are cold enough to draw wisps of sea smoke off the harbour, Haligonians are accustomed to spending much of their winters around the freezing point. Nice spring days are cherished because they are few. But autumn, Nova Scotia's finest season, flatters Halifax. Then, crisp days slant yellowish light, and the city's tree-lined streets blush with colour.

A GARRISON TOWN

Halifax was established in 1749 to counter the military threat posed by the French Fortress of Louisbourg. This century, the city's magnificent harbour has served as a marshalling area for North Atlantic convoys during two World Wars. Halifax's economic fortunes have flowed during conflict and ebbed with peace.

POINT PLEASANT PARK

Today, the Citadel in the heart of the city and the historic fortifications at Point Pleasant Park and York Redoubt are celebrated aspects of Halifax's military landscape, but there is also a contemporary military presence to go along with those reminders of the past. Warships regularly ply the harbour and helicopters fly overhead. A substantial number of military personnel are stationed here, and sailors from the NATO fleet are regular visitors.

Yet, despite the steady thrum of naval activity, Halifax is no longer a primarily military town. In postwar Halifax, rapid growth in the research, transportation, and public service sectors has turned the old garrison town into a vital commercial and government centre. This is Atlantic Canada's largest city. The provincial legislature is here, and a substantial federal bureaucracy works out of the city.

There is a thriving alternative scene here. Five

HMCS *SACKVILLE*, MARITIME MUSEUM OF THE ATLANTIC

universities, including the Nova Scotia College of Art and Design, provide much of the impetus.

So, Halifax serves up some startling contrasts. The same city that annually hosts the popular Nova Scotia International Tattoo, with its

PROVINCE HOUSE, HOLLIS STREET

regimental bands and drill teams, also stages the Atlantic Fringe Festival — alternative theatre that scandalizes the city's conservative element. The military is here but so is Vajradhatu, the headquarters for an international network of Buddhist meditation centres. Burgers and draught beer or bean sprouts and herbal tea — the downtown pubs and bistros cater to a city with multiple personalities.

A walk along Hollis Street, one of the city's oldest, tells some of the story. Government departments and law offices operate cheek by jowl in high-rises that stand along the street's northern end.

DOWNTOWN

You can explore the downtown area by foot, as the heart of the city extends for only a few — but very hilly — blocks.

The Grand Parade, framed by Argyle and Barrington Streets, sits between Citadel Hill and the waterfront. City Hall is situated on the North side and special activities, like the Remembrance Day service and New Year's Eve parties, take place here. On mild nights, people collect in the Grand Parade as they go from bar to bar, and summer days see business people patronizing hot dog vendors in the square.

Completed in 1750, St. Paul's Church still occupies the south side of the Parade. It was patterned on James Gibbs' design for Marybone Chapel, in London. Gibbs apprenticed with Christopher Wren, and his work includes the beautiful

THE GRAND PARADE AT CITY HALL

St. Martin-in-the-Fields on Trafalgar Square. St. Paul's is the oldest Protestant Church in Canada. Local legend has it that the profile of the vicar who died in the Explosion of 1917 (see p. 52) can still be seen in one of the upper windows, on the Argyle Street side of the church. St. Paul's Cemetery (the Old Burying Ground) on Barrington Street was the town's original cemetery. Information on headstones is available at the church.

Nearby, on Hollis Street, is Province House, the seat of provincial government. Opened in 1819, it is a fine example of the Palladian style. During a visit to Halifax in 1842, Charles Dickens described it as "a gem of Georgian architecture." The building really is beautiful remarkably so, given that, as far as anyone can tell, the plans were drawn up by John Merrick, a local contractor. Tour guides are always on hand to take you through the building's splendid interior. Highlights include the Red Chamber, with its tall windows and ornate plasterwork, where you can see the oak table from the *Beaufort*, the ship that brought Edward Cornwallis to Halifax in June of 1749. The Legislative Library, complete with hanging staircases and a three-sided balcony, is also magnificent.

OLD TOWN CLOCK

The city's turn-of-the-century commercial success is reflected in the Barrington and Granville streetscapes. Many of these buildings were of steel beam construction, a new technology that emerged in

PROVINCE HOUSE

HANGING STAIRCASE LEGISLATIVE LIBRARY, PROVINCE HOUSE (TOP); RELIEF ON PROVINCE HOUSE WALL (MIDDLE)

the wake of the Chicago fire of 1871. The walls of these structures were not load-bearing so that they were often build high with lots of windows and decorative arches. Contemporaries questioned their extravagance, but millionaires like George Wright could afford the best. The Wright Building still stands at 1672-4 Barrington Street. (Wright was one of 33 millionaires to go down in with the *Titanic* in 1912.)

This area is also the old stomping ground of Anna Leonowens, immortalized in the Rodgers and Hammerstein musical, *The King and I*, and several movies, including the recently released film starring Jodie Foster, *Anna and the King*. In 1876 Leonowens moved here with her daughter and son-in-law, who took up a position with the Bank of Nova Scotia. Soon after, Leonowens was actively involved in the establishment of libraries, reading clubs, and a Shakespeare Club. Today, the Nova Scotia College of Art and Design represents the culmination of Leonowens's interest in the local artistic community. Halifax jewelers and graphic designers — there are many — share in her legacy.

The Art Gallery of Nova Scotia, located in a heritage building on Hollis Street, houses a varied collection including Mi'kmaq and folk art; paintings by Nova Scotian artists can be purchased at the Art Sales and Rental Gallery. The work of many of the province's best craftspeople and designers is displayed at the Nova Scotia Centre for Craft and Design on Barrington Street.

Unique Nova Scotian wares can also be found in Barrington Place and the shops at Granville Mall,

adjacent to the Delta Barrington Hotel. These open up to a courtyard and feature such stores as Seagull Pewter and Christmas By the Sea.

The International Visitors Centre on Barrington at Sackville holds multi-media displays and videos about Nova Scotia. Multilingual travel counsellors help with vacation planning, reservations, car rentals, tickets to

ART GALLERY OF NOVA SCOTIA

events, and tours. Next door, the Discovery Centre makes science fun for all ages with interactive displays and experiments.

Continue south on Hollis to the Brewery Market, the former home of Alexander Keith's brewery (Keith's beer, now brewed by Labatt, is still sold in Nova Scotia liquor stores). The brewery is frequently

held up as an example of what can be achieved by preservation-minded developers. Its arches and gothic windows provide a comfortable setting for one of Halifax's best restaurants, Da Maurizio's. On Saturday mornings, the Brewery hosts a farmers' market where local crafts, baked goods and produce are available.

Further south, between Hollis and Barrington streets, Government House is another example of a beautiful Georgian building, in the Palladian style. When John Wentworth became Lieutenant-Governor of Nova Scotia in 1792, he sought to upgrade his accommodation. A well-connected family who knew royalty on the most intimate terms was probably justified in doing so. The cornerstone of Government House, the Wentworths' new residence, was

THE BREWERY MARKET, LOWER WATER STREET

GOVERNMENT HOUSE, BARRINGTON STREET

laid in 1800. It has served as the Lieutenant-Governor's residence ever since. Normally not open to the public, the Lieutenant-Governor continues a long-standing tradition of hosting a New Year's Day levee, when everyone is invited inside for a look (and a glass of sherry).

Backtracking on Barrington, you come to Spring Garden Road. There are a number of fine boutiques and craft shops in the Spring Garden Road area. The Halifax Folklore Centre provides the city's best introduction to the traditional music of Nova Scotia. Jennifer's of Nova Scotia sells everything from small souvenirs to the prized works of Nova Scotia's best artisans. Fine foods and wines are available at the Spring Garden Place Market, and at Port of Wines and the Italian Market, on Doyle Street. There are

BARRINGTON STREET

also a number of good bookstores and coffee shops along

the city's most fashionable street. Nearby on the other side of the Public Gardens, the Nova Scotia Museum features the natural history of the province along with a number of other permanent and temporary exhibits.

THE CITADEL

The Halifax Citadel, a national historic site operated by Parks Canada, is Nova

VIEW FROM THE CITADEL

Scotia's most visited attraction.

Built between 1828 and 1856, the fortification is the fourth to occupy the hilltop site, with its commanding view of Halifax Harbour.

The present Citadel was built through the semi-divine intervention of the "Iron Duke", Arthur Wellesley. The Duke of Wellington, a strong proponent of colonial defenses at a time when opinion was sharply divided, used his prime ministerial authority to push approval for the project through the British Parliament. In his view, a strong fortification was needed to defend against the American threat, which remained palpable in the wake of the War of 1812.

The fort was designed to prevent a land-based attack on the naval dockyard, It was left to the harbour defenses to repel an attack from the sea. Whether the Citadel was a necessary discouragement is open to debate. No attack ever came. The Citadel's smooth-bore cannons were never fired in anger.

During the summer months, Citadel staff re-enact the fort's military routines, as they were carried out during the years 1869–71. At that time, the Citadel was manned by

THE 78ᵀᴴ
HIGHLANDERS

85

ENTRY TO THE CITADEL

soldiers from the 78th Highlanders and the Royal Artillery, along with sailors of the Naval Brigade. Today, students take on these roles, drilling according to instructions laid out in the 1860s manuals, hoisting the signal flags, and standing watch at the sentry posts. The firing of the noon gun is heard throughout downtown Halifax. The signal flags flying above the ramparts once told civilians what ships were in the harbour and where they were docked. They were also used to send messages to the other harbour fortifications. At one time, it was thought that a series of signalling stations could be used to reach as far as Quebec!

Tour guides help explain the Citadel's rituals and exhibits, adding anecdotes, in French or English, about the fort's colourful past. "The Tides of History," a 40-minute audio-visual presentation, takes visitors on a dramatic tour through Halifax's military history. Visitors to Halifax are encouraged to find time for the Citadel, where they will discover why it held pride of place for much of the city's long life as a garrison town. And the view of downtown Halifax and the harbour is often reward enough for the steep climb up Citadel Hill.

At the base of the Citadel, along Sackville Street, is the cluster of buildings that make up Royal Artillery Park. Two of these, the residence of the General Commanding Officer and the Officers' Mess, are the sole survivors of the many wooden buildings that once housed army regiments in the early 1800s. Unfortunately, they are not open to the public.

The Old Town Clock has marked the time at the base of Citadel Hill since 1803. Unperturbed by such cataclysmic events as the Halifax Explosion in 1917, the clock has undergone restoration to ensure that it will remain, in the words of Joseph Howe, "a good example to all the idle chaps in town."

From the Citadel, looking east and north, you see Halifax's North End and towards the area demolished in the Explosion. Nearby are some fascinating historical buildings.

The Little Dutch (Deutsche) Church was originally built to accommodate German settlers who were brought to Halifax not long after its founding. Across the street is the beautiful St. George's Round Church, largely reconstructed after a disastrous fire several years ago. It is one of Price Edward's round buildings. Several handsome 19th century town-houses still stand along Brunswick Street. Further from the Citadel in the North End is

ST. GEORGE'S ANGLICAN CHURCH, BRUNSWICK STREET

the Hydrostone area, known to Canadian town planners as the first example of 20th century urban renewal (and a much better precedent than what came later). By the MacKay bridge is the site of the Africville community which was razed by Halifax city hall in the 1960s (see p.36).

THE WATERFRONT AND DARTMOUTH

Along the waterfront is Historic Properties, a 1970s restoration project that revitalized the downtown core. Privateers' Warehouse, one of ten buildings from the Georgian and early Victorian periods, is the most storied. Early in the 19th century, Enos Collins, a wealthy Halifax merchant, used the building to warehouse booty that he seized during legalized privateering raids off the New

England coast. Today, these buildings house a variety of shops and services. Suttles & Seawinds, a local company, has won international acclaim for its

HISTORIC PROPERTIES

NOVA SCOTIA CRYSTAL

MODEL OF THE RMS TITANIC (RIGHT); TITANIC DECKCHAIR REPLICA (BELOW)

distinctive line of clothing; many designs were inspired by traditional quilts. The Upper Deck Restaurant, overlooking the harbour from Privateers' Warehouse, prepares some of the city's best seafood dishes. There is a Visitor Information Centre in the Old Red Store, another building with a long history.

The food court at the Properties is certainly unique, offering, among other things, seafood, Italian dishes and a micro-brewery.

Follow the boardwalk along the harbour's edge to Cable Wharf, named for the transatlantic cable ships that once docked here, where more shops and restaurants can

be found. Nova Scotia Crystal, home of Canada's only mouth-blown, hand-cut crystal has a window that gives visitors a peek at the glass-blowers at work.

Boats operating from Cable Wharf are available for private charter. If you are interested in deep-sea fishing, make careful inquiries before booking your spot, or you may find yourself simply drifting in the harbour off Point Pleasant Park — hardly a deep-sea experience!

The Harbour Queen I and the *Haligonian* offer historical commentaries during their harbour cruises. A private ferry will take you to McNabs Island, where grassy trails lead to secluded coves, overgrown forts and rocky beaches.

Further along the boardwalk from Cable Wharf is the Maritime Museum of the Atlantic. The museum houses over 20,000 maritime artifacts and gives a poignant account of the 1917 Explosion (see p.52). There are

exhibits on shipwrecks and lifesaving, the *Titanic*, the Navy, steamships and sailing ships. The William Robertson & Son ship chandlery has been restored, and there are lots of boats — about 70 in all.

Since the blockbuster Titanic movie, the museum has mounted a permanent display of its fine collection of *Titanic* artifacts. Halifax's connection to the disaster came about because the city was the nearest large port to the site of the sinking. It was from Halifax that efforts were organized to search for the wreckage and to recover the bodies of victims. Funerals were organized, and many lie in graves in Halifax. Crew members on the ships sent out to the site collected memorabilia (a deck chair, for example), and gradually many of these items found their way to the Museum collection.

More recently, scientists from the Bedford Institute were involved in expeditions to the wreck site and in research on the deep ocean environment. Items in the exhibit reflect this work too.

Though modest in size, the exhibit is informative and appealing to visitors of all ages. It has become the museum's leading attraction, and is well worth a visit.

Continue south and visit Pier 21 on Marginal Road. This was the last immigration shed in Canada and a million immigrants, refugees, war brides and children passed through here to their new country. Now a National Historic Site, multimedia presentations, live performances and genealogical records tell their stories.

One of the easiest and least expensive ways for visitors to get out on the water is to take a trip on the Halifax-Dartmouth ferry. In Dartmouth, Ferry Terminal Park affords outstanding views of the Halifax waterfront. The

HALIFAX HARBOUR FERRY

89

World Peace Pavilion on the Dartmouth waterfront displays historical rocks and bricks from countries around the world, including pieces of the Berlin Wall and the Great Wall of China.

Nearby, the Shubenacadie Canal Interpretive Centre tells the canal's story. Following the old Mi'kmaq canoe route cross-country from the Bay of Fundy, the canal took more than 30 years to build. Shortly after it was completed in 1861, the new Intercolonial Railway made it obsolete. But the canal workings remain a source of fascination.

Up by the MacKay Bridge in Dartmouth, the Bedford Institute of Oceanography is one of the world's largest oceanographic establishments. Models and tours explain to visitors the institute's research of fishery science, oceanography and hydrography.

While in Dartmouth, plan to visit the Black Cultural Centre for Nova Scotia on Cherrybrook Road. The history and culture of Black Nova Scotians is preserved here with a library, auditorium and exhibits on life dating back to the 1600s.

The Cole Harbour Heritage Farm is also worth a look. Right in the middle of the suburbs, this 2.5-acre farm includes heritage buildings, farm animals, archival materials, gardens and a tearoom. Special events are held here throughout the year.

PUBLIC GARDENS

PARKS

On February 1, 1793, a 22-year conflict began with the French declaration of war against Britain. A year later, Prince Edward, son of George III and, eventually, father to Queen Victoria, arrived to take command of the garrison in Halifax. He set to work strengthening the town's fortifications. Martello towers were all the rage, and

Edward built three of them. Two of these, one overlooking the western approaches of the harbour at York Redoubt, and the Prince of Wales Tower in Point Pleasant Park (which Edward named after his favourite brother) are national historic sites. Both locations are worth visiting, for their scenic as well as historical value. York Redoubt is a perfect spot for a picnic, affording a wonderful view of the harbour.

CHAIN ROCK BATTERY, POINT PLEASANT PARK

Point Pleasant Park covers 75 wooded hectares (186 acres) in Halifax's South End and is leased by the city from the Crown for a shilling a year. From the park, you can watch ships enter the harbour or see sailboats tack across the Northwest Arm. A series of walking paths makes Point Pleasant ideal for an afternoon stroll. Along the way, you will pass a number of interesting ruins (see the map in the parking lot at the western entrance). From the Chain Rock Battery, a chain boom once stretched across the water to defend against enemy warships. During the First World War, mines were laid between the Point Pleasant Battery and McNabs Island, leaving a narrow channel lit by searchlights. A steel anti-submarine net was added later. Tall pine trees and beautiful harbour vistas now obscure the park's military past.

Returning from Point Pleasant Park towards the downtown, you pass through Halifax's South End. Here are many of the city's grandest homes, and a wonderful collection of unique Victorian townhouses built of wood and painted bright colours.

VICTORIAN ARCHITECTURE (LEFT) AND CRAFTSMANSHIP (BELOW)

If you drive or walk along Young Avenue (which becomes South Park Street) you can explore the Victoria South End by turning east along any one of the streets that run between Inglis and Spring Garden. Of course the Victorian streetscape is regularly interrupted by clumsy, unappealing post-1945 construction including high rise apartments, but

much of the original area remains and there are wonderful architectural details to notice in these houses' porches, windows, gables, and trim. For visitors curious about Halifax's royal

MUSIC BUILDING, BEDFORD HIGHWAY

past, a small park along the Bedford Highway has a wonderfully romantic origin and a beautiful small building to appreciate.

Three months after Prince Edward arrived, his beautiful French mistress followed. Governor John Wentworth lent them his country estate along the shores of the Bedford Basin. The only building still standing is a round ornamental garden temple that is similar in design to several buildings that had been constructed at Kew Gardens, Edward's childhood home. Visible from the Bedford Highway, the building is not open to the public, but visitors are welcome to stroll through the Hemlock Ravine opposite the rotunda. The pond in the 185-acre park is heart-shaped and known as Julie's Pond, in honour of Edward's mistress. Legend has it that the paths that once meandered through the estate spelled out her name.

Many of Halifax's parks evoke a sense of Victorian times, when Halifax "society" took leisurely strolls through Point Pleasant Park and picnicked on McNabs Island. The Royal Nova Scotia Yacht Squadron held regular regattas. Athletic pursuits were thought to be ennobling. By the 1880s, skating parties were held regularly at the rink in the Exhibition Building. In 1882, the Wanderers' Amateur Athletic Association Club was established to foster the growth of cricket, football, and hockey. After a purifying workout on the Wanderers' Grounds, participants could

THE DINGLE

cross Sackville Street and take a relaxing stroll through the Public Gardens.

These formal Victorian gardens are the oldest in North America. Originally owned by a group of prominent Haligonians who constituted the Nova Scotia Horticultural Society, the gardens were opened to the public in 1867. In 1874, the Society sold them to the City, which still maintains them. The Public Gardens were to serve a threefold purpose. They would improve the physical and mental health of the working classes, provide material for polite discourse among the more refined, and be a source of civic pride for all.

The Gardens are outstanding. Pathways wander among beautiful weeping trees, formal flower beds, and subtropical plantings. They lead across classical bridges, past cast iron fountains, and to the elaborate central bandstand. During the summer months, Sunday afternoon concerts are held there. On Saturday afternoons, brides, grooms, and attendants can be seen posing for photographers. If you need a break from the demands of travel, the Gardens are a find oasis.

FIREWORKS OVER THE HARBOUR

Across the Northwest Arm from Point Pleasant is Sir Sandford Fleming Park or, "the Dingle." Fleming, creator of Standard Time Zones and engineer for the Canadian Pacific Railway, donated the park to Halifax in 1908. The 95-acre park features the Dingle Tower, a sandy beach, a frog pond and two walking trails.

Connected to the trails in Shubie Park in Dartmouth, the Trans-Canada Trail winds from Sullivan's Pond along Lake Banook and Lake MicMac for seven kilometres. The paths are wide and wheelchair accessible.

AT THE AFRICVILLE REUNION

BLUENOSE II IN HALIFAX HARBOUR

ENTERTAINMENT

Throughout the summer months, Halifax and Dartmouth host a wide range of festivals and events. What follows is only a small sampling. Dates vary, so call the province's Check In information line (425-5781) or consult the *Nova Scotia Travel Guide* for details.

The Nova Scotia International Tattoo, which draws military bands from around the world, runs for a week each July, at the Metro Centre. The International Buskerfest, held in August on the Halifax waterfront and along city sidewalks, is very popular with both locals and visitors. Children especially enjoy the clowns and jugglers. The Atlantic Jazz Festival began on a shoestring budget and has quickly grown into a first-rate event. Held in July, mainstage and late-night concerts make for crowded downtown bars. The annual Africville Reunion brings together former residents of a Halifax suburb that was razed in the 1960s (see p. 36). Visitors are welcomed, and the Reunion provides a good opportunity to learn about the black community of Halifax.

Evenings, dine out at one of the city's fine restaurants. Not surprisingly, seafood is an ubiquitous specialty. Check the dining section of the listings at the back of this book for recommended dining spots.

If you prefer a raucous tavern evening, try the Lower Deck in Privateers' Warehouse, where Celtic bands are a regular feature. The Economy Shoe Shop complex on Argyle Street is a mecca for the cultural set. The Midtown Tavern, a Halifax institution, offers sturdy fare in a noisy, friendly atmosphere. The late-night cabarets are for the boldly adventurous – when the sailors are in town, these places are reminders of the seamier side of old Halifax.

LIGHTHOUSE ROUTE

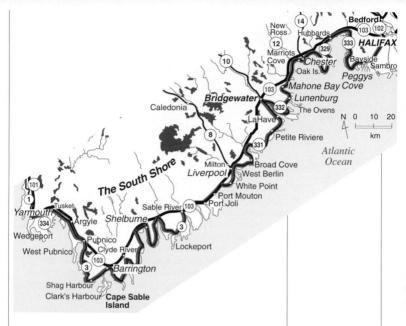

PEGGYS COVE

Peggys Cove is a 30-40 minute drive from Halifax on
Route 333. Along the way, at Bayside, the 18-hole Granite
Springs Golf Course welcomes RCGA card-carrying
members and their guests. The course is usually in great
shape with tight fairways and interesting hazards that offer
a stiff challenge.

Peggys Cove, with its vivid, pitched-roof houses
perched atop a mass of granite overlooking the snug
harbour, has been exposed on miles of film and acres of
canvas. It has become the postcard profile of an east coast
fishing village.

Historian Ian McKay has described what he terms "the
invention of Peggys Cove." A fishing village since the early
1800s, the Peggys Cove that has become the principal icon
of Nova Scotia tourism did not emerge until the 1920s and
'30s. It was born out of the region's
economic hard times. With the failure
of industry in Nova Scotia came the
assertion that quaint fishing villages
and rugged seascapes had always
been more real — more Nova Scotian
— than the illusory progress of the
late 19th and early 20th centuries.
The invention of Peggys Cove was
part of a developing mythology that
idealized the "Golden Age" of Nova
Scotia's seafaring past.

LIGHTHOUSE AT PEGGYS COVE

LIGHTHOUSE AT PEGGYS COVE

Tragedy befell Peggys Cove in September, 1998, when Swiss Air Flight 111 crashed off its shore. Fishermen donated their time and boats to help look for survivors and, when it was apparent there were none, pieces of the wreckage. A memorial has been erected for the 229 people lost.

Canadian journalist J. F. B. Livesay was one of the Cove's chief protagonists. He had discovered the village in the 1920s, and his *Peggys Cove*, based upon a summer visit in 1943, was published posthumously a year later. Livesay presented an unabashedly romantic view of the village: "The Cove on that first glance was still quite perfect, nothing to be added and nothing to be taken away, a little pulsing human cosmos set in the uneasy sea." He characterized the unwillingness of a local woman to purchase a washing machine as an emphatic rejection of modernity. As McKay points out, Livesay did not mention that the same woman also owned the only telephone in Peggys Cove, nor did he make any allowance for the discouragement that solid granite might offer someone who was considering additional plumbing!

SWISS AIR MEMORIAL

What Livesay's prose did for Peggys Cove in the 1940s, the photographs of W.R. MacAskill had been doing since 1921. In that year, MacAskill's Quiet Cove appeared. Tourist promoters seized the opportunity afforded by MacAskill's beautiful photography. Peggys Cove was close enough to Halifax to offer visitors to the city a chance to encounter the "essential" Nova Scotia — the desolate boundary where land meets sea.

The successful promotion of Peggys Cove has led to a curious irony. You are exhorted to discover the unspoiled beauty of Peggys Cove in the company of tens or even hundreds of other people. A mass of glacier-scarred granite cuts an impressive profile against sky and sea, but here you

will also find air-conditioned coaches from all over North America. Artists from far away make their homes here. There is a busy restaurant and gift shop (the Sou'wester) and the old lighthouse now serves as a post office.

WILLIAM DE GARTHE RELIEF SCULPTURE IN PEGGYS COVE

But something truly elemental is still revealed at Peggys Cove — something about the human spirit in the face of adversity. If you visit on a day when a stiff onshore breeze sends waves crashing against the rocks (heed the warnings to keep your distance), you will marvel at the pluck of those who choose to live here.

For an impressive landward view of the cove, Peggys Cove Whale Watching Tours leaves twice-daily from the government wharf. The tour offers frequent sightings of puffins, dolphins, whales and seals.

Upon leaving Peggys Cove, continue along Route 333 through the picturesque villages that dot the eastern shore of St. Margarets Bay. If you time things right, you may arrive at Candleriggs, in neighbouring Indian Harbour, for a Scottish afternoon tea or a fine evening meal.

Route 333 eventually rejoins Highway 3 which takes you back to Halifax or farther along the South Shore towards Chester and Mahone Bay.

CHESTER

Nova Scotia's South Shore is a storied stretch of shoreline. In colonial times, privateers — American, French, and Nova Scotian — plied these waters with letters of marque from their governments, licensing them to plunder enemy

CHESTER WATERFRONT

ships. Later, rum-runners unloaded their illicit cargoes in secluded coves and bays. Tall ships once crowded South Shore harbours. Today, coastal towns like Chester and Mahone Bay have retained the romantic aura of earlier days, and their harbours are still a boating haven.

The village of Chester lies across three fingers of a

CHESTER HARBOUR

peninsula that overlooks Mahone Bay. With its 365-odd islands ("one for each day of the year") the bay is a sailor's paradise. The village itself is a New England coastal town that just happened to end up in Nova Scotia.

Appropriately, Chester's first settlers (it was called Shoreham then) sailed from Boston in 1759; much of the rest of the Mahone Bay area was colonized by Germans, French, and Swiss. Although Chester is also increasingly the haunt of yachtsmen from Halifax, Toronto, and beyond, its predominantly Cape Cod-style architecture and the Yankee accents of many of its summer residents still give the town an unmistakable New England flavour.

Despite its New England roots, Chester was unable to avoid the attention of American privateers. It is believed that "Blockhouse," a private dwelling near the government wharf, on the village's Front Harbour, was the focus for the community's defenses. This was the site of a curious

THE CAPTAIN'S HOUSE

happening in 1782. Apparently, three American privateers were on their way to sack Chester, when the commander of the local forces came up with an inspired plan. Since all the local men were away gathering firewood, this chap gathered a brigade of broom-wielding women from the village to march back and forth on the hill overlooking the harbour with the red linings of their cloaks exposed. The Americans, so the story goes, were fooled into thinking there were British Redcoats guarding Chester and sailed down the coast to take out their frustrations on Lunenburg.

Most Americans came to Chester with friendlier intentions. In 1822, the Reverend John Secombe, a Harvard graduate, sailed to the village from Boston with several friends. His home, now the Captain's House Inn on Central Street, is a Chester

landmark. The inn offers fine meals — Sunday brunch is especially popular with Chesterites — in grand surroundings.

As the 19th century moved along, a growing number of wealthy Americans discovered Chester. The town's magnificent Front and Back Harbours provided a scenic refuge for yachtsmen and retired naval brass.

They came — to sail, fish, and get

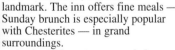

away from it all. American admirals joined their Canadian counterparts. There were bankers, doctors, and oilmen from Boston, Baltimore, and Pittsburgh. Students from Yale came to Chester to unwind following their studies.

Their houses are among Chester's main attractions, especially those along "The Peninsula" at the western boundary of Front Harbour. Chester homes have names like Sea Chest, Wisteria, and Lordly.

Early this century, American families would travel by steamer from Boston and Philadelphia to Yarmouth, Halifax, or Digby, where they would catch a train or take another boat to Chester. Several gruelling days later, their chauffeurs would arrive with their fancy cars. Of course, this annual pilgrimage changed Chester. Chesterites, who traditionally fished and farmed, began working as guides on the trout and salmon streams, and crewed on splashy sailboats.

Visitors who arrive at Chester by boat will find a range of yachting services without equal in Atlantic Canada. South Shore Marine, in nearby Marriots Cove, is the region's largest marina. Not surprisingly, the facility's restaurant, The Galley, specializes in seafood, and window tables provide an unforgettable view of Mahone Bay.

Chester Race Week, held in early August, is the height of the summer social season. Then, the Front and Back Harbours are filled with sleek yachts. Some participants race to win; others are happy to be a part of the hoopla. The Parade Grounds off South Street, site of the Yacht Club, a bandstand, a war memorial, and a salt-water swimming pool (the Lido), provide the best vantage point for non-sailors who are interested in viewing the races.

CHESTER GOLF COURSE

For those who want to get out on the water but lack a boat, cruises and charters are available. There is also a 45-minute ferry trip (pedestrians only) from the government wharf to Tancook Island, the largest in Mahone Bay.

Chester offers a number of landward diversions. Nearby, an 18-hole golf course is characterized by its short, tight fairways and wonderful views of the ocean and nearby islands. Live

CHESTER PLAYHOUSE

theatre is presented at the Chester Playhouse year-round. Those who like to shop should visit the Warp and Woof between Water and Duke streets. The shop includes a sweater annex and an art gallery, and sells gift items such as fine stationery and handcrafts. The handmade quilts are a special draw.

As a special treat and highlight of your Nova Scotia holiday, stay at Chester's magnificent Haddon Hall Inn. Built in 1905 as a summer home, the inn sits atop Haddon Hill and affords unrivaled views of Mahone Bay. Choose from the luxurious suites in the main house or the chalets that are scattered throughout the grounds of the 90-acre estate.

Leaving Chester and driving towards the nearby town of Mahone Bay, you pass Oak Island (now joined to the mainland by a causeway), reputed to be the hiding place of Captain William Kidd's treasure. Since 1795, when a pit was discovered on the island, fortune-seekers have sought in vain for the booty. And for just as long, people have tried to explain the ingenious method by which the famous pirate is thought to have hidden his treasure in an elaborate network of underground tunnels. The story is well told by Mark Finnan in *Oak Island Secrets*, and by Graham Harris and Les MacPhee in *Oak Island and its Lost Treasure* — both are available in local bookstores and gift shops. The Oak Island Coastal Inn & Marina, a recently renovated oceanfront hotel, is a good jumping off point from which to explore the area.

MAHONE BAY

Be sure to take the old road, Route 3, from Chester to Mahone Bay. The road dips and winds its way along the shore until a long, sweeping bend brings one of Nova Scotia's most recognizable landscapes into view. Colourful buildings and wharves, monuments to Mahone Bay's seafaring past, line the waterfront of the town's near perfect harbour. Sailboats and other pleasure craft are moored offshore. And three fine 19th-century churches — United, Lutheran, and Anglican — stand side-by-side by side at the head of the harbour.

THREE CHURCHES AT MAHONE BAY

The area's original inhabitants were Mi'kmaq. The

Mushamush River on the edge of town bears the name of an early encampment. The village of Indian Point is only minutes away. The bay was also a haven for French fishermen and pirates. The name Mahone is derived from the French *mahone*, a low-lying vessel that kept French pirates hidden from their prey.

The present town was established by "Foreign Protestants" in 1754 (see p. 42). A display at the Settlers Museum, on Main Street, tells their story.

Mahone Bay had its own encounters with American privateers. During the War of 1812, the *Young Teazer* was chased into Mahone Bay by a British warship. One of the privateer's crew was a British deserter. Rather than risk capture, he set fire to the ship's powder magazine; 28 died in the explosion that followed. Today, the Teazer, on Route 3, is an upscale gift shop carrying both fine local crafts and imported goods.

Mahone Bay was once a flourishing shipbuilding centre. Many Main Street businesses now occupy buildings formerly used in the trade. Upstairs, at the Settlers Museum, the town's shipbuilding heritage is revealed. It is also visible in the architecture of Mahone Bay. A "Walking Tour" brochure is available at the museum and will steer you towards some of the beautiful Cape Cod, Georgian, and Victorian homes that used to belong to local shipbuilders. The Sou'Wester Inn, once the home of a Victorian shipbuilder, is one of many bed-and-breakfasts in the area.

In mid-summer, the town holds its Wooden Boat Festival. Inaugurated in 1990, the festival is already one of Nova Scotia's best. The quality of craftsmanship of many of the boats displayed at the festival reaches Mahone Bay standards.

Fine shops abound — the kind of shops that have given way to malls in so many other places. Kathi Thompson, one of several potters in Mahone Bay, makes and sells beautiful blue-green, sea-inspired pottery out of her Main Street studio and shop. Just down the road is Amos Pewterers. Now an economuseum, interpretive plaques and an open workshop allow visitors to see Greg and Suzanne Amos at work fashioning pewter items — vases, candleholders, goblets, sculptures, picture holders, Christmas ornaments, earrings, pins, and pendants. Boats

SEA KAYAKING

were once built in the waterfront store. Still on Main Street, but away from the water, Suttles and Seawinds is one of Mahone Bay's most successful enterprises. Vicki Lynn Bardon is responsible for the explosion of colour that greets you upon entering the store. Inspired by traditional quilts, her line of distinctive clothing has won international acclaim.

Three local restaurants reach the high standard for quality set by Mahone Bay's shops. The Innlet Café, with a harbour view that includes the three churches, emphasizes stylish seafood dishes in casual surroundings. Mimi's Ocean Grill serves up interesting and unusual dishes on Main Street.

LUNENBURG

Make time for Lunenburg during your visit to Nova Scotia. With the possible exception of Annapolis Royal, Lunenburg is the province's prettiest and most interesting town. Its architectural integrity has been preserved to a remarkable degree. Lunenburg's "Old Town" — first laid out by the province's chief surveyor in 1753 — has been designated a National Historic District by the Government of Canada and a World Heritage Site by UNESCO.

Lunenburg's beautiful harbour, its outstanding architecture, its seafaring tradition, and its proximity to Halifax have attracted many visitors over the years. Some have stayed. Lunenburg is home to a vital artistic community and has long been at the centre of Nova Scotia's fishing industry. The demand for wooden ships has declined, but waterfront companies continue to outfit and repair local boats.

Lunenburg represents the second attempt made by British authorities to colonize Nova Scotia (Halifax was the first). This site had a number of advantages. It offered the best agricultural land along Nova Scotia's Atlantic coast, some of which was already cleared, though not nearly as much as was promised. There was a fine harbour, the narrow peninsula could be easily defended by a palisade,

LUNENBURG

and the site was close to Halifax, and distant from the French settlements at Ile-Royale (Cape Breton) and along the Bay of Fundy.

In 1753, a group of German-speaking "Foreign Protestants" arrived by boat from Halifax (see p. 42). Surveyor General Charles Morris measured off blocks and streets in a gridiron pattern along the slope overlooking the harbour. The Old Town was a 48-block rectangle, rows of six blocks running parallel to the shore, and columns of eight blocks running up the hill. A central core of four blocks was reserved for public purposes.

The settlers overcame the adversities of hostile French and Mi'kmaq in the area, and Their endeavours eventually flourished. Surpluses in timber, boards, and root vegetables were sent to Halifax. Settlement reached southwest as far as West Berlin, and northeast to Mahone Bay and beyond. Prime land along the banks of the LaHave River drew people farther and farther upriver, from Bridgewater to New Germany.

It was inevitable that some of the new settlers would turn to the sea for their livelihoods. Towards the end of the 18th century, the inshore fishery began to flourish. Cod, mackerel, dogfish, salmon, herring and gaspercaux were easily caught from small boats close to shore.

Lunenburg's waterfront still reflects the importance of its shipbuilding industry and the fishery. At the eastern end of Montague Street, Scotia Trawlers has been outfitting and repairing fishing vessels since acquiring the Smith and Rhuland boatyards in 1976. Smith and Rhuland, established in 1900, had built both the *Bluenose* (1921) and the *Bluenose II* (1963). Lunenburg shipbuilders were renowned long before the *Bluenose* was launched, but it was this 285-ton racing schooner, never defeated in Nova Scotia waters, that won them international recognition. In addition to the *Bluenose II*, the same shipyard also launched replicas of *HMS Bounty* (1960) and *The Rose*.

DORY BUILDING AT LUNENBURG

The fishery spawned other industries. The buildings of the old Adams & Knickle outfitting company can still be seen. Nearby, Thomas Walters and Sons' blacksmith company, established in 1893, has been the sole survivor of a once-

thriving Lunenburg trade.

Farther west on Montague Street, the Fisheries Museum of the Atlantic occupies buildings that were once a part of National Sea Products' processing plant (now located at Battery Point). The museum, one of Nova Scotia's best, has many excellent exhibits relating to Lunenburg's fishing and shipbuilding heritage. The aquarium of Atlantic fishes is especially popular with children; adults may find the rum-running display more to their taste. An exhibit on the Banks fishery and the Age of Sail includes meticulously crafted models. Various demonstrations take place throughout the summer. Moored alongside the museum's wharf, the *Theresa E. Connor*, a salt-bank schooner, and the *Cape Sable*, a steel-

hulled trawler, welcome visitors aboard. You may also find the *Bluenose II* here (she sails out of Halifax as well).

In recent years, careful planning has preserved Lunenburg's architectural character. Before that, good fortune was largely responsible.

FISHERIES MUSEUM OF THE ATLANTIC

Lunenburg's failure to industrialize in areas other than the fishery is one explanation for the absence of major fires in the downtown area. And significant redevelopment in the Old Town was averted when "New Town" was established in 1862. With a few minor exceptions, Old Town remains remarkably similar in both form and function to Morris's 1753 plan. Public buildings still stand where they did in the

settlement's early days. The original frame of St. John's Anglican Church, built between 1754 and 1763, is still within the walls of the present structure. Lunenburg's courthouse was built in 1775, and is now used by St. John's parish as a church hall. Predictably, the new courthouse, built in 1902, also stands on the Grand Parade, in the heart of the town.

There are a number of other 18th-century structures. Typically, these are one-storey Cape Cod-style houses or two-storey dwellings in the British Classical tradition.

"LUNENBURG BUMP"

Nineteenth-century buildings dominate Old Town. Although architecturally conservative, Lunenburgers permitted themselves one extravagance in the latter half of the 19th century. Scottish dormer windows were added to British Classical houses. Over time, these were moved down the slope of the roof until they hung over central doorways. The "Lunenburg Bump" can be quite ostentatious, and probably was a reflection of the town's success in the salt fish trade.

Built just before the turn of the 20th century, the second Lunenburg Academy (the first was destroyed by fire in 1893) is one of the town's architectural gems. It stands outside the Old town, atop Gallows Hill, and the four towers that jut from its Mansard roof are visible for miles. Young Lunenburgers are still educated at the Academy.

Lunenburg hosts a series of first-rate festivals during the summer. Its growing reputation as a centre for arts and crafts is reflected in the quality of work displayed at the Craft Festival (mid-July) and the Nova Scotia Folk Art Festival (early August). The Lunenburg Folk Harbour Festival (August) features top North American performers

LUNENBURG
ACADEMY

and attractive waterside venues. For many, the highlight of the summer season is the Lunenburg Fishermen's Reunion and Picnic (August). The fisherman's competitions, including dory racing and scallop shucking, are hotly contested by highly skilled

LUNENBURG

participants. They also are great fun.

The town boasts a number of fine shops and galleries, and across the harbour you can shoot nine holes of golf at Bluenose Golf and Country Club, while enjoying the spectacular view.

To the south of Lunenburg, the privately run Ovens Natural Park has a series of coastal caves. A cliff-side hiking trail leads down a concrete stairway to the mouth of Cannon Cave — so named because of the dramatic boom created by the surge of waves into the narrow cavern. Zodiac tours of the caves are available between late June and early September (weather permitting).

BRIDGEWATER

Follow the coastline south to the LaHave River, and then go up river to Bridgewater, the thriving town which prides itself as the "Main Street of the South Shore." Bridgewater offers its visitors numerous services and conveniences, including restaurants, accommodations, bustling malls, banks, a regional hospital, museums, recreational facilities and a visitor information centre.

Built in 1860, the Wile Carding Mill displays machines that once carded wool for spinning and weaving. Bridgewater hosts its rural neighbours each July at the South Shore Exhibition and International Ox Pull.

A pleasant drive down the western banks of the LaHave leads to the dock where a cable ferry provides a transportation link across the river, and on to the Marine Museum on Bell's Island Nearby is the Fort Point Museum, a former lighthouse keeper's house, and site of the Fort Sainte-

Marie-de-Grâce National Historic Site, where Isaac de Razilly, the first governor of New France, landed with his settlers in 1632. At Rissers Beach, supervised swimming, picnic areas and change facilities are provided.

More beaches, museums, and

inviting villages can be found at such shoreline communities as Cherry Hill, Broad Cove, Petite Rivière, Green Bay and Crescent Beach.

LIVERPOOL

Situated at the estuary of the Mersey River, Liverpool was settled by New England Planters in the 1760s (see p. 24).

Much of Liverpool's colonial past has been popularized in the historical fiction of Thomas Raddall. Raddall was far and away Nova Scotia's best-selling novelist, with millions of copies sold in the United States, Great Britain, and Canada. In *His Majesty's Yankees,* he told the powerful story of a fictional Liverpool family caught up in the events surrounding the American Revolution. To give his novel life, Raddall relied heavily on the diaries of an 18th-century Liverpool merchant, Simeon Perkins.

Perkins' diaries give a unique account of colonial Nova Scotia. They describe the dilemma faced by the Planters, who had spent most of their lives as New Englanders, when the American Revolution polarized loyalties. Perkins was among those community leaders who eventually called for armed resistance to the attacks of American privateers.

Today, Perkins House on Main Street is one of Liverpool's chief attractions. Built in 1766, the house was acquired by the Queens County Historical Society in 1936 and is now a part of the Nova Scotia Museum Complex. Like Raddall's novels, Perkins House and the adjacent Queens County Museum tell a romantic story of Liverpool's tumultuous early days. Much is made of privateers — hardly surprising in a town that styles itself "Port of the Privateers." Liverpool hosts a Privateer Days celebration at the end of June. The town also stages a summer program of concerts and plays at the beautiful Astor Theatre, once the

PERKINS HOUSE

Liverpool Town Hall. This is also the venue for the Liverpool International Theatre Festival, a biennial springtime series of high-calibre performances.

Logging has been the backbone of Liverpool's economy almost from the beginning. Some of the lumber was used to build ships,

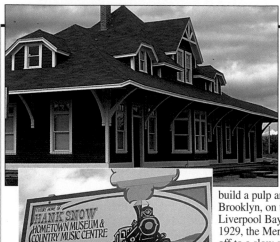

HANK SNOW MUSEUM

which often took on additional lumber for export to Great Britain.

In the 1920s, the forest industry in Queens County was given a major boost by the decision of Yarmouth-born financier Izaak Walton Killam to build a pulp and paper mill at Brooklyn, on the north side of Liverpool Bay. Completed in 1929, the Mersey Paper Mill got off to a slow start but soon picked up speed. When Killam died in 1955, he held approximately three-quarters of the company's common stock and his estate was valued at around $200 million. The Killam trusts are still used for university endowments and the construction of public buildings across Canada. Bowater Mersey continues to be the major employer in the Liverpool area.

The Sherman Hines Museum of Photography and Galleries, located in Liverpool's historic Town Hall, is the only photographic museum east of Montreal. It features artifacts and vintage photographs by the likes of Karsh and MacAskill.

The former Liverpool train station is now the Hank Snow Country Music Centre, honouring the Queens County-born country music legend. The centre has rotating displays and memorabilia from well-known Nova Scotia musicians, interactive exhibits, railway memorabilia, workshops and a gift shop. In August, the Hank Snow Society hosts a weekend of classic country music at the fairgrounds.

FORT POINT LIGHTHOUSE PARK

Nova Scotia's fourth oldest surviving lighthouse is the centrepiece of Fort Point Lighthouse Park. Once a welcome sight for seafarers entering Liverpool's busy harbour, the lighthouse now contains an exhibit area with models, interpretative panels and an audio-visual presentation.

South of Liverpool, Route 3 leads to White Point Beach Lodge. A full-service resort, the Lodge has wide-ranging facilities including a playground, pool, nine-hole CPGA-rated golf course, tennis courts, freshwater paddling, and of course, a long stretch of fine, white, sandy beach (warm water enthusiasts will prefer the pool for swimming). Continue along Route 3 towards some of the province's best beaches. Summerville Beach Park, with its salt-water lagoon, is a great spot for a picnic and swim. The Quarterdeck Beachside Villas & Grill is situated along this white sand beach. The resort offers all the amenities including full kitchen facilities, jacuzzis, and fireplaces.

For a more secluded setting, drive on to Carters Beach at Port Mouton. The beach is actually three crescent-shaped stretches of the finest white sand imaginable. It's worth the trouble to ford the small stream that separates the first of these beaches from the last two. Here you will find magnificent dunes and unmatched views of Port Mouton Bay.

PIPING PLOVER

The endangered piping plover has also taken advantage of the relative seclusion of this coastline. Kejimkujik National Park's Seaside Adjunct protects key nesting areas between Port Mouton and Port Joli. Two hiking trails lead to isolated beaches, sections of which are closed from late April to late July so that nesting birds remain undisturbed. Both hikes offer spectacular coastal views. There are still more wonderful beaches at Lockeport, just off Route 3. Crescent Beach, one of five in the area, is a fully-serviced 1.5-km (1-mi) long stretch of fine, white sand. It is a short drive from here, up the indraft of Jordan Bay, and across the peninsula to Shelburne.

SHELBURNE

Shelburne is Nova Scotia's Loyalist town. Drawn by the outstanding harbour, one of the largest in the world, 3,000 Loyalists settled along the shores of the Roseway River estuary in 1783 (see p. 30). Within a year, nearly 10,000 people were there, making Shelburne the largest town in British North America.

LOYALIST DAYS, SHELBURNE (ABOVE AND BELOW)

A number of Loyalist-era structures have survived in Shelburne. Ross-Thomson House is operated by the Shelburne Historical Society for the Nova Scotia Museum. Built around 1784, the store was soon occupied by business partners and brothers Robert and George Ross (Robert

Thomson would become their clerk). The old store has since been refurbished with period furnishings and merchandise. The comfortable, solid building, no doubt the work of a shipbuilder, impresses on its own.

The Cooper's Inn, also on Dock Street, is one of several waterfront restoration projects that grew out of the visit of the Prince and Princess of Wales to Shelburne in 1983. The former owners received an award from Heritage Trust Nova Scotia for their work on this 18th-century Loyalist home (c. 1785). The dining room is superb — everything from scratch using fresh local ingredients. Five rooms, some with harbour views, are available for overnight guests.

South on Dock Street, the Shelburne County Museum tells more of the Loyalist story. For a small fee, the museum will provide a walking tour brochure that points out several other Loyalist buildings in town. Most points of interest are along the waterfront, on or near Dock Street.

THE DORY SHOP MUSEUM

Like other fishing communities along the South Shore, Shelburne also has a rich shipbuilding heritage. The town

is renowned for its dories. In 1877 Isaac Coffin Crowell, a native of nearby Barrington, invented and patented a metal clip for joining the floor futtocks with those of the sides. In Lunenburg, dory builders continued (and continue) to use naturally crooked tamarack roots for the job. A debate still rages as to whose method is better, but Crowell's clip allowed Shelburne builders to undersell their Lunenburg competitors. At one time, Shelburne had seven dory shops.

The Shelburne Historical Society operates The Dory Shop Museum, which was a going concern from 1880 to 1970. It demonstrates the building and outfitting of a Shelburne dory and explains the crucial role that these boats played in the fishery. The museum has a dory builder and is well worth visiting.

SHELBURNE HARBOUR

BARRINGTON

Between Shelburne and Yarmouth lies Barrington. Just four years after Barrington was founded by Planter families from Cape Cod in 1761, the new township had its New England-style meeting house. Now part of the Nova Scotia Museum Complex, the unadorned structure that served both religious and secular purposes is Canada's oldest extant nonconformist place of worship.

Nearby, the Barrington Woolen Mill, built in 1884, is also operated by the museum. The mill houses original machinery and includes exhibits on sheep raising and wool processing. The Seal Island Lighthouse Museum was constructed in Barrington to commemorate the light and keepers that steered countless sailors past Seal Island's notorious shoals for 160 years (built in 1830, the lighthouse was automated in 1990). Exhibits relate to lighthouse life. There is a good view of Barrington Bay from the top of the five-storey museum.

Reached by causeway from Barrington Passage, Cape Sable Island, in Barrington Bay, is also steeped in maritime lore. The island was home to Ephraim Atkinson, who first built the boat that became the workhorse of the North Atlantic lobster fishery. Typically, the Cape Islander is about twelve metres long with a three-to-four metre beam. You'll find them in working harbours throughout Atlantic Canada. Learn more about the Cape Islander and this storied fishing community at the Archelaus Smith Museum in Centreville.

At West Pubnico, the oldest Acadian settlement still inhabited by descendants of its founders, an historic Acadian Village honours the perseverance and generosity of Acadian people. Original structures and artifacts donated by local residents were used to create vintage Acadian buildings, including houses, a forge, a barn and a lobster peg mill. Guides in period costume welcome visitors to a reception centre, a restaurant serving traditional Acadian dishes, and an arts and crafts shop.

ALONG THE CLYDE RIVER

111

OLD YARMOUTH HOME

YARMOUTH COUNTY MUSEUM

YARMOUTH

Take a stroll through the town of Yarmouth and you'll be struck by the houses. On the slope rising up from the ferry terminal are lavish 19th-century homes — Georgian, Gothic, and Italianate, among others. Some have costly frills, like the one on Parade Street, not far from the Yarmouth County Museum, which is trimmed with wooden rope and comes complete with portholes. Fish-processing plants along the waterfront attest to a fairly healthy fishery (a rarity in Nova Scotia these days) and the town is well serviced, but there are few clues as to where the extravagant wealth came from that built these homes.

That is because Yarmouth's century was the 19th — first as Nova Scotia's most prosperous "wood, wind, and sail" community, and then as a thriving industrial centre.

The County Museum is a good place to begin a tour of the town. Here are many paintings of the fleet, commissioned by Yarmouth captains in ports like New York, Belfast, and Hong Kong.

During the middle of the 19th century, Yarmouth families like the Killams and Lovitts, who traced their roots back to the New England Planters who first settled Yarmouth in the 1760s, became powerful shipping magnates. Their ships, flush with lumber and salt fish, made for the West Indies. There they laded rum, sugar, and molasses bound for Boston. Thence, back to Yarmouth with manufactured goods. They reinvested profits in shipping. For a time, Yarmouth boasted the largest per capita concentration of registered shipping tonnage in the world.

By the 1860s, huge ships were being built for the international bulk trade. Yarmouth's wealthiest families entered into partnerships to finance their construction. All along the French Shore — the string of Acadian communities between Yarmouth and Digby — shipyards were kept busy.

The Killam Brothers Building, part of the County Museum and located along the waterfront, attests to the wealth of the ship owners. Look for the hand-worn grooves in the cash tray of the huge, stand-up chestnut desk.

And, then, so the story usually gets told, sail was replaced by steam, and it was over. The worldwide slump in trade in 1873 is often cited as the turning point. The golden age of wooden ships and iron men had passed. Yarmouth's mercantile class was left to languish in the face of progress.

But that's not what really happened. A visit to Yarmouth's excellent Firefighters Museum on Main Street provides some insight into the real story. Among the exhibits is a horse-drawn hose reel that was built in Yarmouth by the Burrill-Johnson Iron Company in 1891.

The threat of fire was real because Yarmouth industry boomed until the turn of the century. In addition to the Burrill-Johnson foundry, which had been expanded during the 1880s in order to supply more products to national and international markets, the Yarmouth Duck and Yarn Company was started in 1883. It was one of several cotton mills established in the Maritimes to take advantage of the federal government's National Policy.

That policy, implemented in 1878, sought to stimulate the Canadian manufacturing sector by slapping tariffs on foreign manufactured goods while allowing certain raw materials, including cotton, to enter the country duty-free. So, Yarmouth merchants did not suddenly abandon shipping in a fit of panic. Rather, they scaled back operations in light of the advent of steam and sought to take advantage of the new technologies by investing in land-based manufacturing. The National Policy provided the economic stimulus, and the newly completed Western Counties Railway linked Yarmouth to the national market.

COUNTY MUSEUM, YARMOUTH (TOP); THE CAT FERRY IN YARMOUTH HARBOUR

But regional manufacturers could not compete with their central Canadian counterparts. The transfer of local capital to larger Ontario and Quebec interests was a problem experienced in all of Nova Scotia's industrial towns. Yarmouth's decline was as dramatic as its rise. By 1900 little industry was left. The cotton mill was still around but was soon controlled by outsiders.

Today there are some wistful reminders of Yarmouth's heyday. But there is a bright side to today's story. The town still thrives as the service centre for southwestern Nova Scotia and a key entry point for the province. The *MS Scotia Prince*, a combination cruise ship and car liner, connects Yarmouth to Portland, Maine. Bay Ferries operates another car ferry, the *Cat*, from Yarmouth to Bar Harbour, Maine.

The Yarmouth Arts Centre (Th'YARC) stages a variety of entertainment, including summer theatre, in its 380-seat theatre on Parade Street. Dory races are a highlight of Seafest, a week-long community festival held each July.

For the most part Yarmouth offers hotel/motel-style accommodation, but there are notable exceptions. Murray Manor (c. 1820) is a beautifully restored heritage property with lovely gardens and tasteful rooms (Acadian French is spoken). The Manor Inn, in nearby Hebron, features all the amenities (dining room, pub, tennis courts and more) on nine acres of attractively landscaped waterfrontage.

If you are looking for a good meal in a hurry, visit Harris's Quick and Tasty, a Yarmouth institution since the 1960s. The simple diner-style fare, including fishcakes and lobster sandwiches, will not disappoint.

Yarmouth's lobster fishery still flourishes. Take a drive out to Cape Forchu between the spring and fall lobster seasons and you'll see thousands of traps piled along the roadside.

EVANGELINE TRAIL

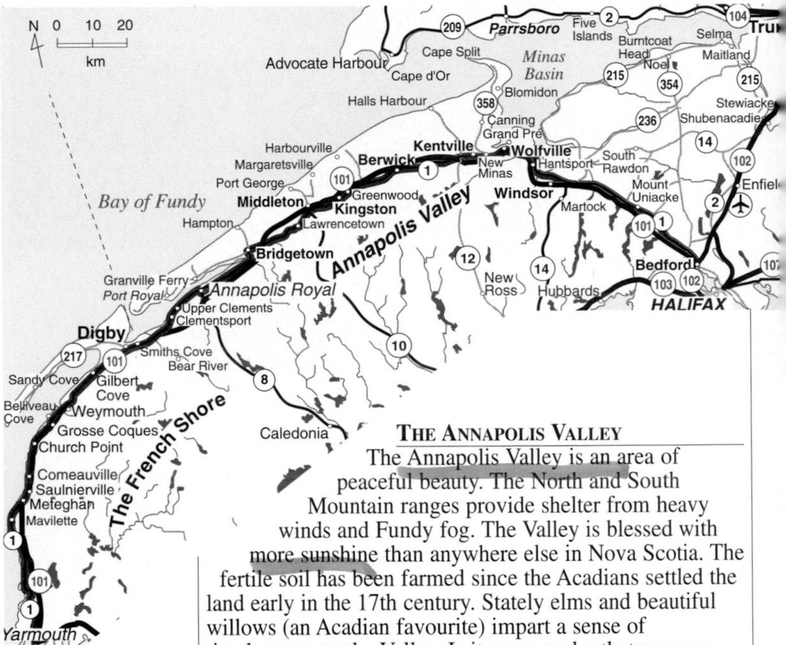

THE ANNAPOLIS VALLEY

The Annapolis Valley is an area of peaceful beauty. The North and South Mountain ranges provide shelter from heavy winds and Fundy fog. The Valley is blessed with more sunshine than anywhere else in Nova Scotia. The fertile soil has been farmed since the Acadians settled the land early in the 17th century. Stately elms and beautiful willows (an Acadian favourite) impart a sense of timelessness to the Valley. Is it any wonder that you can find a village named Paradise here?

The Valley is an ideal setting for a tragic romance. And history obliged with a suitable cast of characters — the Acadians, deported by the British in 1755, their lands, houses, and livestock all confiscated (see p. 19). All that was needed was for someone to write the story.

Henry Wadsworth Longfellow's epic poem *Evangeline* was published in Boston in 1847. It was immensely popular, running through five editions in its first year. Other publications followed which further aroused the curiosity of New Englanders in the "Land of Evangeline."

A rail link between Halifax and Yarmouth, completed in 1891, provided a convenient way of getting here. The Yarmouth Steamship Company added a new ship to its Boston run, and the Windsor and Annapolis Railway inaugurated the "Flying Bluenose." Since then, the Valley has been a popular destination for visitors from New England and beyond.

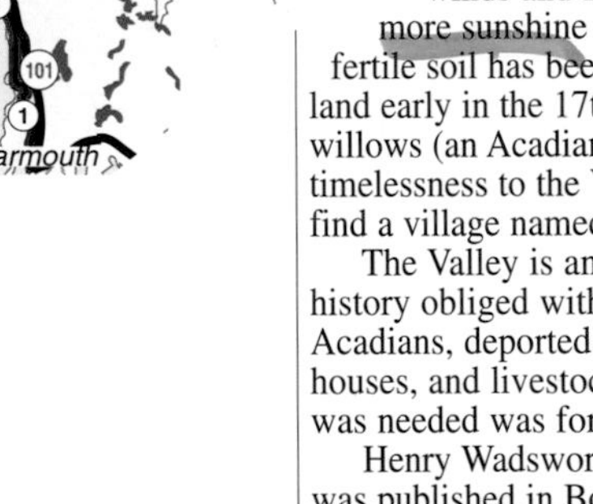

If you approach the valley from Halifax, on Highway 101, you will pass near Mount Uniacke, where Richard John Uniacke built an impressive Georgian mansion, Uniacke House, in 1813. After fighting on the rebel side of the American Revolution, Uniacke

CAPE BLOMIDON

bounced back nicely to become one of Nova Scotia's wealthiest and most influential men. As Attorney General and Advocate General to the Admiralty Court during the War of 1812, he made a fortune — a chunk of which went into the building of his country home. The Uniacke Estate Museum Park is now part of the Nova Scotia Museum Complex, and features many original furnishings, along with Uniacke family portraits.

As you continue your journey toward Windsor, the lush Valley landscape makes a dramatic appearance. Spread out before you are the rich farmlands that skirt the Avon River. If the tide is out, the river is an expanse of red mudflats. The Tidal View Farm in Newport offers one of the best views of the tide coming in. Remnants of Acadian dykes are here, although it is impossible to distinguish the originals from later reconstructions.

Windsor, is a service centre for Hants County farmers. The town was also home to Thomas Chandler Haliburton, the Nova Scotian humorist who created the character Sam Slick, the Yankee clockmaker with the acerbic wit. Haliburton House, a provincial museum, features Victorian furnishings and an attractive 10-hectare (25-acre) estate. Windsor is the home of Howard Dill, the farmer who developed the Atlantic Giant pumpkin that has produced pumpkins weighing more than 450 kilograms (1000 pounds). Visitors flock to the Dill farm on College Road, particularly in late summer and early fall, to marvel at the monster vegetables.

The Dill farm also is the site of Long Pond, where residents are convinced students at King's College School played the first-ever game of hockey. Downtown, the Windsor Hockey Heritage Centre tells the story of how Canada's great winter sport began.

Close by, at Falmouth, the Saint-Famille winery, which provides tours, and the well-kept greens and fairways of the Avon Valley golf course, both attest to the fine Valley weather.

Hantsport, once a prosperous shipbuilding centre, is now home to a busy pulp and paper products plant,

115

SAINT-FAMILLE
WINERY, FALMOUTH

and serves as a depot for export of gypsum. As you travel west, fields and orchards appear, reminders that agriculture has always been the mainstay of the area. During harvest season, roadside stands do a brisk business as locals and visitors load up on fresh fruit and vegetables.

In late May, the Annapolis Valley is in full bloom — orchards and orchards of apple trees laden with delicate pink and white blossoms. Since the 1930s, Valley residents have celebrated the start of the growing season with an Apple Blossom Festival.

Before the mid-nineteenth century, there was not much of an apple industry in the area. Poor roads and contrary winds made the shipment of perishable goods a dubious enterprise.

Railways and steamships changed all that. By the 1880s, Valley apples were being regularly shipped to Great Britain. In 1905, the Nova Scotia Fruit Growers' Association convinced the federal government to locate an experimental farm in Kentville. Valley farmers successfully lobbied rail and shipping interests for favourable rates that strengthened their position in the British market. For their part, the British cooperated by gobbling down more apples than any other people in the world. By the 1930s, Britain regularly consumed three-quarters of Nova Scotia's commercial crop. When that market suddenly dried up with the outbreak of war — the British could not use Nova Scotian apples to fight the Germans — the problem was thought to be temporary. It was not. A sluggish post-war economy forced Britons to severely limit the number of pounds that they could convert for dollar purchases. Valley apples were not a high priority. Currency restrictions were eventually relaxed but the British market was never recovered. Now, much of the crop is bought by multi-national corporations for processing; relatively few apples are grown for export.

But there are plenty of apples for the local market. In early fall, roadside stands brim with apples — Cortland, McIntosh, Gravenstein, Delicious, and more. Visitors with their own favourite apple recipes can spend an afternoon at one of the Valley's many "U-Pick" orchards.

Grand Pré National Historic Site is nearby. Hundreds of Acadians were deported from here in 1755, and the village became the setting for Longfellow's *Evangeline*. The grounds are beautiful, with gardens and winding paths shaded by old willow trees. A memorial church built in 1922 houses an exhibit on the Expulsion. Bilingual tours are provided.

Today, an increasing number of Valley residents live in towns, most of which are service centres for the agricultural hinterland. Magnificent elm trees and elegant Victorian homes give a peaceful, settled quality to these towns.

Wolfville is the cultural and academic centre of the Annapolis Valley. Acadia University, established as Acadia College in 1838, is situated on one of Canada's prettiest

STATUE OF EVANGELINE AND MEMORIAL CHURCH, GRAND PRÉ NATIONAL HISTORIC SITE

campuses. The university gives Wolfville a slightly more cosmopolitan feel than other Valley towns.

Not surprisingly, when organizers (including Christopher Plummer) were looking for a home for their new classical theatre festival, they chose Wolfville. Inaugurated in 1995, the Atlantic Theatre Festival stages top-quality traditional performances in a beautifully renovated, 500-seat, thrust stage theatre. The festival has won widespread acclaim and attracts fine actors from

ACADIA UNIVERSITY, WOLFVILLE

across North America. The season runs from June to September.

In addition to being the Valley's cultural centre, Wolfville is also one of its prettiest towns. Beautiful Victorian homes line elm-shaded streets. The visitor information centre at Willow Park, on Main Street, will provide you with a brochure for the Heritage Home Walking Tour.

Several of Wolfville's grandest homes are now among the province's best hostelries. The Blomidon Inn features 26 rooms in a lavish 1877 mansion. The entrance and public spaces are especially impressive, as are the Blomidon's best rooms. The Tattingstone Inn is a special place — you'll find four-poster beds and marble-tiled bathrooms, but also a swimming pool and tennis court. There is a carriage house and a cottage for honeymooners. Victoria's Historic Inn and Carriage House Bed & Breakfast (1893) is another registered heritage property. The main house includes three honeymoon suites, complete with jacuzzis.

Wolfville offers fine dining as well. Two of the inns mentioned have excellent dining rooms, and two more restaurants — Chez La Vigne and Acton's, where a popular lunch buffet features fresh Valley produce and Fundy seafood — make dining out in Wolfville a pleasure.

There are a number of interesting shops in town. Box of Delights is a good general bookstore with the Valley's best selection of local titles. Treasures is a quirky gift shop where you will find out-of-the-ordinary gardening supplies and Victorian housewares alongside local jewellery and crafts.

Wolfville's Robie Tufts Nature Centre (Tufts' bird books are available at most Nova Scotia bookstores) provides summer visitors with a rare spectacle. From May to late August, chimney swifts gather here for a startlingly acrobatic descent down a chimney.

Randall House, another grand Wolfville home, features a collection of historical materials relating to the

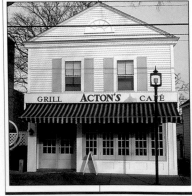

Planters who settled Mud Creek before it became Wolfville. (Across the street, a path leads to a series of dykes that are ideal for walking and offer great views of the town and surrounding countryside.)

In an area renowned for its agriculture, it may surprise you to learn that many of Wolfville's elegant homes, including the Blomidon Inn, were built with wealth earned from the shipping trades. Nearby Kingsport, Hantsport, and Port Williams were all important shipping centres. After 1928, some independent growers shipped Valley apples directly from Port Williams.

Three kilometres (2 mi.) away, at Starrs Point, Prescott House was built in 1815 by Charles Prescott, a businessman and horticulturist who introduced several varieties of apples, including the Gravenstein, to Nova Scotia. The house is filled with period furnishings, and the garden and grounds are especially attractive. Not far from the museum is the Planters' Barracks Country Inn, the oldest authentically restored inn in the province. Late in the 1770s, British soldiers were stationed here to protect the new Planter settlement at Starrs Point. Today, the barracks has nine rooms (all en suite); guests are invited to stroll through the heritage gardens or take afternoon tea in the adjacent Acacia Croft Tearoom.

Back at Port Williams, Route 358 continues north across Acadian dykes, through Canning, then on to The Lookoff. From high atop Cape Blomidon, you can survey the Minas Basin and six river valleys. In autumn, the view is made even more beautiful by the fall foliage that spreads out beneath you.

At the end of Route 358, hikers can carry on to the end of Cape Split (the continuation of Cape Blomidon) along a 13-kilometre (8-mi.) marked trail that yields spectacular views of the Bay of Fundy (see also p. 62).

Kentville services the richest farming area in the Valley and has been a long-time leader in the apple industry. The Agriculture Canada Research Station assists fruit growers with an ongoing program of scientific research. Blair House is an on-site museum with exhibits relating to the history of the apple industry and the Research Station's

CAPE BLOMIDON DOMINATES THIS FUNDY VIEW

involvement in it. Guided tours of the station are available by prior arrangement during the summer months. In town, the Old Kings Courthouse Heritage Museum on Cornwallis Street devotes much of its space to the social history of the area — especially to the arrival of the New England Planters in the 1760s (see p. 24). A good walking tour brochure is available from the visitor information centre. The tour lasts about three hours and will take you past several outstanding heritage homes.

Back towards Wolfville, the Ken-Wo Golf Club is one of the Valley's best courses. The sheltered fairways are well maintained, and the casual atmosphere makes green-fees feel more than welcome.

Villages and towns run into one another as you continue west through the Valley along Route 1. Road-weary travellers can choose from the many rural bed-and-breakfasts in places like Berwick, Middleton, and Lawrencetown. At Aylesford, families will enjoy the Oaklawn Farm Zoo, which features over 100 species of mammals and birds. The 18-hole Paragon golf course at Kingston is usually less crowded than other Valley courses and almost always drier (a nuisance at the height of summer, but a blessing at other times). Its wide-open fairways make it a forgiving course for novices.

A short side trip over North Mountain takes visitors to picturesque fishing villages hugging the shores of the Bay of Fundy. At places like Halls Harbour, Harbourville, Margaretsville or Hampton, fishing boats dramatically demonstrate the rise and fall of the tides, as they alternately ride high at their moorings, or sit on the mud flats awaiting the next high tide.If you have time, take a detour through Bridgetown and see for yourself why it is billed as "the prettiest little town in Nova Scotia." While a resident here, Canadian artist Kenneth Tolmie painted his "Bridgetown series." His work can be viewed at the Saratoga Gallery, one of three galleries in the town. Bridgetown was also the setting for Ernest Buckler's *The Mountain and the Valley*, probably the best work of fiction to come out of Nova Scotia.

OAKLAND FARM ZOO

PORT ROYAL

The communities along the shores of the Annapolis Basin are a treasure trove of history. All Nova Scotia school children know the story of the coming of Sieur de Monts and Samuel de Champlain to Port Royal at the beginning of the 17th century. They also learn how a second Port Royal, established on the opposite shore of the Basin in 1635, became Annapolis Royal in 1710 and served as the seat of British colonial government in Nova Scotia until Halifax was established in 1749. Here was the first successful European settlement in what is now Canada — and the genesis of British rule in Nova Scotia.

Off Route 1, about ten kilometres (6 mi.) southwest of Granville Ferry, is the reconstructed Port Royal Habitation. Close to here, de Monts and Champlain

established a fur-trading post in 1605. The reconstruction is based on Champlain's sketch of the site. Like Normandy farms of that time, buildings form a rectangle around a central courtyard.

THE HABITATION AT PORT ROYAL

A good deal is known about the French stay at Port Royal through the writings of Champlain, Marc Lescarbot, and Father Pierre Biard. Lescarbot, a disenchanted lawyer with literary aspirations and an ebullient personality, wrote extensively about his year at the Habitation. His frivolous Neptune pageant, now celebrated as Canada's first theatrical presentation, was played out along the shores of Port Royal in November of 1606. Even Champlain, no great fan of Lescarbot, was entertained.

The winter that followed was a relatively mild one, made even more bearable by Champlain's *Ordre de Bon Temps* (Order of Good Cheer). Champlain sought to ward off the

121

17TH CENTURY CARPENTRY

ravages of scurvy by promoting feasting and fellowship among the Order's members.

In 1607 de Monts' fears were realized when his monopoly was revoked; the Habitation was abandoned until 1610. Father Biard, a Jesuit priest, arrived the following year. His frequent clashes with the Biencourts, the father and son who now ran the Habitation, and the difficulties he encountered in his mission work with the Mi'kmaq, were well suited to Biard's acid pen. When Port Royal was sacked by a group of Virginians led by Samuel Argall in 1613, Biard may well have breathed a sigh of relief had he not been wrongfully accused of complicity in the raid by Biencourt the younger. For those who want to learn more about the Port Royal years, Elizabeth Jones offers a lively, narrative history in *Gentlemen and Jesuits*.

The present-day Habitation evokes Canada's first European settlement. Costumed interpreters, employed as 17th-century artisans, go about their tasks. Visitors can imagine Marc Lescarbot scribbling away in his reconstructed dwelling. Other buildings at the site, which include the Governor's House, the Priest's Dwelling, the Chapel, the Blacksmith's Shop, and the Trading Room, may well inspire 17th-century reveries.

FORT ANNE, ANNAPOLIS ROYAL

ANNAPOLIS ROYAL

At Granville Ferry, pause long enough to look across the river at the Annapolis Royal waterfront. On a calm, clear day this is one of Nova Scotia's special views. Also worth a look is the fine collection of Georgian furniture, ceramics, glass, and silver housed at the North Mills Museum in Granville Ferry.

At the Annapolis River Causeway is a prototype tidal power installation. An on-site interpretive display shows how the generators work, but the power house itself is underground and off-limits to the public. From here, Route 1 leads directly to Annapolis Royal.

Beautiful Annapolis Royal, on the shores of the

Annapolis Basin, is a showcase of heritage restoration. A reconstruction project launched in 1979 spruced up some of the town's fine old buildings, attracting both business and tourists. Before the project, visitors to Annapolis Royal had to leave town to get a good meal. Now three local restaurants — the Garrison House, Newman's, and Leo's Café — are listed in *Where to Eat in Canada*. All three

occupy buildings of historic interest. (The Adams-Ritchie House, site of Leo's, was built by a New England merchant in 1712.) Since 1984, the restored King's Theatre has featured the Annapolis Royal Arts Festival, a September celebration of local, regional, and national talent. The same venue hosts a summer theatre festival during July and August. The work of local artists and artisans, many of them recent arrivals to Annapolis Royal, can be seen in waterfront shops and galleries.

HISTORIC GARDENS, ANNAPOLIS ROYAL

In the centre of town, Fort Anne National Historic Site represents the fourth and last fort built by the French at this location. Governor Subercase's powder magazine (1708) is the one extant building from the French era. The story of the struggle for supremacy between the French and English is told in the museum building, which was constructed as officers' quarters by the Duke of Kent in 1797. A stroll along the earthworks affords some beautiful views of the Annapolis Basin.

The Annapolis Royal Historic Gardens were opened in August 1981 as part of the heritage restoration project. Abutted by reclaimed marshland and a 20-hectare (50-acre) wildfowl sanctuary, the stunning 4-hectare (10-acre) gardens display much of the area's natural history. Among the more than 200 varieties in the Rose Garden are several which were grown by Acadian settlers in the

BEAR RIVER IS HOME TO A FLOURISHING ARTISTIC COMMUNITY

area in the 17th century (the roses are at their peak from late June until August). Next to the replica of an Acadian cottage, willow and apple trees shade an Acadian potager, or vegetable garden, wherein can be found the makings of an outstanding pot of soup. Other highlights include the Governor's Garden, which was modelled after 18th-century gardens in southern New England, and the carefully ordered Victorian Garden with its 300-year-old elm tree.

Annapolis Royal bustled during the late 18th and 19th centuries. Ships left waterfront wharves loaded with apples, potatoes, and lumber, and returned with sugar, molasses, and rum from the West Indies. Packet boats from Digby, Saint John, and Boston made Annapolis Royal a regular port of call. The town was a popular overnight stop.

Today, the O'Dell Inn Museum, dating from the 1860s, recreates the cosmopolitan atmosphere of a busy 19th-century inn. It catered to well-off travellers, the nicer rooms going for $1.50 a night. The museum also houses collections of Victorian costume and furnishings, artifacts of childhood, as well as the ubiquitous relics of a shipbuilding past.

Bonnett House, also on Lower St. George Street, is a research centre for local history and genealogy. The centre is open year-round by chance or appointment.

Several other outstanding Georgian and Victorian structures are along or just off St. George Street. (The de Gannes-Cosby House, built in 1708, is thought to be the oldest wooden house in Canada.) "Stroll Through the Centuries," a brochure put out by the Historical Association of Annapolis Royal, provides an interpreted walking tour of the town. During the summer months (except Sundays) the association offers regular guided tours from its headquarters at the lighthouse on Lower St. George Street.

TOWARD DIGBY

From Annapolis Royal, Route 1 meanders along the shore of the Annapolis Basin towards Digby (Highway 101 provides a faster, less scenic alternative). At Upper Clements, the 10-hectare (25-acre) Family Vacation Park is popular with children. The flume ride, roller coaster, and carousel are special favourites. Across the highway, the Upper Clements Wildlife Park offers visitors a chance to see native Nova Scotian animals — lynx, cougar, porcupines, foxes, ground hogs, skunks, deer, and moose — along winding, wooded trails.

To the southwest, Route 1 eventually crosses Bear River into Digby County. The work of Nova Scotia artisans, many from Bear River, is showcased at Flight of Fancy on Main Street. Featured downstairs arc striking bird paintings on stone, Mi'kmaq crafts, sculptured hardwood burls, pottery, weaving, jewellery, stained glass, and carved birds. The upstairs gallery displays paintings, photographs and sculpture by well-known Nova Scotia artists. Bear River's Cherry Carnival, held in mid-July (blossom time) includes an auction, parade, and woodsmen's show.

Back on the main drag is the resort community of Smiths Cove. Outstanding views of the Annapolis Basin and Digby Gut make Smiths Cove a good choice for an overnight stay. The Mountain Gap Resort offers waterside accommodation (including cottages) at a reasonable price — especially for families, who will appreciate the resort's beach, swimming pool, tennis court, and playground.

GARRISON HOUSE INN, ANNAPOLIS ROYAL

From there it is a short drive to Digby, home of the world's largest scallop fleet. Scallops and Digby Chicks (smoked herring) are served in local restaurants. From the deck of the Fundy Restaurant on Water Street, you can enjoy Digby seafood with a view of the boats that caught your meal. Golfers rave about Stanley Thompson's championship course at the Digby Pines Resort. The par-71, 18-hole course plays through mature stands of spruce and pine while affording some beautiful views of the Annapolis Basin. The hotel, built in 1929, features a Norman-style chateau and 30 cottages strung out along a bluff which rises from the shores of the Basin. A regular ferry service shuttles across the Bay of Fundy between Digby and Saint John, New Brunswick.

ACROSS THE ANNAPOLIS BASIN TO DIGBY GUT

Whale- and seabird-watching tours are just some of the reasons to enjoy a drive and two short ferry rides along Digby Neck, to Long Island and Brier Island. Along the way are spectacular panoramas of rocky headlands that have been carved by the powerful Fundy tides. Brier Island Lodge offers food and accommodation as well as breath-taking ocean views.

THE FRENCH SHORE

Between Digby and Yarmouth, along the margin of St. Marys Bay, runs a string of Acadian villages. There is no mistaking Nova Scotia's "French Shore"; it is distinctly Acadian. Every few kilometres, a steeple soars from one of the magnificent Catholic churches. Colourful houses adorned with curious whirligigs and gizmos line the road at Mavilette or Grosses Coques. Yet, for generations after their arrival from France, the original Acadian settlers ignored this area. Most preferred the fertile land of the Annapolis Valley.

BRIER ISLAND, AT THE ENTRANCE TO ST. MARY'S BAY

The British paid no heed to Acadian preferences in 1755. The Acadians were deported, their houses and barns put to the torch, and their lands seized by the Crown (see p. 19). Soon after, the governor began granting these lands to new settlers, many of them from New England, whose loyalty he trusted.

Some Acadians managed to escape the Deportation. They withdrew to the forests or fled to remote corners of the province. They lived as refugees. Many died during that first winter. Others were caught and imprisoned at Halifax, Windsor, or Annapolis Royal. Still, there was a group of Acadians in Nova Scotia who somehow persevered. When the Treaty of Paris ended the war between France and England in 1763, these people began looking for a home. Sadly, the Annapolis Valley was lost to them.

Eventually, Lieutenant-Governor Michael Francklin responded to their plight. Land was surveyed along St. Marys Bay. In 1768 the Township of Clare, named after the Irish county, was created for settlement by the Acadians.

The villages of St. Bernard, Belliveau Cove, Grosses Coques, Church Point, and Little Brook fall within the boundaries of that original grant. As families grew and others returned from exile, Acadian settlement extended southward to Salmon River. Today, this entire stretch is part

of the Municipality of Clare.

Life along the shore was much different from the life the Acadians had known in the Valley. They still kept gardens, although the soil was poorer, but the forest and the sea were irresistible forces. Acadian farmers became woodsmen, shipbuilders, and fishermen — jacks of all trades.

Today their self-reliance is revealed by a drive along Route 1, sometimes called "the longest main street on earth." Family-run businesses crowd the shore. U. J. Robichaud and Sons run a lumber business at Meteghan Centre. A. F. Theriault and his sons have a shipyard at Meteghan River. The Comeaus and Deveaus seem to be everywhere. Comeau's Sea Foods in Saulnierville is a huge operation. The Deveaus are into fish at Belliveau Cove and insurance at Meteghan. Few businesses along the French Shore are run by outsiders.

The French Shore has long served as a centre for Acadian culture in Nova Scotia. Both in terms of size and population density, it is the largest Acadian region in the province. In villages all along St. Marys Bay, people gather each July to celebrate their Acadian heritage during the Festival Acadien de Clare. Festivities are fuelled by Acadian music and food. (For a special treat try rappie pie, a savoury casserole of potato and chicken, at the Cape View Restaurant, overlooking Mavilette Beach.)

L'ÉGLISE SAINT BERNARD

Mavilette, one of several wonderful beaches in the area, has 5 kilometres of magnificent shore.

In 1890, a group of Eudist priests established Collège Sainte-Anne at Church Point. Over the years, Saint-Anne, which became a university in 1977, has made enormous contributions to Acadian culture in Nova Scotia. *Evangeline*, a musical drama based on Longfellow's poem, is staged here during the summer months (an English synopsis is supplied). The Magasin Campus (campus bookstore) has a wide selection of books on Acadian themes.

A large, fairly homogeneous Acadian population has benefited the people of the French Shore in other ways. The area also has a long tradition of political representation by Acadians, both at the federal and provincial levels. And recent studies have shown that the French spoken in this part of the province has retained more 17th-century features than that spoken elsewhere in Nova Scotia.

But the most visible expressions of the cultural vitality along the French Shore are the beautiful churches. Acadians pride themselves on their Catholic faith, and parishioners of modest means went to great pains to

FESTIVAL ACADIEN DE CLARE

L'ÉGLISE SACRÉ COEUR, SAULNIERVILLE

demonstrate this pride. Hidden behind the graceful exteriors of these churches are surer signs of Acadian faith, workmanship, and resourcefulness. Two churches — L'Église Sainte Marie at Church Point and L'Église Saint Bernard at St. Bernard — should not be missed.

The plans for Sainte Marie were drawn up in France, but construction of the church was left in the skillful hands of Leo Melanson, a master carpenter from nearby Little Brook. Between 1903 and 1905, he and many others laboured. They must have been in awe of their achievement.

Sainte Marie is the largest wooden church in North America. Its steeple rises 56 metres (185 ft.) above the community of 318 people. It is anchored by 40 tons of stone ballast to keep it from blowing off in hurricane force winds.

Other things impress. The interior of the church belies its size. A wooden floor softens the stained glass light,

lending a warm and comfortable feeling to the entire nave. The "stone" pillars that support the roof are not stone. They are huge tree trunks that have been lathed and covered in plaster. Overhead, the "marble" arches are wooden as well.

The parishioners of St. Bernard were not to be outdone. They hired an architect from Moncton, New Brunswick, who had visited France. He sent down the plans, but again the work was left to locals. Between 1910 and 1942, they built a huge stone church that seats over 1,000.

Visitors to the French Shore will receive a warm welcome in French or English. All but a handful of the Acadian population speak both languages. However, it is their French, like their magnificent churches, through which the Acadians of Clare express pride in their culture.

The Evangeline Trail continues to Yarmouth (see pages 112-3).

GLOOSCAP TRAIL

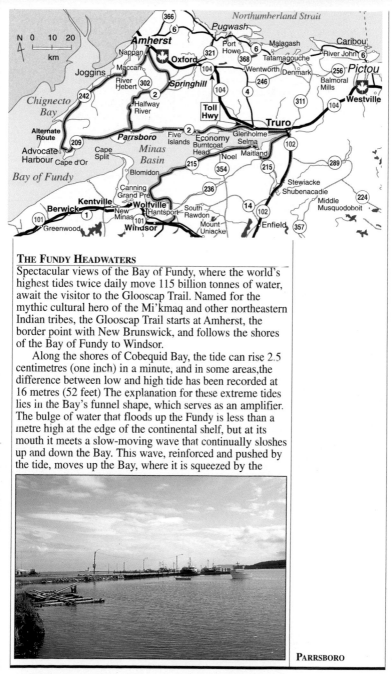

THE FUNDY HEADWATERS

Spectacular views of the Bay of Fundy, where the world's highest tides twice daily move 115 billion tonnes of water, await the visitor to the Glooscap Trail. Named for the mythic cultural hero of the Mi'kmaq and other northeastern Indian tribes, the Glooscap Trail starts at Amherst, the border point with New Brunswick, and follows the shores of the Bay of Fundy to Windsor.

Along the shores of Cobequid Bay, the tide can rise 2.5 centimetres (one inch) in a minute, and in some areas, the difference between low and high tide has been recorded at 16 metres (52 feet) The explanation for these extreme tides lies in the Bay's funnel shape, which serves as an amplifier. The bulge of water that floods up the Fundy is less than a metre high at the edge of the continental shelf, but at its mouth it meets a slow-moving wave that continually sloshes up and down the Bay. This wave, reinforced and pushed by the tide, moves up the Bay, where it is squeezed by the

PARRSBORO

129

RAFTING ON THE SHUBENACADIE

rising ocean bottom and the narrowing Fundy shores.

This produces some dramatic effects. Tidal bores occur when a wave of water moves upstream and collides with the current, making it appear as though rivers are flowing backwards. Depending on the phase of the moon and other factors such as wind direction, the tidal bore can be either a barely detectable ripple or a wall of water a metre high. Tidal bores can be viewed along a number of rivers in the upper Fundy region, including the Salmon River near Truro (the Palliser Restaurant provides an ideal vantage point and great home-style cooking); the Shubenacadie River at various locations; and from the Maccan and River Hebert bridges. Several companies offer upriver rafting trips on the Shubenacadie. These are safe but can be exciting, as small craft go down river, then return on the crest of the incoming tide.

AMHERST AND SPRINGHILL

Join the Glooscap Trail at Amherst, where some truly grand homes, especially along Victoria Street, and shells of old factories stand as evidence of past industrial glory. The Cumberland County Museum tells some of Amherst's industrial and labour history. Amherst was one of the towns

GRAND HOMES WERE BUILT DURING AMHERST'S INDUSTRIAL HEYDAY

FIRST BAPTIST CHURCH, AMHERST

able to take advantage of the steam-based technologies that fueled the new industrialism of the 19th century. "Busy Amherst" boomed, as textile milling, boot and shoe manufacturing, gas-boiler production and railway car construction drew hundreds of people to the town.

A choice of routes to Parrsboro is offered at River Hebert. One can either follow Route 209 along a sparsely populated section of the Fundy shore or continue along Highway 2 to enjoy a stop at Springhill, which remembers the bustle and tragedy of its coal mining history and celebrates the success of its contribution to the continent's entertainment industry. Over the years, more than 400

people have died in local mines. The "Springhill Bump" of 1958, remembered more for the miraculous survival of 18 men who had spent a week trapped underground than for the 75 who did not make it, brought an end to large-scale mining in the town. But it did not bring an end to tragedy. In 1975, fire ravaged the town's mainstreet business district. Today, retired miners give underground tours at the Springhill Miners' Museum, where exhibits include poignant accounts of the mining accidents. The museum is built on the site of a small mine that closed in 1970.

The Anne Murray Centre pays tribute to the Springhill-born recording artist and offers a surprisingly candid look at her life — including report cards and baby pictures. Fans of "Canada's Country Sweetheart" should definitely drop in.

ANNE MURRAY CENTRE

SPRINGHILL MINERS' MUSEUM

PARRSBORO

Those who choose Highway 209 to get to Parrsboro will see a part of the province that has long been recognized as a treasure trove of fossil remains. The Fossil Centre at

Joggins, an old coal mining town on Chignecto Bay, offers guided tours of the famous fossil cliffs. Fossil finds, usually plant material, date from the time when Nova Scotia's vast coal deposits were formed about 300 million years ago. The cliffs themselves are off-limits, but they erode quickly so that new fossils are always falling to the beach. Children will enjoy the outing, and are almost always assured of finding something. As you search the beach beneath the cliffs, take an occasional peek behind you; you will be surprised to see how quickly the tide is falling — or rising!

OTTAWA HOUSE, PARRSBORO (LEFT)

The Bay of Fundy, like most large bodies of water, has its share of marine folklore, and one of these stories, that of the saga of the ghost ship *Mary Celeste*, is recounted at a cairn at Spencers Island. It was in December, 1872, that the brigantine was discovered at sea with sails set and everything in order, but no one was on board, or was ever found. It would turn out to be one of the great sea mysteries of all time.

UNUSUAL ROCK FORMATIONS AT CAPE D'OR

Along the stretch of coastline between Advocate and Parrsboro, the scenery rivals the coastal views along Cape Breton's Cabot Trail. Across the Minas Channel, Cape Split and North Mountain loom large on a clear day, and Cape d'Or is just as spectacular. There is a lookoff at the Cape d'Or lighthouse (just off Route 209) with an unforgettable view — east toward the Minas Basin, south across the Minas Channel, and west to the Bay of Fundy.

In Parrsboro, the Fundy Geological Museum houses a display on the effects the giant Fundy tides have had on the people and the land. Museum exhibits also detail the geological and fossil history of the area.

GLOOSCAP STATUE, PARRSBORO

Good opportunities for rock-hounding are plentiful in the Parrsboro area. The town holds Nova Scotia's Gem and Mineral Show each August. Zeolites — semi-precious stones such as agate and amethyst — are common finds along the beaches and cliffs of the Minas Basin. Eldon George, Parrsboro's most famous rock hound, has a rock shop at the edge of town. In April, 1984, George found a rock with some very tiny — and soon to be highly celebrated — dinosaur footprints on its surface.

Parrsboro's Ship's Company Theatre stages innovative productions aboard the *MV Kipawo*, a beached ferry boat that once serviced Parrsboro, Kingsport and Wolfville. The acclaimed company features many plays by Maritime writers during a season that runs from mid-June to Labour Day.

PARRSBORO TO WINDSOR

The road from Parrsboro to the TransCanada Highway at Glenholme offers an opportunity to visit several quaint and historic hamlets such as Economy, Bass River, Portapique/Highland Village, Great Village and Londonderry. If you stop at Five Islands Provincial Park, you can see where the

WENTWORTH FALLS

legendary Glooscap threw handfuls of sod at Beaver, creating Moose, Diamond, Long, Egg and Pinnacle islands. There are also a number of hiking trails in the Park.

Five Islands Lighthouse – a "pepper pot" wooden structure – also has a

LAWRENCE HOUSE,
MAITLAND

terrific view of the islands. Scenic falls in
the region are popular destinations for
hikers. A novel opportunity to observe the
evolution of nature can be enjoyed at
Economy Falls, where a major rock fall
changed the appearance of that popular
attraction in late 1997.

From Truro, there are the options of heading towards
Halifax or continuing along the Fundy shore to Maitland.

The village of Maitland, located at the mouth of the
Shubenacadie River, flourished during the Age of Sail. At
one time, 11 shipyards bordered an 11-kilometre (7-mile)
stretch of shore near Maitland. Fortunes were made and
lavish homes were built. Close to 50 of these have
survived, prompting the provincial government to
designate Maitland as Nova Scotia's first Heritage
Conservation District. A walking tour brochure is
available at the local visitor information centre. The Frieze
and Roy General Store, established in 1839, displays a
number of interesting historical items.

On October 27, 1874, more than 4,000 people gathered
in Maitland to see the launching of the *W. D. Lawrence*, the
largest full-rigged ship ever built in Canada. (The village
commemorates the event with a Launch Day Festival in
September.) The *Lawrence* was nearly 2,500 tonnes, and
turned a handsome profit for her owners. At Lawrence
House, designated a National Historic Site in 1965, the
signs of wealth are everywhere. English iron-work radiators
are topped with Italian marble. At the back of the house,
you can see the huge blocks that were used to step the
masts of Lawrence's ships. Not surprisingly, William
Lawrence, elected to the Nova Scotia Assembly in 1863,
strongly opposed Confederation, and fought for repeal of

BURNTCOAT HEAD

the Union Act. The Intercolonial
Railway, the linchpin of Confederation
and a symbol of future prosperity,
would not run through Maitland.

Continuing west from Maitland,
along coastal Route 215 toward Windsor,
one soon begins enjoying the scenic Noel
Shore, one of the prettiest spots in the
province when the horse chestnuts are in
bloom in late June. At Burntcoat Head,
during the Saxby Tide in 1869, the
highest tides in the world were recorded.
Gale-force winds helped generate a high
tide of 16.5 metres (54 feet).

SUNRISE TRAIL

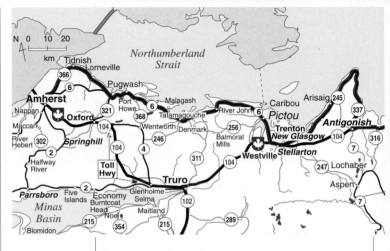

AMHERST TO PORT HOWE

The Sunrise Trail follows the north shore, from Amherst (see p. 130) to the Canso Causeway. With its picturesque towns, gentle farmland and seaside views, this route is a recommended alternative to the TransCanada Highway. Several fine beaches and the warm waters of the Northumberland Strait help make it a popular summer holiday destination.

The Nova Scotia Information Centre at the provincial gateway displays information on the Chignecto Ship Railway, the ambitious 19th-century venture that would have transported ships from the Bay of Fundy to the Northumberland Strait by rail. A 4-kilometre walking trail follows the remnants of the railbed to Tidnish Dock Provincial Park.

Not much further, near Lorneville, is the Amherst Shore Country Inn run by the son and daughter-in-law of Jim and

Donna Laceby who also operate the Blomidon Inn in Wolfville (see page 118). The inn offers four rooms and four suites, as well as a rustic seaside cottage and memorable dining. In Port Howe, Chase's Lobster Pound offers fresh live and cooked lobsters.

SEAGULL PEWTER, PUGWASH

PUGWASH AND THE SHORELINE

Pugwash, with street signs in both Gaelic and English, is one of several North Shore communities with a rich Scottish heritage. (The village holds a Gathering of the Clans Festival in early July.)

During the 1950s and '60s, wealthy Cleveland industrialist Cyrus Eaton hosted a number of Thinkers Conferences at his Pugwash estate, to which he invited Western and Soviet intellectuals. Albert Einstein was among the attendees.

Today, Pugwash is home to several silver and pewter manufacturers who ship pewter jewellery, dishes, and picture frames to worldwide markets. Seagull Pewter has a large shop on the main road. Canadian Sterling Silversmiths sell fine silver and gold jewellery from their retail craft outlet. The jewellery is made on site, and daily tours are offered from June to October. High-quality Maritime handcrafts are also featured at the shop.

Just outside town, serious golfers can enjoy 18 challenging holes on the Northumberland Sea Shore Golf Links. The open, tree-lined fairways are well-maintained. Several holes play along the water, and the views of the Strait can be quite a distraction.

The views are just as striking at Sunrise Beach Golf & Country Club, overlooking Brule Harbour near Tatamagouche. But unlike the Pugwash course, this wide-open, nine-hole round of golf is well-suited to beginners.

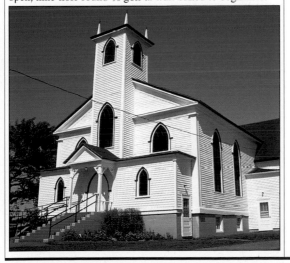

In addition to a modest fishery, Tatamagouche is a service centre for local dairy farms. (Appropriately, Highland cattle are beginning to catch on in the area as well.) And the favourable climate sustains some other, more exotic enterprises. The Josts, one of several German families to settle along the North Shore since the Second World War, have a wine-making operation in nearby Malagash. Tours of the vineyards are provided and visitors are invited to sample Jost wines at the on-site retail store. There are some good quality, inexpensive wines.

Farther along, two restored mills give a glimpse of earlier times. The Balmoral Grist Mill, at Balmoral Mills (Route 256) grinds wheat, oats, and buckwheat into flour using 19th-century water-powered milling techniques. The Sutherland Steam Mill, in nearby Denmark (Route 326) began sawing logs into lumber in 1894. The steam boilers are fired up occasionally in the summer months; the rest of the time, the mill is inoperative.

The Northumberland Strait is a choice area for the lobster fishery. The season runs from early May to late June. Then, communities like River John bustle. The village holds frequent lobster suppers during the season, and visitors are invited to take part.

The good beaches — such as the one at Caribou, northwest of Pictou — attract cottagers to this shoreline. For a shorter stay, you might choose the Pictou Lodge on Braeshore Road, just east of town and four kilometres (2.5 mi.) from the Prince Edward Island Ferry. Built in the mid-1920s as an exclusive retreat, the lodge was originally managed by the Canadian National Railway. Its log construction is typical of many CNR resorts including the Jasper Park Lodge in the Canadian Rockies. The cabins include several dating from the 1920s plus many more modern units. Ocean views can be spectacular, especially at sunset, from the sunporch bar.

PICTOU

Pictou's Scottish culture, scenic harbour, and fine architecture make it the North Shore's most popular destination for visitors. And for those Nova Scotians who take great pride in their Scottish heritage, Pictou is a kind of Plymouth Rock. The *Hector,* which landed Nova Scotia's first Scots (excluding the few that had come and gone during the 1620s and '30s) on the shores of Pictou Harbour in 1773, has been called the "Scottish Mayflower" (see p. 38). For a Nova Scotia Scot, the ability to put ancestors aboard the *Hector* accords special status.

Today, the showpiece of Pictou's waterfront is the *Hector,* at the Hector Heritage Quay. The 33-metre (110-ft.) full-rigged West Indian trader was reconstructed on site, and as of September 2000, was to begin its career as a floating museum exhibit. Although no plans for the original *Hector* exist, engineers went to some trouble to ensure that the

reconstructed ship closely resembled its predecessor. The story of 18th-century Scottish immigration and the *Hector* voyage is told in the Quay's Interpretation Centre.

The site also includes a carpentry shop, a blacksmith shop, and a gift shop. You can nip into a nearby pub for a wee dram. During August, the Hector Festival features Scottish music, dance, and food, with Celtic musical performances being held at the de Coste Centre on Water Street. (This venue also serves as Northeastern Nova Scotia's centre for the performing arts throughout the year.)

PICTOU IS A CENTRE OF SCOTTISH CULTURE

Next to the Hector National Exhibit Centre, on old Haliburton Road, is McCulloch House, a restored home dating from 1806.

Pictou's architecture is another Scottish legacy. Throughout the town you can see 19th-century neoclassical buildings, mostly of stone. Typically, these have gabled walls that extend above the plane of the roof at either end of the house. The "Scottish dormer," recognizable by its bay window, is another prominent feature. Fine trim and mouldings lend elegance to houses that would otherwise appear stark. Some Pictou streets, especially those with row houses, could easily run through towns in western Scotland.

The tourist bureau, located at the rotary just outside town, can direct you to the town's historic buildings. Several are open to visitors. The Walker Inn (c. 1865) the Willow House Inn (c.1840) and the Consulate Inn (c. 1810) are Registered Heritage Properties that offer bed-and-breakfast style accommodation in the downtown area. The Customs House B&B offers carefully restored rooms in what was Pictou's Customs House. The Braeside Inn, though built this century, also impresses from its hilltop

MCCULLOCH HOUSE

perch overlooking the harbour. It offers fine harbour views from the inn's two large dining rooms (seafood is a specialty) and from several of its 20 guest rooms.

Pictou's archi-tecture and landscape also reflect its historic importance as a shipbuilding centre. The Consulate Inn, so named because it housed the American Consulate during

PICTOU'S SCOTTISH ARCHITECTURE

the last half of the 19th century, is one sign of this legacy. The shipyard, where visitors who arrive on the right day may still see a large vessel in dry-dock, is another. The lobster fishery also makes this a working harbour. Here, and in countless other villages along the Strait, fishermen spend May and June mornings setting and unloading traps. Since 1934, the town has celebrated this fishery during the Pictou Lobster Carnival, held in early July. (Local boat races highlight the festival.)

While in town, you can also visit Grohmann Knives, known to outdoor enthusiasts as the manufacturer of the world-renowned D.H. Russell Belt Knife. Grohmann offers free factory tours (some restrictions apply) and the gift shop often has good buys on seconds. Nearby gift shops offer a range of crafts from local craftspeople. The Pictou Golf Club, over-looking the harbour, is a fairly easy nine-hole course despite all the downhill, uphill, and sidehill lies that you'll encounter.

Melmerby is the best of several good warm-water

beaches in the Pictou area. Take Exit 25 off Highway 104 (the TransCanada) to get to this 2 kilometre (1.2-mi.) stretch of broad, sandy beach. Melmerby is supervised and offers canteen, shower, and change facilities.

MELMERBY BEACH, NEAR NEW GLASGOW

NEW GLASGOW AND STELLARTON

Most of the area's heavy industry sprang up in the towns across the harbour, to the southeast of Pictou. Coal mining transformed the landscapes of Westville and Stellarton. Canada's first integrated metal-making and metal-working complex did the same to New Glasgow and Trenton. These towns, with their long history of industrial activity, have fascinating stories to tell, including the 1992 disaster at the Westray coal mine.

There was nothing exceptional in the rise of the Pictou County coal industry; similar growth was taking place in Cape Breton and Cumberland County. It was the metals industry that relied heavily on the entrepreneurial spirit of the Pictou County elite. When shipbuilding became

unprofitable in the 1880s, New Glasgow's wealthy merchant families began looking for somewhere else to put their money. What they found, the Nova Scotia Steel and Coal Company, changed Pictou County. The populations of New Glasgow and Trenton exploded as people came to work in one of the country's foremost industrial enterprises. During the First World War, "Scotia" employed close to 6,000 miners and steelworkers. Many other Pictou County operations were busy converting Scotia's steel into a wide range of secondary metal products.

But Scotia's story is a familiar one. During the 1920s, increased freight rates, competition from central Canada, and outside ownership led to a rapid decline. Pictou County industry has been teetering on the brink ever since. The story of industrial boom and bust is told at the Nova Scotia Museum of Industry, just off the TransCanada Highway at Stellarton. Exhibits include two of the world's oldest steam locomotives. Children, especially, enjoy working on the museum's toy train assembly line.

MUSEUM OF INDUSTRY IN STELLARTON

New Glasgow celebrates its Scottish, not its industrial, legacy. The Festival of the Tartans, an annual gathering that features Highland music and games, is held here in mid-July. New Glasgow's Abercrombie Country Club is a challenging 18-hole course that punishes wayward tee shots. It is essential to book tee-times in advance.

ANTIGONISH

Antigonish, along the eastern section of the North Shore, is home to St. Francis Xavier University and the Highland Games. The Games, held in mid-July, include piping, Highland dancing, heavy events, and track and field, making for one of Nova Scotia's best Scottish festivals. Festival Antigonish offers live theatre on the university campus throughout the summer months. The Antigonish Golf Club is the North Shore's best 18-hole bet for spur-of-the-moment golf. It is rarely crowded on summer weekdays and provides a stiff test, playing 6100 yards from the men's tees.

If you have time to dawdle, take Route 337 north from Antigonish along the western shore of St. Georges Bay. Like many of the roads along the North Shore, this drive takes you off the beaten track. The views from Cape George are beautiful, and there are more good beaches along the way.

ST. FRANCIS XAVIER UNIVERSITY, ANTIGONISH

MARINE DRIVE

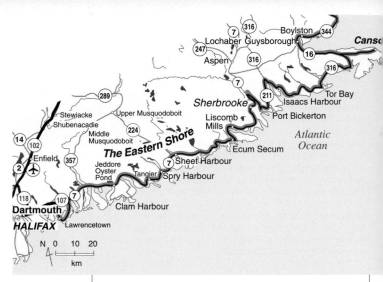

The Eastern Shore, which extends along the Atlantic coast between Halifax and Canso, is rugged and relatively undeveloped. A vast network of wilderness lakes and rivers makes the area a favourite with canoeists and campers. Coastal kayaking is popular, especially in the area around Tangier (see p. 60). Outdoor enthusiasts can explore five Nature Zones: the Eastern Shore Beaches; Harbours and Islands; the Canso Barrens; the Guysborough Lowlands and the Mulgrave Plateau.

But to those who choose the Eastern Shore's Marine Drive as an alternative to the TransCanada Highway for the trip from Halifax to Cape Breton, take heed. Here you will find some spectacular coastal scenery, but the 400-kilometre (250-mi.) drive along winding roads is best spread over two days.

SURFERS AT LAWRENCETOWN BEACH

BEACHES
Lawrencetown Beach is just east of Dartmouth. A provincial park, this steep, sandy beach is supervised and has change and canteen facilities. Lawrencetown is relatively exposed, and large waves make it a favourite with Nova Scotia surfers.

Farther along, to the south of

Musquodoboit Harbour, is Martinique Beach. (The name is tropical, but the crystal-clear water is not.) Because of its distance from Halifax, on some summer days you will have this 5-kilometre (3-mi.)-long stretch to yourself. The **MARTINIQUE BEACH**

fine sand hardens at the waterline, making Martinique ideal for long walks. Nearby, the Martinique Beach Game Sanctuary is the northernmost wintering ground of the Canada Goose. The Salmon River House Country Inn, at Salmon River Bridge, offers six well-appointed guest rooms in an area where accommodations are scarce. On-site outdoor activities include hiking, boating, hunting and fishing. The Fisherman's Life

Museum, in neighbouring Jeddore Oyster Pond, recalls the lives of a turn-of-the-century inshore fisherman and his family. The museum interpreters have some wonderful stories to tell.

Clam Harbour Beach comes next. Its fine, white sand is ideal for sand-castles. In mid-August, thousands come here for the Clam Harbour Beach Sand-Sculpting Contest, with group and individual competitions for young and old. Some of the sculptures are extremely intricate. On Route 224 toward Middle Musquodoboit is the Moose River and Area Museum, telling of gold mining in the area and the famous mine disaster in 1936.

TAYLOR HEAD PROVINCIAL PARK

Highway 7 continues east through Tangier on its way towards Sherbrooke Village. Tangier is home to Willy Krauch's Danish Smokehouse. Open year-round, Krauch's wood-smoked salmon, eel, and mackerel have won

customers from around the world.

Farther along Highway 7, on a peninsula that juts into the Atlantic, is Taylor Head Provincial Park, where there are a number of boardwalks and trails. The beach and the views of the ocean are both spectacular.

SHERBROOKE VILLAGE

Sherbrooke Village has been restored to appear as it was during the last half of the 19th century. Area residents work there, and take pride in its history. The result is a low-key living museum, where the past rubs shoulders comfortably with the present.

The site along the banks of the St. Marys River has attracted many people over the centuries. The Mi'kmaq were drawn by the large runs of salmon in the river, and New England fishermen frequented the area. In 1755, the French established a fur trading post here (Fort Sainte Marie) where they traded with the Mi'kmaq, fished, and cultivated the soil, until they were driven out by an English force in 1669.

Around 1800, about 50 settlers from the Truro and Pictou areas moved cross-country to establish new homes. The new arrivals took advantage of the area's most valuable resource, timber, and sawmills began producing lumber for small shipbuilding operations. Sherbrooke, so named in 1815 after Sir John Coape Sherbrooke, Lieutenant-Governor of Nova Scotia, exported timber to

Great Britain in locally built ships. Families like the Cummingers and the MacDonalds were involved in both ends of the operation, and grew quite wealthy. During the 1860s and '70s, their shipyards turned out several barques in excess of 500 tons for the carrying trade, as well as many smaller boats for the fishery.

The contributions of these families feature prominently

SHERBROOKE VILLAGE

in the restored village. The general store was operated by the Cumminger brothers, Samuel and John. You need look only at the store's elaborate counters to gain some appreciation of their wealth and the woodworking skills associated with shipbuilding. Superior craftsmanship also is apparent at Greenwood Cottage, built by John and Sarah Cumminger in 1871.

The reconstruction of the MacDonald Brothers water-powered, up-and-down sawmill is located a few minutes away from the main village, but do not miss it. The sawmill is wonderful. You can feel the power of the water-wheel, and see it in the rise and fall of the huge saw blade. All the workings — great belts and pulleys — are exposed.

There is much more. Sherbrooke Village has a blacksmith shop which has operated continuously since it was built in 1870. The Sherbrooke Drug Store was given most of its stock by

SHERBROOKE VILLAGE RECAPTURES LATE-19TH CENTURY LIFE

the Nova Scotia Pharmaceutical Society and has a wonderful display of turn-of-the-century medicines. Among the many other buildings on site are a Temperance Hall, a boat-building shop, a village potter, a Presbyterian church, and a courthouse. Tea and more substantial meals are served at the What Cheer Tea Room.

Another smokehouse has opened in St. Mary's River near Sherbrooke Village.

A few minutes away, at modern-day Sherbrooke Village, you can enjoy teas, lunches and dinners at the Bright House, a lovely circa 1850 home. The provincially-run Liscombe Lodge, at nearby Liscomb Mills (about 20 minutes from Sherbrooke Village) offers first-rate accommodation in lodge, cottage or chalet style surroundings.

LIGHTHOUSE AT PORT BICKERTON

PORT BICKERTON

The lighthouse at Port Bickerton that protected the region's seafaring folk since the 1920s has been refurbished to its original decor, and has been re-opened as an interpretive centre. Panels inside show the history behind the 166 lights which dot Nova Scotia's

143

coastline. Visitors can also find detailed information on the Sable Island and Sambro lighthouses, along with local history concerning the 16 lights in Guysborough County. Stepping from old to new, there is a CD-ROM in English and German, detailing all Guysborough County lights.

CANSO AND GRASSY ISLAND

Near the end of a peninsula that juts far out into the Atlantic is the fishing village of Canso, one of Nova Scotia's oldest communities. It was the rugged and beautiful nature of this area that inspired some of the most memorable songs of Stan Rogers. His music and his place in local folklore are celebrated at the Stan Rogers Folk Festival, in July. Other events include the Seafood Festival in July and the Canso Regatta and Tuna Cup in August.

Offshore, Grassy Island is the site of a once prosperous community of New England fishermen and merchants until the fishing station was sacked by a French force from Louisbourg in 1744.

In Canso, a Parks Canada visitor centre tells the story through a brief audio-visual presentation and a series of life-size exhibits detailing the interiors of three Grassy island properties — a tavern, a merchant's house, and the home of a military officer. Between June and September, a daily boat service takes visitors to the island, where an interpretive trail links eight designated sites.

GRASSY ISLAND

144

CAPE BRETON AND THE CABOT TRAIL

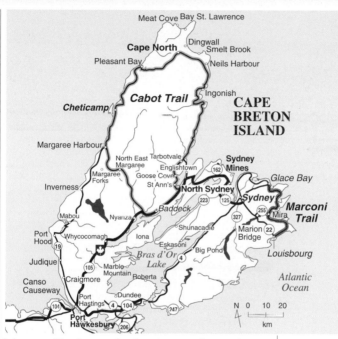

It is a rare thing for a road to become more famous than any of the places it passes through, but that is what has happened with Cape Breton's Cabot Trail. Its hairpin turns, ear-popping climbs and descents, and spectacular cliff-side views have been thrilling motorists since the 1930s.

If we take A. S. MacMillan (Minister of Highways during the 1920s) at his word, the decision to undertake the costly and ambitious construction of the Cabot Trail was, quite literally, the result of one man's dream. In August 1924, MacMillan went to Cheticamp to look into the possibility of building a road that would extend northward to the community of Pleasant Bay and beyond.

Apparently, the trip along the northwestern shore of Cape Breton left quite an impression on the minister. He recalls in a 1952 document, reproduced in the June 1992 issue of *Cape Breton's Magazine,* what took place upon his return to Baddeck:

"Some time near morning I fell asleep and dreamed about a wonderful development that I could see underway, numerous houses, cottages and tourist homes in the many bays

THE CABOT TRAIL, ONE OF THE WORLD'S SPECTACULAR DRIVES

145

CORNEY BROOK, CAPE BRETON HIGHLANDS NATIONAL PARK

and inlets as well as sail boats and all kinds of pleasure craft, apparently everybody enjoying themselves."

MacMillan was inspired and the rest, he would have it, is history. Today, the 300-kilometre (186-mi.) Cabot Trail, named for the famous explorer who reputedly landed on the shores of Aspy Bay in June of 1497, is a loop that takes you along most of the coastline of northwestern Cape Breton. Contrary to MacMillan's vision, much of that coastline remains undeveloped. The Trail can be comfortably driven in a day, ideally a sunny one in late September or early October when fall colours blaze. But visitors who prefer not to spend most of their time in the car should plan on at least two days for the trip. Outdoor adventurers will want to take most of their vacation to explore the beautiful wilderness areas in Cape Breton Highlands National Park.

BADDECK

Baddeck is generally considered to be the beginning and end of the Cabot Trail. However, the village was attracting summer visitors long before it earned this distinction. In 1879, Charles Dudley Warner's *Baddeck, and That Sort of Thing* was published. Though not very popular with Cape Bretoners — they were mockingly portrayed as backward and primitive — the book's description of Baddeck's

ALEXANDER GRAHAM BELL NATIONAL HISTORIC SITE, BADDECK

146

splendid isolation struck a chord with many American readers. Among those was the inventor of the telephone, Alexander Graham Bell. Seeking refuge from the hot summers of Washington, D.C., Bell and his wife, Mabel, decided to stop in at Baddeck on their way to Newfoundland for a holiday in 1885. They fell in love with the place. Eight years later, they built their estate, Beinn Bhreagh (Beautiful Mountain) on a headland overlooking the Bras d'Or. There, Alexander and Mabel spent many happy summers, until his death in 1922.

HYDROFOIL HALL AT THE BELL MUSEUM

Today, Alexander Graham Bell National Historic Site, Nova Scotia's finest indoor museum, offers visitors to Baddeck a chance to learn a great deal about the inventor's life. The site's collection of Bell's artifacts, written materials, and personal mementoes is the most comprehensive in the world. Provided you have the time (a

complete tour takes several hours) the exhibits give a surprisingly complete and intimate account of Bell's life.

Bell was a compulsive inventor. He may have left the Washington heat behind, but Bell brought his passion for invention and experimentation to his summer home. Among his lesser-known efforts were attempts to develop a multi-nippled sheep for Cape Breton farmers, and a device that would relieve the plight of Banks fishermen by converting fog into drinking water. During his last years, the hydrofoil was Bell's special interest. Several models were built and tested in Baddeck.

FLIGHT WAS ONE OF BELL'S PASSIONS

Baddeck's status as a resort and tourist centre has grown since the Bell era. The village of 1000 offers more quality accommodation than any other place along the Cabot Trail. (Even so, it is advisable to book early.) The Inverary Inn Resort has 125 rooms in five main buildings along with 13 cottages. This full-service resort offers tennis, an indoor pool, canoeing and boat cruises, and a host of other

147

BADDECK

activities. MacNeil House, on the grounds of the Silver Dart Lodge, has six luxurious suites with jacuzzi, fireplace, and kitchen facilities. Other amenities include live entertainment in the dining room, boat and bicycle rentals, and a lakeside beach. For those who prefer quieter surroundings, the Duffus House Inn (c. 1830) features antique furnishings and English gardens in a waterside setting. Telegraph House offers motel-style units or rooms in the old-fashioned inn. (The Bells stayed in Room No. 1 before they built Beinn Bhreagh.) Auberge Giselle's Inn, Broad Water Inn and Lynwood Country Inn and Ceilidh Country Lodge also offer fine accommodation. Ask for a room overlooking the Bras d'Or Lakes.

Baddeck's shops carry a variety of upscale handcrafts and folk art. Fine wool sweaters are sold at Seawinds Chandlery, on the Government Wharf. Up from the water, Kidston Landing features a wide selection of Nova Scotia crafts, woolens, and country clothing. Chebucto Place is a mini mall that houses other craft and clothing shops, as well as a coffee shop where you can relax from your day of shopping. The Outdoor Store sells quality outdoor clothing and camping supplies. It's a worthwhile stop for those who plan to spend time in the wilderness areas of Cape Breton Highlands National Park.

Baddeck is full of summertime activity. The Murray Road concert series is a new event featuring area musicians. Since 1904, Baddeck has held its annual regatta in early August. Throughout the summer months, yachts are berthed at the government wharf or at private anchorages along the shores of Baddeck Bay.

Some distance inland, near Baddeck Bridge, is Uisge

BEINN BHREAGH, WHERE BELL'S DESCENDANTS STILL SPEND THEIR SUMMERS

Ban Falls Park, one of the prettiest spots in all of Cape Breton. A network of maintained hiking trails leads through hardwood forest to a dramatic gorge and waterfalls. This is a great place for a picnic. (You'll find all the fixings for a delicious lunch at the Highwheeler Café in Baddeck or the Herring Choker Deli & Bakery, a kilometre west of the Cabot Trail entrance at Nyanza.)

MARGAREE RIVER

When leaving the Baddeck area, you have a choice. You can head for Hunter's Mountain and the Margaree Valley, which would take you in a clockwise direction around the Cabot Trail, or you can take the counter-clockwise route along the shores of St. Anns Bay and north to Ingonish.

The clockwise route takes you away from the salt water and through the beautiful Margaree Valley. The Margaree has been nominated as a Canadian Heritage River. Anglers should not pass it by, especially during August and September. Guides are

available for salmon and backwater trout fishing. The Margaree Salmon Museum, near North East Margaree, is one of the best privately run museums in Nova Scotia. If you plan on fishing the river, you should drop in for sure. Fly fishermen will have heard of John Cosseboom. (The Cosseboom fly has fooled many Atlantic salmon.) Cosseboom was an ardent disciple of Izaak Walton (*The Compleat Angler*) and spent many summers on the Margaree. His is one of several stories well told by the museum's wonderful collection of fishing memorabilia.

MARGAREE SALMON MUSEUM

NORMAWAY INN IN THE MARGAREE VALLEY

Nearby, along the mysteriously named Egypt Road, is the Normaway Inn, which has catered to anglers and others since the 1920s. The main lodge and 19 cabins (4 with jacuzzi!) are

DISTINCTIVE ACADIAN ARCHITECTURE (TOP) AND ART (ABOVE) ARE EVERYWHERE IN CHETICAMP

within easy striking distance of some of Nova Scotia's best salmon pools. The dining room offers four-course country gourmet dinners.

The Trail follows the Margaree until the river spills into the Gulf of St. Lawrence. There is a small sand beach to the south of Margaree Harbour and a larger sand and gravel beach to the north. The larger beach is part of a narrow sand-spit that serves as a natural breakwater for the colourful fishing boats of Margaree Harbour. From here, the road bends to the northeast towards Cheticamp. At Cap Lemoine, one of several tiny Acadian villages that dot this shore, Joe's Scarecrow Theatre has been giving visitors the willies for a number of years.

CHETICAMP

Cheticamp is the largest and oldest Acadian village along this shore (see p. 19). Cheticantins take special pride in the large cooperatives that dominate the waterfront. They represent the culmination of a long struggle for independence.

When the Treaty of Paris forced the French to abandon the Gulf of St. Lawrence fishery in 1763, merchants from the English Channel Islands were quick to take their place. Charles Robin, a French Huguenot from the Isle of Jersey, set up his operation at Le Chadye (Cheticamp). He

A CHETICAMP CRAFT SHOP

encouraged exiled Acadians who had spent time near the French port of St. Malo (just to the south of Jersey) to settle in Cheticamp, where they could work for him.

And that's just what they did for more than a century. The Charles Robin Company ruled Cheticamp. It owned boats and fishing gear. Fishermen were paid in provisions from the company store. Indebtedness to the "Jerseys" was a way of life from the time the Acadians first settled Cheticamp in the 1780s until late in the 19th century.

Then Father Pierre Fiset arrived. He devoted himself to the spiritual well-being of the Cheticantins — Cheticamp's beautiful Saint-Pierre

Church was built under his direction, but he also took a special interest in the worldly affairs of his parishioners. Determined to loosen the Jerseys' grip on the community, Father Fiset purchased a store in 1883. He traded in fish and livestock, and in 1888 he built a wharf on the harbour. Five years later, Father Fiset bought Cheticamp Island from the Robins. The extent of his involvement in worldly affairs troubled some clergy, but they did not question his motives.

L'ÉGLISE SAINT-PIERRE, CHETICAMP

Fiset died in 1909. Six years later, a group of fishermen founded Cheticamp's first sales cooperative. During the 1930s, they were greatly assisted by another Catholic clergyman — Reverend Moses Coady, a professor at St. Francis Xavier University in Antigonish who was appointed by the government to help Maritime fishermen organize cooperatives. The so-called Antigonish Movement had its greatest successes in Antigonish County and Cape Breton.

Today there are seven cooperatives in the Cheticamp area — the most in any Acadian region of Nova Scotia. The Cheticantins jealously guard the management of their own affairs; hardly surprising, given their history.

One of the groups to organize a cooperative in Cheticamp during the 1930s was the rug hookers. Rug hooking is an industry with a peculiar connection to the Bells and Baddeck. Cheticamp women had been hooking rugs from old rags for ages when, in 1922, Lillian Burke, an American friend of the Bells, suggested that they would be able to sell their rugs if they switched from rags to wool and began using softer colours. A cottage industry was born. Burke did well selling Cheticamp rugs in New York until 1936, when Alexandre Boudreau, a leader of the local co-op movement, suggested that the women organize themselves.

RUG HOOKING IS A MAINSTAY OF THE CHETICAMP ECONOMY

Now, the Coopérative Artisanale de Cheticamp Ltée. runs the business. Cheticamp rugs are world famous — especially those of Elizabeth LeFort, whose works can be found at the Vatican, the White House, Buckingham Palace and the Dr. Elizabeth LeFort Gallery & Museum at Les Trois Pignons (The Three Gables) in Cheticamp. Rug hooking is still a cottage industry, but it is no longer

quaint. The computerized cash system in the Co-op Artisanale attests to that. Some rugs retail for two thousand dollars. At Le Motif, a local gift shop featuring needlework and folk art, there are some original rag-style rugs for sale. Asked if they were coming back, the woman working at the store replied, "We'll see, if people buy them then they're coming back." Cheticantins are not novices when it comes to the business of art.

There are plenty more rugs (and a wide selection of Cape Breton and Nova Scotian crafts) at Flora's, one of the province's largest craft shops. But Cheticamp area artisans do more than hook rugs. Some of Nova Scotia's most interesting folk art is produced here. You'll see colourful whirligigs and gizmos in shops and front yards throughout the Acadian villages along this coast. One of Canada's best folk artists, Bill Roach, works out of the Sunset Art Gallery in Cheticamp. His whimsical, brightly-coloured wood carvings — birds, fish and people among them — are prized by collectors worldwide.

BILL ROACH AT WORK IN HIS CHETICAMP STUDIO (BOTTOM)

Local artists and artisans draw strength from Cheticamp's rich Acadian culture (Acadian flags are everywhere). Locals still speak French with a 17th-century accent. Cheticantins are justifiably proud of Father Fiset's magnificent church. Saint-Pierre, overlooking the village and the bay, anchors the community. Each August, a special mass is held here during the Festival de l'Escaouette, a week-long cultural celebration that brims with Acadian food, song and dance.

The waterfront bustles during summer. Several whale-watching cruises, deep-sea fishing charters and water tours leave from the Government Wharf and the Quai Mathieu waterfront boardwalk. Pilot whales and minkes are frequently sighted (fin whales less often) and the landward views of Cheticamp and the Cape Breton Highlands are spectacular.

There are a number of restaurants along the water side of Main Street that feature Acadian cuisine. Savoury meat pies

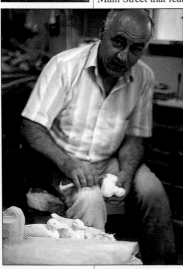

and rich seafood chowders are served with thick slices of homemade bread at the Restaurant Acadien in the Co-op Artisanale. Fruit pies are made the traditional way, with flaky biscuit crusts. Several establishments on the waterfront boardwalk have outdoor patios where you can enjoy a drink and watch the sun set behind Cheticamp Island.

If you plan an overnight stay in Cheticamp, book well in advance. For the most part, the village offers motel-style accommodation along its busy Main Street. Laurie's Motor Inn has many guest amenities, including a whale-watching cruise. Across the harbour, the Cheticamp Island Resort features two-bedroom cottages with housekeeping facilities and ocean swimming. The resort offers weekly rates and is ideal for those who plan an extended stay in the Cheticamp area.

CAPE BRETON HIGHLANDS NATIONAL PARK

Just to the northeast of Cheticamp is the entrance to Cape Breton Highlands National Park. Established in 1936, the park protects about 950 square kilometres (367 sq. mi.) of coastline, wooded valleys, and barren plateaus. If you plan to hike, cycle, fish, or camp in the park, then stop at the Cheticamp Information Centre for permits and advice. Vehicle permits should be purchased at the centre by anyone intending to use park facilities. Exhibits, including interactive games for children, will introduce you to the park. To get better acquainted, visit the centre's well-stocked bookstore.

Hikers, especially, will find useful resources here. *Walking in the Highlands*, a guide to the park's 27 hiking trails, can be purchased at the centre. So can David Lawley's *Cabot Trail*, an interpretive naturalist's guide to hiking in the area. There are hikes well-suited to a family stroll (like the Lone Shieling Trail near Pleasant Bay) and those with more challenging terrain (the Franey Trail, near Ingonish Beach, ascends 366 metres in only four kilometres). Some offer spectacular coastal scenery (like the Coastal Trail that leaves from Black Brook Beach); others climb to the barren highland plateau (the Lake of Islands Trail, near Ingonish, is a 26 km-long back-country adventure). To truly appreciate the grandeur of the Cape Breton Highlands, park the car and go for a walk.

The 106-kilometre (66-mi.) stretch of road between Cheticamp and Ingonish is what made the Cabot Trail famous. Soon after entering the park, the roller coaster ride begins — up French Mountain to a height of 455 metres (1500 ft.) then down the other side, then another ascent, this time 372 metres (1220 ft.) to the top of MacKenzie Mountain, and down to Pleasant Bay. Stop at the lookoffs along the way. The view from Fishing Cove Lookoff is breathtaking. On a crystal clear day you might be able to spy the Magdalene Islands to the northwest, across more than 80 kilometres (50 mi.) of water.

Pleasant Bay, following a serpentine descent of MacKenzie Mountain (you can imagine the difficulty of a landward approach to this community before the road was built) is a scenic fishing village with a variety of visitor services. Two whale-watching cruises leave from the Pleasant Bay wharf. The coastline north of Pleasant Bay is spectacular and pristine (a community of Tibetan Buddhist monks is located here); pilot whales, grey seals and bald eagles are regularly sighted. You'll find plenty of whales and seabirds among the beautiful folk art creations of Reed Timmons, a local lobsterman and gill-netter. His Pleasant Bay studio is also filled with colourful roosters.

From Pleasant Bay, the Trail moves inland towards North Mountain. At the mountain's base is the Lone Shieling, a replica of a Scottish crofter's hut. The hut is the result of an outpouring of Scottish sentiment from a rather unlikely source. Donald MacIntosh, a native of Pleasant Bay, was a geology professor at Dalhousie University in Halifax. When he died in 1934, he left 40.5 hectares (100 acres) at Pleasant Bay to the Crown. His will expressed the desire that the government use the land for a small park where they would construct a cabin modelled after the lone shieling on the Isle of Skye. That is how a Skye crofter's cottage came to be tucked among a stand of 350-year-old sugar maples. While the cottage may leave you scratching your head, the massive trees — some are more than 36 metres (120 ft.) tall — along the Lone Shieling hiking trail make the stop worthwhile.

THERE ARE PLENTY OF CLIFF-SIDE VIEWS ALONG THE CABOT TRAIL

From the top of North Mountain (445 m, 1,460 ft.), the Trail descends into the Aspy River valley, passing some spectacular gorges along the way. At the bottom, a dirt road leads to Beulach Ban Falls, an ideal spot for a picnic. Nearby, Arts North is a fine craft store that features the functional and decorative pottery of Linda and Dennis Doyon, and the deceptively simple designs of jeweller Johanna Padelt. The work of other local artisans is on display in the loft.

PLEASANT BAY

Here, if you have time, leave the Trail at Cape North and head still farther north to Cabot's Landing (site of a picnic park and long, sandy beach) and Bay St. Lawrence. To boldly go where few tourists have gone, continue along the shores of Bay St. Lawrence to Capstick and follow the winding dirt road to Meat Cove, a drive you'll not soon forget! For a landward view of the wild beauty of Cape Breton's northern tip, take a bird- and whale-watching boat tour from either Bay St. Lawrence or Dingwall, on Aspy Bay.

Back in the village of Cape North, the Cabot Trail bends to the southeast, towards Ingonish. Many prefer the alternative coastal route, which takes you through the fishing villages of Smelt Brook, White Point, New Haven, and Neils Harbour. For an up-close view of the rugged

CABOT'S LANDING, NEAR CAPE NORTH

MEAT COVE, AT CAPE BRETON'S NORTHERN TIP

scenery along this exposed shoreline, you can rent mountain bikes at the Sea Spray Cycle Centre in Smelt Brook. The Doyons, who also operate Arts North, display their pottery in a small studio here. At Neils Harbour, the Chowder House restaurant makes good use of the village's active fishery in its thick, seafood chowders. You can see the fishing fleet from the restaurant, and walk down to the edge of the North Atlantic after your meal.

From Neils Harbour, the Trail heads south towards Ingonish. On a hot day, stop at Black Brook Beach along the way. The water is reasonably warm and there are usually great waves for body surfing (the left side of the beach is less rocky).

NEILS HARBOUR IS ONE OF SEVERAL SCENIC FISHING VILLAGES ALONG THIS SHORE

The Ingonish area is the resort centre on the Trail's Atlantic shore. The beaches are wonderful. The challenging Highlands Links Golf Course was recently rated by *Golf Magazine* as the best course in Canada, and the 75th worldwide. The Middle Head hiking trail runs the length of the narrow peninsula that separates South Bay Ingonish from North Bay Ingonish. Cliff-side views, including an offshore colony of nesting terns at the trail's end, are ample reward for a relatively easy hike. This same promontory is also the site of the provincially owned Keltic Lodge. Other accommodations in the Ingonish area are more modestly priced, but some visitors are willing to pay a premium for the Lodge's commanding view of Ingonish Beach and South Bay. There is a fine dining room at Keltic which features fresh seafood and local produce, elegantly presented. There

is ample opportunity to survey the waters of South Bay Ingonish. Whale-watching cruises leave from the ports of Ingonish Beach, Ingonish Harbour and Ingonish Ferry. Minke and pilot whales are frequently sighted and the coastline is pocked with sea caves and unusual rock formations. While most whale cruises use converted fishing vessels, Sea Visions, out of Ingonish Ferry, allows you to hear as well as see the Atlantic from the 35-foot sailing vessel *Resplendent*.

After Ingonish, the Trail snakes its way up and down Cape Smokey — steel yourself for yet another spectacular lookoff, before heading south on the home stretch. In Indian Brook, you can see the creations of one of Cape Breton's best artisans at Leather Works. John Roberts got

KELTIC LODGE

his start at historic leather working when someone from Louisbourg approached him to do reproductions for the fortress. Leather buckets and less antiquated leather goods — belts, wallets, work aprons and bags — are hand made on the premises.

At the Barachois River Bridge, the road forks. Route 312 takes you to Englishtown via a short ferry ride across St. Anns Harbour. (While waiting for the ferry, you can visit Sea Shanty Crafts and Antiques where the quilts — old and new — are of special interest.) Englishtown was home to Angus MacAskill, Cape Breton's famous 2.4-metre (7-ft. 9-in.) 193-kilogram (425-lb.) giant.

From the Barachois River Bridge, the Cabot Trail twists its way toward South Gut St. Anns. Beginning at Tarbotvale, the road passes by several interesting craft shops. Wild Things features the wood turnings and carvings of Claire Ryder and Juan Prieto. Unique gifts and clothing (including period costume) are displayed at Sew Inclined. The School on the Hill, at North River Bridge, stocks top-quality Atlantic crafts and a good selection of regional books. And Carole MacDonald sells beautiful stoneware and porcelain pottery (including many "raku" pieces) from her roadside studio at Goose Cove.

LEATHER WORKER JOHN ROBERTS, INDIAN BROOK

The Gaelic College of Celtic Arts and Crafts teaches traditional Highland music, dance and craft on the shores of South Gut St. Anns. The Gaelic language is also taught during the six-week summer session. The Gaelic Mod, a week-long festival of Celtic culture, is held here each August.

Ironically, St. Anns, the centre of Scottish revivalism in Nova Scotia, was the site of a mass exodus of Scottish settlers during the middle of the 19th century. Norman MacLeod, a Presbyterian minister, led 800 followers on an extraordinary odyssey to New Zealand. MacLeod thought, and others believed, that they could do better than the grinding poverty that had been their experience at St. Anns. This is a story that does not get told in the Gaelic College's Hall of the Clans.

GAELIC COLLEGE OF CELTIC ARTS AND CRAFTS, SOUTH GUT ST. ANNS (ABOVE)

BRAS D'OR LAKES

The Bras d'Or Lakes form Cape Breton's 1165-square-kilometre (450-sq-mi.) inland sea. Two narrow channels — Great Bras d'Or and St. Andrews — and a canal at St. Peter's link this sailors' Mecca to the North Atlantic. Myriad islands, harbours, coves and salt-water ponds provide shelter from ocean storms, and the region is virtually fog-free. Although roads skirt almost the entire coastline of the Bras d'Or, the geography of the lakes makes circumnavigation impractical. The attractions mentioned below can be reached from a number of points along the TransCanada Highway to the north of the lakes, and from Route 4 to the south.

Its favourable climate, abundant wildlife and outstanding natural beauty have long drawn people to the shores of the Bras d'Or. The Mi'kmaq have been here for centuries. Today, there are four reserves in the area, including the largest in the province at Eskasoni. At Whycocomagh, the Googoo family has been running the Negemow basket shop for more than 30 years. (Before that, baskets were sold door-to-door.) The craftsmanship is exceptional; so is the smell of sweet grass.

The Bras d'Or also attracted European settlers — mostly Scots, like the MacNeils from the Hebridean Island of Barra who came to Iona towards the end of the 18th century. In 1956, Iona was chosen by the Association of Scottish Societies as the site for a proposed village that would depict the evolution of Scottish settlement in this part of Nova Scotia. Overlooking the Barra Strait, the Nova Scotia Highland Village tells its story through a series of structures, beginning with a Hebridean Black House and ending with an early 20th-century home. Interpreters are used to hearing complaints about the steep climb that a tour of the village requires, but once they see the view, most visitors come around.

Perhaps the best view of the Bras d'Or is from Marble Mountain, overlooking West Bay. A steep trail to the abandoned quarry (750 men once mined this hillside) starts from the main road, directly across from a small lookoff and picnic area. Interesting old workings provide a good excuse to stop and catch your breath on the way up. The view from the top — islet-studded West Bay and the wide open waters of the Bras d'Or — will stay with you long after you descend the mountain. Back at the lookoff on the main road, a steep path leads downhill to a beach of crushed marble sand. The water is ice-cold (several spring-fed brooks flow down the hillside) and crystal-clear.

The Dundee Resort is at the head of West Bay. The resort's 60 hotel rooms and 39 cottages are spread out over 550 acres. Dundee has all the amenities, including an 18-hole championship golf course. The course was built on a steep slope overlooking the bay, making for great views and difficult golf. The resort also has a large marina where you can arrange a cruise on the Bras d'Or.

At Roberta, not far from Dundee, Kayak Cape Breton

DUNDEE RESORT

offers guided sea-kayaking trips on the Bras d'Or and along the Atlantic Coast. The sheltered waters of the Bras d'Or are ideal for beginners. Keep your eyes open for bald eagles; the lakes are an important breeding area.

Guided eagle tours are provided at Big Pond, on the shores of East Bay. Sightings are frequent during the two-hour walking tour that includes an introduction to the plant life and trees of the area. Big Pond is also the home of Cape Breton singer Rita MacNeil. Many of her awards and records are on display at Rita's Tea Room, in a converted one-room schoolhouse. You may well see Rita here or at the Big Pond Festival, a week-long celebration of folk music held each July.

At the Atlantic entrance to the Great Bras d'Or Channel are two islands, Ciboux and Hertford. Each summer the "Bird Islands" host Nova Scotia's largest colony of breeding sea birds — razorbills, guillemots, gulls, kittiwakes, cormorants and the feature attraction — Atlantic puffins. Bird Island Tours operates out of Big Bras d'Or. The two-and-a-half hour boat trip trims the shores of both islands and the Van Schaiks, long-time operators of the tour, provide a lively and informative narrative.

ATLANTIC PUFFINS ARE AMONG THE THOUSANDS OF SEA BIRDS THAT COLONIZE THE "BIRD ISLANDS"

THE CEILIDH TRAIL

Those who have travelled the Cabot Trail in a counter-clockwise direction might consider bypassing the Margaree Valley by turning onto Route 19 (the Ceilidh Trail) at Margaree Forks, and heading for Inverness and Mabou. Each summer, communities along this shore play host to a number of accidental tourists — would-be Cabot Trailers who have gone astray. Few are disappointed. The landscape is more pastoral than it is along the Cabot Trail, but just as beautiful — especially between Inverness and Mabou, and along the Colindale Road, between Mabou and Port Hood. And there is great saltwater swimming at Inverness, Mabou, and Port Hood beaches. (The water of the Northumberland Strait is comfortably warm during summer.)

**PASTORAL
LANDSCAPE ALONG
THE CEILIDH TRAIL**

The Glenora Inn & Distillery Resort offers nine comfortable rooms in a unique complex. Glenora is North America's only distiller of single malt whisky. Tours are provided and the single malt, Kenloch, is on sale in the gift shop. The Duncreigan Country Inn, overlooking Mabou Harbour, has eight spacious guest rooms with bay windows. The menu at the inn's excellent dining room includes seafood and local lamb seasoned with garden-fresh herbs. An on-site gift shop features the work of Maritime artists and artisans. Other accommodations includes cottages available to rent or the Mabou Hostel.

Periodically, there are spirited requests from western shore residents to make the Ceilidh Trail a part of the Cabot Trail. But the same isolation that prompts these complaints from tourist-driven enterprises has helped to preserve the western shore's strong Scottish identity. Mabou offers Gaelic at its school — but not to attract tourists. *Am Braighe*, the village's Gaelic newspaper, stands on its own. The series of summer ceilidhs held along the shore at Broad Cove, Mabou, and Judique would likely go ahead with or without visitors. The steady stream of talented Celtic musicians — from John Allan Cameron to the Rankin Family — also speaks to the strength of Scottish culture in the area. Perhaps it is a good thing that the Cabot Trail does not run through all of Cape Breton.

MABOU HARBOUR

MARCONI TRAIL

CAPE BRETON ISLAND

North East Margaree · Tarbotvale · Englishtown · (162) · **Sydney Mines** · Glace Bay · Goose Cove · St Ann's · **North Sydney** · (223) · (125) · **Sydney** · **Marconi Trail** · *Cabot Trail* · Baddeck · (327) · (255) · Mira · Mabou · Nyanza · Shunacadie · Marion Bridge · (22) · Whycocomagh · Iona · Eskasoni · Big Pond · Louisbourg · (19) · *Bras d'Or Lake* · (4) · *Atlantic Ocean* · (105) · Marble Mountain · Roberta

N 0   10   20
km

LOUISBOURG

A trip to Louisbourg, where the reconstructed Fortress of Louisbourg brings history to life, provides one of the province's most rewarding experiences.

Tourism has replaced the fishery as the economic mainstay of the modern town, which is situated at the sheltered northern end of the harbour. Louisbourg Lighthouse is adjacent to the ruins of Canada's first lighthouse, which dates back to 1734. Visitors can enjoy a stroll along the harbourfront boardwalk, and nearby are Louisbourg Market Square, shops, museums, a ship chandlery, accommodations, and post office.

Visitors can take in live theatre and concerts at Louisbourg Playhouse during the summer and fall, and in August, the Louisbourg CrabFest celebrates the bounty of the sea. The S&L Railway Museum houses the visitor information centre, along with exhibits that tell the story of the Sydney and Louisbourg Railway and railway technology.

A few minutes drive from the town you will find the entrance to the 18th-century fortress and the gateway to a living museum.

By the Treaty of Utrecht, in 1713 the French agreed to

THE QUAY, FORTRESS OF LOUISBOURG NATIONAL HISTORIC SITE

BENOIST PROPERTY

leave their fishing station at Placentia, in Newfoundland, and give up Acadia (which included present-day mainland Nova Scotia) to the British. In exchange, France was allowed to hold on to the islands in the Gulf of St. Lawrence. Ile-Royale (Cape Breton) would emerge as the most important of these, and within a short time, the French had established the Fortress of Louisbourg on its southeastern shore. There they were soon landing 13,600,000 kilograms (30,000,000 lb.) of cod a year, worth two to three times the value of the fur trade at Quebec and Montreal. They also had an imposing fortress that lay between the British colonies of Newfoundland and Nova Scotia and, in the fishery, a ready-made nursery for their navy. It is no wonder that the French said of the bargain that they had received an ingot of gold for a bar of silver.

As an entrepot — a clearinghouse for commodities from France, New England, Nova Scotia, Canada, and the West Indies — Louisbourg flourished. Outbound ships, their holds brimming with cod, would return to Louisbourg laden with West Indian rum and sugar, cloths from

FRÉDÉRIC GATE

Carcassonne, and the wines of Provence. Enticed by such rich cargoes, wealthy New England merchants supplied wood products and foodstuffs in exchange for them. To a lesser extent, traders from Nova Scotia and Quebec did the same. Atlantic trade filled Louisbourg's harbour and quickened its waterfront.

The quay was a lively place. Scores of shallops (small boats) maneuvered between large traders so that fishermen could bring their codfish to shore, where they would soon be drying on flakes. Sailors on leave crowded into the inns and taverns that lined the south side of the quay; Louisbourg fathers made sure their daughters were accounted for. Commercial necessity overcame the difficulty of haggling with someone who spoke a different language. Goods flowed back and forth between ship and shore.

By 1760 it was over — the town deserted, the fortress destroyed. Louisbourg's commercial promise had been fulfilled, but its military promise had not.

Twice in its short history, Louisbourg fell. When France declared war on Britain in 1744, Louisbourg's commander went on the offensive in the New World, and the British outpost at Canso was captured. A campaign against Annapolis Royal was less successful, but reprisals seemed unlikely. Louisbourg was too well defended and the British seemed unwilling to expend much effort against it.

An attack did come in 1745 — from an unexpected quarter. William Shirley, Governor of Massachusetts, succeeded in raising a force of 4000 New England militiamen for the purpose. Shirley was strongly supported by wealthy merchants, and the proposed campaign was, in part, a reflection of their desire to take over control of the rich Louisbourg fishery. The militia, under the leadership of General Pepperell, and with the help of a British naval squadron from the West Indies, succeeded in taking the fortress after a 46-day siege.

During the intense negotiations that followed the end of the war in 1748, the British sacrificed Louisbourg in order to hold on to some of their European gains. The following year, Louisbourg was returned to the French. New Englanders were outraged.

In 1756, when war broke out again, the British strategy was to attack France through its colonies and foreign trade. Louisbourg was an obvious target. The town endured several blockades until 1758, when an irresistible combination of British land and sea power overwhelmed the fortress. The French surrendered Louisbourg in July. Two years later, rather than run the risk that Louisbourg would be returned to the French by future negotiations, British engineers were ordered to blow up the fortifications.

The town barely survived. A few people settled in the sheltered northern end of the harbour. Daily, fishermen made the melancholy trip out the harbour, past the Royal Battery, around

Careening Point, to gaze upon the desolation of the fortress on their way to the fishing grounds.

The reconstruction of Fortress of Louisbourg began in 1963 as a creative response to severe unemployment in Cape Breton's coal mines. More than 150 out-of-work coal miners were employed in the project, as stonemasons, labourers, and carpenters. Researchers had found the original drawings for the military buildings in Paris. Archaeological and graphic evidence was used to reconstruct civilian buildings. The entire effort was characterized by a meticulous devotion to Louisbourg's past.

Proof of this devotion abounds. Buildings sit on their original foundations. Dormer windows jut from gabled roofs, as they did in Poitou, Saintonge, and Brittany in the 18th century. Plank siding and a clutter of chimneys speak to an ongoing struggle with cold and damp. Everywhere, timber, sod, stone, mortar, and mud have been used to resurrect one quarter of the original town — over 50 buildings in all.

CHAPEL IN THE CITADEL (BOTTOM)

Details help convince. The sculptured trophies atop the Dauphin Gate were quarried from the same French limestone as the originals. In the Carrerot property, mortar laced with glass in the south cellar was used to keep out rats.

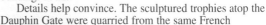

Louisbourg's authenticity goes beyond architecture. Bread is baked in the Royal Bakery; savoury dishes simmer in the Engineer's House. The Governor's Apartments are appointed according to Governor Jean-Baptiste-Louis Le Prevost Duquesnel's inventory. They are comfortable and luxurious, well suited to sipping fine Bordeaux. This, in marked contrast to the Hotel de la Marine — a sturdy tavern run by a fisherman where rum and sapinette (spruce beer) flowed freely.

Finally, there are the people. Parks Canada has endeavoured to recreate a moment in the summer of 1744, and the players know their roles. And, by design or not, they seem to fit them. The woman who plays the 18th-century harpsichord in the Ordonnateur's Property does not look out of place. Neither do the soldiers who bear precise reproductions of 1734 French-made flintlock muskets. The man

carting firewood to houses along the quay looks just right.

Plan on taking an entire day to fully appreciate the Fortress of Louisbourg. Ask questions of those who work there. Their answers do more than just inform — they lend flavour to this 18th-century French garrison town.

Until recently, most visitors to Louisbourg chose not to stay overnight. That's changing. Two outstanding inns have led the way in upgrading the town's accommodations. The Louisbourg Harbour Inn is a century-old sea captain's

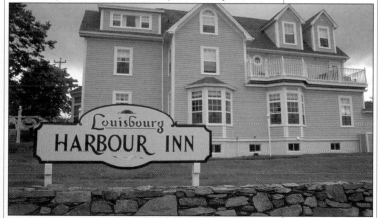

house with balconies overlooking the fortress and the harbour. Five of the inn's eight rooms have jacuzzis. Close to the fortress entrance, the Cranberry Cove Inn is another restored turn-of-the-century home. It, too, combines antique furnishings and other traditional touches with modern conveniences like gas fireplaces and jacuzzis. With North America's largest historic reconstruction at hand, the town's other visitor services will continue to improve.

SYDNEY AND GLACE BAY

The former city of Sydney, now the hub of Cape Breton Regional Municipality, has long prided itself on being the "industrial heart of Cape Breton." Founded in 1785 by Col. J. E. W. DesBarres, Sydney was first settled by Loyalists from New York State, who were followed by immigrants from the Scottish Highlands. The construction early in this century of the Dominion Steel and Coal Company steel plant (now Sydney Steel) took full advantage of the large

protected harbour and provided the mainstay of the city's economy for more than 75 years.

Wentworth Park, a narrow green area near the city centre, with duck ponds, walking paths, picnic areas and a bandstand, is a favorite respite for residents and tourists. Cossit House, built in 1787 on Charlotte Street, is the city's oldest, and now is a provincial museum. Nearby are St. Patrick's Church, Jost House, and the Cape Breton Centre for Heritage and Science. Action Week, during the first week in August, is the time to celebrate Sydney's heritage. Centre 200 is the venue for sports and culture events throughout the year.

In other parts of this area there are still places that reveal the pride and prosperity that were such a part of the island's past. The Gowrie House in Sydney Mines was built in 1830 for Samuel Archibald, agent-general of the General Mining Association which ran the coal mines. It remained in the Archibald family until 1975, when the present owners, Clifford Matthews and Ken Tutty, purchased it. For an overnight stay in industrial Cape Breton, there is no better spot. Guest rooms and common areas have since been furnished with beautiful things — Staffordshire figurines, Chippendale chairs, and more. A four-course dinner prepared by Matthews is served each evening; reservations are a must. Visitors to and from Newfoundland find the Gowrie House especially convenient, as it is only minutes away from the ferry terminal in North Sydney.

In Glace Bay, the Savoy

GOWRIE HOUSE,
SYDNEY MINES

Theatre on Union Street is another reminder of a time when Cape Breton industry boomed and the population of coal-mining towns exploded. Built in 1901, the theatre quickly became the venue for a host of cultural activities that Glace Bay residents demanded and could easily support. When the entire Union Street block burned to the ground in 1927, Glace Bay's prosperity was on the wane, but still sufficient to quickly rebuild the Savoy — this time, with ornamental touches that included the iron rococo chandeliers that hang from the ceiling today. The 761-seat theatre stages theatrical and musical productions throughout the year and is considered one of the finest performance venues in the Atlantic region.

At the edge of town, a national historic site commemorates Guglielmo Marconi's experiments with wireless communication. After he received the first trans-Atlantic signal at St. John's, Newfoundland in 1901, several Canadian communities courted Marconi. He chose to conduct his experiments in Glace Bay. In December of 1902, Marconi successfully transmitted signals from here to Poldhu, Cornwall. His story is well told at the museum.

Visitors to Glace Bay should also take an underground tour at the Miners' Museum. Retired coal miners tell of the dangerous and gritty life below the surface, and of the men who died in explosions, cave-ins, floods, and even in union clashes with company police. The Men of the Deeps, a choir of Cape Breton coal miners which has gained world wide recognition, performs weekly at the museum during the summer.

ABOUT THIS BOOK AND ITS CONTRIBUTORS

Nova Scotia is astonishing in its diversity. Whether it's the land itself, the plants, animals, birds, and fishes, or the mix of peoples, places, and cultures, you encounter something different at every turn. We've tried to reflect the range and wealth of that diversity in these pages.

Historian **Brian Cuthbertson** is former Head of Heritage for Nova Scotia and the author of several books on Nova Scotia history.

Elaine Elliot and **Virginia Lee** are the authors of *Maritime Flavours Guidebook and Cookbook* and numerous other cookbooks.

Al Kingsbury is a journalist and author who lives in the Annapolis Valley.

Ron Foley MacDonald writes a regular column on culture for *The Daily News*.

Robert J. McCalla is a geographer and author of *The Maritime Provinces Atlas*, published by Formac.

Stephen Poole is a historian, law school graduate, and freelance writer who enjoys mixing his interest in Nova Scotia's heritage with the experience of visiting every part of the province.

Terrence M. Punch is Past President of the Royal Nova Scotia Historical Society and has written numerous books and pamphlets on genealogical research in Nova Scotia.

Alan Ruffman is a marine geophysicist who has had a long interest in the 1917 explosion in Halifax Harbour.

David Stephens and **Susan Randles** are travel writers and authors of *Lighthouses of Nova Scotia*.

Chris Tyler is Head, Production Crafts at the provincial government's Nova Scotia Centre for Craft and Design.

Photographer **Keith Vaughan** has won numerous photography prizes and medals at local, national, and international competitions.

We welcome any comments you could offer us that might help us in the preparation of future editions of this guidebook. You can reach us at the address shown on page 200.

—The Publishers

Other great Colourguides include:

CONTENTS

GETTING THERE

BY LAND

The Trans Canada Highway enters Nova Scotia from New Brunswick. Visitors from the United States must pass through Canada Customs checkpoints before entering the country.

Greyhound from New York (1-800-231-2222) and *Voyageur* from Montreal (613-238-5900) connect with SMT bus lines in New Brunswick (506-458-6000). SMT connects with Acadian Lines (902-454-9321) which offers bus service to most Nova Scotia destinations from Amherst.

VIA Rail Canada (1-800-561-3952) provides train service to Halifax via Montreal.

BY SEA

There are several options for car-ferry trips to Nova Scotia.

Portland, Maine, to Yarmouth, Nova Scotia

Daily service by MS *Scotia Prince* from early May through October. Reservations required. In Canada: Box 609, Yarmouth, N.S., B5A 4B6. In the U.S.A.: Prince of Fundy Cruises Limited, Box 4216, Station A, Portland, Maine, 04101. In U.S.A. and Canada call toll-free 1-800-341-7540; in Maine, 1-800-482-0955; www.princeoffundy.com.

Bar Harbor, Maine, to Yarmouth, Nova Scotia

Service from May to October aboard the *Cat*. Contact: Bay Ferries Ltd., P.O. Box 634, Charlottetown, PE, C1A 7L3. In U.S.A. and Canada call toll-free 1-888-249-7245; www.nfl-bay.com.

Saint John, New Brunswick, to Digby, Nova Scotia

Daily service across the Bay of Fundy aboard the MV *Princess of Acadia*; additional service during peak season. Bay Ferries Ltd., P.O. Box 634, Charlottetown, PE, C1A 7L3; In U.S.A. and Canada call toll-free 1-888-249-7245; www.nfl-bay.com.

Prince Edward Island to Nova Scotia

Daily service between May 1 and December 20 from Wood Islands, P.E.I., to Caribou, N.S.. Northumberland Ferries, Box 634, Charlottetown, P.E.I., C1A 7L3; 1-800-565-0201 in N.S. or P.E.I., Elsewhere, 902-566-3838. No reservations.

The 12.9-kilometre (8 mile) Confederation Bridge joins Borden-Carleton, Prince Edward Island, and Cape Jourimain, New Brunswick near the Nova Scotia border.

Newfoundland to North Sydney, Nova Scotia

Daily service from Port-Aux-Basques to North Sydney (additional service during peak). Monday, Wednesday and Friday service from Argentia to North Sydney, mid-June through mid-September only. Marine Atlantic/Reservations, 355 Purves St., North Sydney, N.S., B2A 3V2. In the U.S.A. and Canada, 1-800-341-7981; www.marine-atlantic.ca.

BY AIR

Although Canada's largest airlines have merged, both Air Canada (1-800-563-5151) and Canadian Airlines International (1-800-665-1177) provide daily flights to Nova Scotia from most Canadian cities. Affiliated regional carriers Air Nova and Air Atlantic offer scheduled connections within Atlantic Canada and flights to select destinations in the eastern United States.

Air Canada in partnership with Continental Airlines services destinations in the United States and worldwide through Houston, Newark, and Boston.

Other carriers that service U.S. destinations include: Northwest Air Link (Boston to Halifax); Northwest Airlines (Halifax from Detroit); and American Eagle (Halifax from New York).

Several airlines offer regularly scheduled flights between Halifax and a number of European destinations (ask about charters as well).

Most air traffic to Nova Scotia touches down at the Halifax International Airport, with connecting flights to Yarmouth and Sydney. Car rentals may be arranged at all three airports.

Limousine service is available from the terminal buildings. The Halifax airport is located about 40 kilometres (25 mi.) northeast of the city, and the 30–40 minute cab ride costs about $30. An airport bus service to downtown hotels costs $18 round-trip, $11 one-way.

TRAVEL ESSENTIALS

MONEY

American currency can be exchanged at any Nova Scotia bank at the prevailing rate. There are also currency exchange booths at the Visitor Information Centre in Yarmouth and at the Halifax International Airport. Units of currency are similar to those of the United States excepting the Canadian two-dollar and the one-dollar coins .

Traveller's cheques and major U.S. credit cards are accepted throughout Nova Scotia, although you may require cash in some rural areas. Traveller's cheques in Canadian funds can be purchased in the U.S.. Cheques issued by Visa, American Express, and Thomas Cook are widely recognized.

American visitors may also use bank or credit cards to make cash withdrawals from automated teller machines that are tied into international networks such as Cirrus, Interac and Plus. These can be found in larger centres throughout the province.

PASSPORTS

Passports and visas are not required for American visitors although some proof of citizenship or residency might be (a birth certificate or Alien Registration Card will serve). At the border, expect to be asked where you live, why you are coming to Canada, and for how long.

Citizens of other countries should check with the nearest Canadian embassy or consulate regarding entry requirements.

CUSTOMS

Arriving
Visitors to Canada may bring certain duty-free items into the country as part of their personal baggage. These items must be declared to Customs upon arrival and may include up to 200 cigarettes, 50 cigars, 400 grams of manufactured tobacco, and 400 tobacco sticks. Visitors are also permitted 1.14 litres (40 oz.) of liquor or wine, or 8.2 litres (24 12-ounce cans or bottles) of beer.

Gift items—excluding tobacco and alcohol products—for Canadian residents that do not exceed $60 are also duty-free. Packages should be marked "Gift" and the value indicated.

Boats, trailers, sporting equipment, cameras, and similar big-ticket items may enter Canada free of duty. However, Canada Customs may require a refundable deposit to ensure that these goods are not sold for profit. It might be better to register such items with customs officials in your own country, so that when you re-enter you have evidence that they were not bought in Canada.

Some items are strictly controlled in Canada. Firearms are prohibited, with the exception of rifles and shotguns for hunting purposes. Plant material will be examined at the border. Veterinarian's certificates are required for all pets.

For further information on Canadian customs information, contact Customs Border Services, Box 3080 South, Halifax, NS, B3J 3G6; (902) 426-2911 (Canada 1-800-461-9999)

Departing
To find out about U.S. customs regulations and what other restrictions and exemptions apply contact your local customs office or the U.S. Customs Service, Box 7407, Washington, DC, 20044; 202-927-2095. Ask for a copy of *Know Before You Go*.

Travellers from other countries should also check on customs regulations before leaving home.

TAXES

Harmonized Sales Tax (HST)
Most goods and services sold in Nova

Scotia are subject to the Harmonized Sales Tax, a 15 percent federal/provincial tax which may be either included in or added to the price.

Out-of country visitors are eligible for rebates of the HST paid on short-term accommodations, and also on goods purchased for use outside Canada, if removed from Canada within 60 days of purchase. Rebate forms are available from Visitor Information Centres, Revenue Canada offices, Canada Customs ports, and many hotels and inns.

GUIDES

The Nova Scotia Travel Guide (*The Complete Guide for Doers and Dreamers*) is an indispensable aid to visitors. To obtain a copy write to Nova Scotia Information and Reservations, Box 130, Halifax, NS, B3J 2M7 or call toll-free 1-800-565-0000. The Guide is also available at Visitor Information Centres throughout Nova Scotia.

GETTING ACQUAINTED

TIME ZONE

Nova Scotia falls within the Atlantic Time Zone, which is one hour later than the Eastern Time Zone. Daylight Saving Time, when the clocks are advanced one hour, is in effect from early April until late October.

CLIMATE

Nova Scotia's climate is influenced by the sea. Summers are cooler and winters milder than in central Canada. Average daily maximum temperatures for Halifax:

Jan.	1°C	33°F
Feb.	1°C	33°F
Mar.	4°C	39°F
Apr.	9°C	48°F
May	14°C	58°F
June	19°C	67°F
July	23°C	73°F
Aug.	24°C	74°F
Sept.	19°C	67°F
Oct.	14°C	58°F
Nov.	9°C	48°F
Dec.	3°C	37°F

GETTING AROUND

BUS TOURS

Seasonal bus tours of the province are available through a number of tour operators, including Cabana Tours, Halifax (455-8111), Atlantic Tours GrayLine, Halifax (423-6242), and Nova Tours, Halifax (429-3702). Several tour operators will arrange customized itineraries for groups.

BY CAR

Nova Scotia highway maps are available at Visitor Information Centres throughout the province. Highways are generally well maintained. Gasoline prices are approximately 60-80 cents per litre (about $2 per U.S. gal.). Speed limits vary depending on the type of highway, with the 100-level controlled access highways having the highest limit, 110 km/hr (65 mph). The speed limit is 50 kilometres per hour (30 mph) in cities and towns. In Nova Scotia, seat belt use is compulsory for driver and passengers.

A valid United States driver's license is also valid in Nova Scotia. Evidence of the car's registration is required (a car rental contract will also serve). U.S. motorists may obtain a Non-Resident Inter-Province Motor Vehicle Liability Insurance Card through their own insurance companies as evidence of financial responsibility within Canada.

Car Rentals
All major car rental agencies are represented in Nova Scotia. Representatives at the Halifax International Airport are listed below:
- Avis:
In the U.S.: 1-800-331-1084
In Canada: 1-800-879-2847
- Budget:
In the U.S.: 1-800-527-0700
In Canada: 1-800-268-8900
- Hertz:
In the U.S.: 1-800-654-3131
In Canada: 1-800-263-0600
- Thrifty:
In the U.S. and Canada:
1-800-367-2277
- Tilden (affiliated with

National Rent-a-Car in the U.S.):
In the U.S.: 1-800-227-7368;
In Canada: 1-800-387-4747

Consult the Yellow Pages of local telephone directories for local agencies which may offer lower rates.

LODGING

For a complete listing of accommodations in the province, including campgrounds, consult the *Nova Scotia Travel Guide* (see Travel Essentials). Hostellers should contact Hostelling International–Nova Scotia, Box 3010 South, 5516 Spring Garden Road, Halifax, NS, B3J 3G6; 425-5450. Visitors who are interested in bed and breakfast style accommodation in Nova Scotia can consult *Atlantic Canada Bed & Breakfasts*, a comprehensive listing of B&B's published by Formac and updated frequently. Other resources available at local bookstores include an illustrated guide to Nova Scotia's most distinctive inns — Elaine Elliot and Virginia Lee's *Maritime Flavours* (4th ed. Formac Publishing, 2000).

Many establishments are members of Nova Scotia's Check In Reservation and Information Service (see Travel Essentials). Membership is indicated by a check mark in the *Nova Scotia Travel Guide*. In general, the accommodations listed below are the best of their kind in Nova Scotia. Most have distinguishing features that will enhance your stay.

Approximate prices are indicated, based on the average cost, at time of publication, for two persons staying in a double room (excluding taxes): $ = under $70; $$ = $70-$100; $$$ = more than $100.

HALIFAX

- Cambridge Suites Hotel, 1583 Brunswick St., Halifax, B3J 3P5; 1-888-417-8483. At the foot of Citadel Hill in downtown Halifax. Suites with fridge and microwave, guest laundry, exercise room. Complimentary continental breakfast. Open year-round. $$$
- Citadel Inn, 1960 Brunswick St., Halifax, B3J 2G7; 1-800-565-7162. A couple of blocks from the clock

tower and in the downtown area. Complimentary continental breakfast. All amenities. Open year-round. $$/$$$
- Delta Barrington, 1875 Barrington St., Halifax, B3J 3L6; 1-800-268-1133. Close to Historic Properties and most attractions. Adjoins Barrington Place Mall, restaurants and pubs. Open year-round. $$/$$$
- Delta Halifax, 1990 Barrington St., Halifax, B3J 1P2; 1-800-268-1133, 425-6700. Top-floor restaurant with sweeping view of the city and harbour. All amenities. Adjoins Scotia Square shopping mall. Open year-round. $$$
- Halliburton House Inn, 5184 Morris St., Halifax, B3J 1B3; 420-0658. Small, elegant hotel. Registered Heritage Property incorporating three 19th-century townhouses in downtown Halifax. Open year-round. $$$
- Inn-on-the-Lake, Box 29, Waverley, B0N 2S0; 1-800-463-6465. Two hectares (5 acres) of parkland with private freshwater beach and outdoor pool, courtesy shuttle to airport (10 minutes away). Open year-round. $$/$$$
- Prince George Hotel, 1725 Market St., Halifax, B3J 3N9; 1-800-565-1567; reservations@princegeorgehotel.ns.ca; www.princegeorgehotel.com. Central downtown location with all the amenities. Open year-round. $$$
- Sheraton Hotel, 1919 Upper Water St., Halifax, B3J 3J5; 1-800-325-3535; www.ittsheraton.com. Luxury accommodation on the Halifax waterfront (ask for a room on the harbour side). Indoor pool, sauna, whirlpool. Casino with slot machines and table games. Adjacent to Historic Properties. Open year-round. $$$
- Westin Nova Scotia, 1181 Hollis St., Halifax, B3H 2P6; 1-800-228-3000; 1-888-679-3784; sales@halifax.newcastlehotels.com. Comfortable rooms, short walk south of downtown at old train station. Indoor pool, sauna, tennis court. Open year-round. $$$

LIGHTHOUSE ROUTE

Chester and Mahone Bay

- Bayview Pines Country Inn, 678 Oakland Rd., Indian Point, Mahone Bay, B0J 2E0; 624-9970; www.bayviewpines.ns.ca. 8.5-hectare (21-acre) property with hilltop view of Mahone Bay; century-old farmhouse and converted barn with stylish furnishings. Gift shop and tea room. Open year-round. $$
- Captain's House, 129 Central St., Chester, B0J 1J0; 275-3501; www.atlanticonline.ns.ca/captainsh ouse. On the Chester waterfront, close to the yacht club. Dining room and lounge. Open year-round except January. $$
- Haddon Hall Inn, 67 Haddon Hill Road, Box 640, Chester, B0J 1J0; 275-3577; haddon@tallships.istar.ca; www.destination–ns.com/lighthouse/ haddon. Spectacular country estate with panoramic ocean view. Luxury suites and chalets. Gourmet dining. Open April to December. $$$
- Oak Island Inn & Marina, Western Shore, B0J 3M0; 1-800-565-5075; oakisland@istar,ca; www.oakislandinn.com. Recently renovated oceanfront hotel. All-inclusive packages include horseback riding, golfing, sailing, and whale-watching. Open year-round. $$/$$$

Lunenburg

- Bluenose Lodge, Falkland Ave. & Dufferin St., Box 399, Lunenburg, B0J 2C0; 1-800-565-8851; fox.nstn.ca/~bluenose. Restored 1863 inn. Nine guest rooms, breakfast included. Licensed dining room during summer season. Open year-round. $$
- Boscawen Inn, 150 Cumberland St., Box 1343, Lunenburg, B0J 2C0; 1-800-354-5009; boscawen@ns.sympatico.ca; www3.ns.sympatico.ca/boscawen. Victorian mansion in the heart of old Lunenburg. One-of-a-kind rooms and an upscale dining room. Open Easter to year-end (other times by arrangement for groups). $$/$$$
- Lunenburg Inn, 26 Dufferin St., Box 1407, Lunenburg, B0J 2C0;

1-800-565-3963; luninn@auracom.com; www.lunenburginn.com. 1893 heritage inn with sun deck and covered verandah, complimentary full breakfast. Open year-round. $$/$$$
- Ovens Natural Park Oceanview Cottages, Box 38, Riverport, B0J 2W0; 766-4621; ovenspark@ns.sympatico.ca; www.ovenspark.com. Two-bedroom cottages, some with whirlpool and fireplace. Nature trails and sea caves. Pan for gold on the gravel beach. Open May 15 to October 15. $$/$$$
- Schoolhouse by the Sea & Beach House, 963 Kingsburg Beach Rd., Kingsburg, B0J 2X0; 766-4670; www.duckworth–realestate.com/rent al.html. 160-year-old former schoolhouse and new beach house. Schoolhouse sleeps 9, beach house sleeps 8. Open year-round. $$/$$$

Liverpool and Shelburne

- Cooper's Inn, 36 Dock St., Box 959, Shelburne, B0T 1W0; 1-800-688-2011; www3.ns.sympatico.ca/coopers. Loyalist home built around 1785. Five guest rooms in main building and adjoining cooperage, with views of Shelburne Harbour. Open April to October. $$/$$$
- Quarterdeck Beachside Villas & Grill, Summerville Beach, Box 70, Port Mouton, B0T 1T0; 1-800-565-1119; qdvilla@auracom.com; www.quarterdeck.ns.ca. Beachside resort with all the amenities including jacuzzis, fireplaces, and kitchen facilities. Open year-round. $$$
- White Point Beach Lodge Resort, Hunt's Point, B0T 1G0; 1-800-565-5068; resort@atcon.com; www.whitepoint.com. Off Route 3 at White Point. Resort with extensive recreational facilities, including golf, tennis, boating, swimming pools, and kilometre-long white sand beach. Summer dinner theatre. Open year-round. $$$
- Whitman Inn, RR2, Caledonia, B0T 1B0; 1-800-830-3855; inn@whitman.ns.ca; www.whitman.ns.ca. Close to Kejimkujik National Park. Turn-of-

the-century homestead with indoor pool and sauna. Park-related recreational packages for canoeing, bicycling, and cross-country skiing. Open year-round. $/$$

Yarmouth
- Manor Inn, Route 1, Box 56, Hebron, B0W 1X0; 1-888-626-6746; manorinn@istar.ca; www.manorinn.com. Inn, coach house and adjacent motel set on 3.6 hectares (9 acres) of landscaped grounds on Doctor's Lake. Open year-round (no evening dining in the winter months). $$/$$$
- Murray Manor, 225 Main St., Yarmouth, B5A 1C6; 742-9625; mmanor@auracom.com; www.auracom/cts/mmanor. Three large rooms in c. 1820 Gothic style home. Full breakfast and afternoon tea. Acadian French spoken. Open year-round. $
- Rodd Grand Hotel, 417 Main St., Box 220, Yarmouth, B5A 4B2; 1-800-565-RODD. Full-service modern hotel with indoor pool. Open year-round. $$$

Evangeline Trail

- Blomidon Inn, 127 Main St., Box 839 Wolfville, B0P 1X0; 1-800-565-2291; innkeeper@blomidon.ns.ca; www.blomidon.ns.ca. Sea captain's home from the grand shipbuilding era of the 1870s. Open year-round. $$/$$$
- Bread and Roses Country Inn, 82 Victoria St., Box 177, Annapolis Royal, B0S 1A0; 1-888-899-0551. Restored Victorian mansion with antique furnishings, Nova Scotia folk art, and contemporary Canadian and Inuit art. Homemade breakfast included. Not suitable for children under 12. Open year-round. $$
- Brier Island Lodge, Box 1197, Westport, Brier Island, B0V 1H0; 1-800-662-8355; brierisl@atcon.com; www.brierisland.com. Modern rooms with ocean view, excellent opportunities for whale- and bird-watching. Open April 1 to October 31. $$/$$$

- Fairfield Farm Inn, 10 Main St., Box 1287, Middleton, B0S 1P0; 1-800-237-9896; griffith@glinx.com; www.valleyweb.com/FairfieldFarm Inn. Working fruit and vegetable farm. Five rooms in century-old farmhouse; trout fishing on site. Open year-round (by reservation only November to March). $
- Garrison House Inn, 350 Saint George St., Box 108, Annapolis Royal, B0S 1A0; 532-5750; www.come.to/garrison. Small inn, built in 1854, with fine dining. Open April 1 to December 31. $/$$
- Milford House, Box 521, Annapolis Royal, B0S 1A0; 1-877-532-5751; www.chebucto.ns.ca/Recreation/Milford_House. Route 8, South Milford. Secluded 19th-century inn amidst 600 wooded acres between Annapolis Royal and Kejimkujik National Park. Also, 27 lakeshore cabins with fireplace. Country breakfasts and dinners in the main lodge (MAP). Open mid-June to mid-September. $$$
- Mountain Gap Inn, Box 504, Digby, B0V 1A0; 1-800-565-5020; mtngap@tartannet.ns.ca; www.mountaingap.ns.ca. At Smith's Cove. Resort complex with beach, pool, tennis, and other outdoor recreation. Large garden and grounds. Open May 1 to October 31. $$$
- Planters' (Barracks) Country Inn, 1464 Starrs Point Rd., Port Williams, B0P 1T0; 1-800-661-7879. 18th-century restored officers' barracks. Afternoon teas, attractive grounds. Open year-round. $/$$
- Pines Resort Hotel, Shore Rd., Box 70, Digby, B0V 1A0; 1-800-667-4637; pines@gov.ns.ca; www.signatureresorts.com. Full-scale luxury resort with championship golf course and all other amenities. Hotel rooms and suites plus 30 cottages with stone fireplaces. Open mid-May to mid-October. $$$
- Queen Anne Inn, 494 Upper Saint George St., Box 218, Annapolis Royal, B0S 1A0; 532-7850; queenanne@queenanneinn.ns.ca; www.queenanneinn.ns.ca Registered Heritage Property. Open year-round. $$

175

- Tattingstone Inn, 434 Main St., Wolfville, B0P 1X0; 1-800-565-7696; tattingstone@ns.sympatico.ca; www.tattingstone.ns.ca. Tastefully decorated inn with tennis court, outdoor pool, library, and music room. Elegant teas and dinner. Open year-round. $$$

- Victoria's Historic Inn and Carriage House B&B, 416 Main St., Box 308, Wolfville, B0P 1X0; 1-800-556-5744; victoria.inn@ns.sympatico.ca; www.valleyweb.com/victoriasinn. Picturesque 1893 Registered Heritage Property. Luxury suites with jacuzzi whirlpool bath; breakfast and evening dinner. Open year-round. $$$

GLOOSCAP TRAIL

- The Cobequid Inn, RR1, Maitland, B0N 1T0; 261-2841; www.bbcanada.com/cobequidinn. Restored 1828 farmhouse with three guest rooms. Fine licensed dining. Open April 1 to October 31. $

- Four Seasons Retreat, 320 Cove Rd., RR1, Economy, B0M 1J0; 1-888-373-0339; www.fourseasonsretreat.ns.ca. Six beautiful housekeeping cottages on the cliffs overlooking Minas Basin. Near skiing and hiking trails. Open year-round. $$/$$$

- The Palliser, Box 821, Truro, B2N 5G6; 893-8951; palliser@auracom.com. Highway 102 at Exit 14. Comfortable motel-style accommodation, with good view of tidal bore on the Salmon River (viewing area lighted in evening). Complimentary buffet breakfast; dining room serves all meals. Open May to October. $

SUNRISE TRAIL

- Amherst Shore Country Inn, Box 889, Lorneville, B0P 1X0; 1-800-661-2724; innkeepr@ascinn.ns.ca; www.ascinn.ns.ca. Route 366. Small inn with lovely ocean view and renowned dining room. Open May to mid-October. $$/$$$

- Braeside Inn, Front St., Box 1810, Pictou, B0K 1H0; 1-800-613-7701; braeside@north.nsis.com; www.nsis.com/~braeside. Twenty rooms, dining with harbour view. Open year-round. $/$$

- Consulate Inn, 157 Water St., Pictou, B0K 1H0; 1-800-424-8283; www.pictou.nsis.com/consulateinn. Bed and breakfast-style accommodation in a restored c. 1810 property overlooking Pictou harbour. Open year-round. $/$$

- Pictou Lodge Resort, Box 1539, Pictou, B0K 1H0; 1-888-662-7484; www.MaritimeInns.com. Braeshore Road. Rustic 1920s resort with modern amenities. Standard hotel accommodation or multiple-bedroom log cottages with huge stone fireplaces and screened-in sunporches. Open mid-May to mid-October. $$$

MARINE DRIVE

- Liscombe Lodge, Liscomb Mills, B0J 2A0; 1-800-665-6343; www.signatureresorts.com. Full-service resort featuring sport fishing packages (guides available), boat rentals and marina. Hotel and cottage-style accommodations, some overlooking the beautiful Liscomb River. Fine dining. Open May 15 to October 31. $$$

- Marquis of Dufferin Seaside Inn, RR1, Port Dufferin, B0J 2R0; 654-2696. Route 7, eight units with ocean view(six more in motel annex). Sport fishing, boating, sun lounge and deck in lodge. Open May 1 to October.31 $/$$/$$$

- Salmon River House Country Inn, 9931 #7 Highway, Salmon River Bridge, B0J 1P0; 1-800-565-3353; salmonrh@istar.ca;www.highway7.com. Six well-appointed guest rooms along with on-site hiking, boating, hunting, and fishing. Licensed dining. Open year-round (November to April by reservation only). $$/$$$

CAPE BRETON AND THE CABOT TRAIL

- Cheticamp Island Resort, Box 160, Dominion, B0A 1E0; 224-2711. Two-bedroom housekeeping cottages on Cheticamp Island. Ocean swimming. Daily and weekly rates. Open May 1 to November 30 (off-season by arrangement). $$$

- Duffus House Inn, Water St., Box 427, Baddeck, B0E 1B0; 295-2172; www.capebreton.com/Baddeck/DuffusHouse. Circa 1830 home with antique furnishings. B&B. Private wharf, saltwater swimming. Open mid-June to mid-October. No smoking, no pets. $$/$$$

- Duncreigan Country Inn, Box 59, Mabou, B0E 1X0; 1-800-840-2207; mulldci@ns.sympatico.ca; www3.ns.sympatico.ca/mulldci. Four spacious guest rooms with antique furnishings. Fine dining. Open year-round. $$/$$$

- Dundee Resort, RR2, West Bay, B0E 3K0; 1-800-565-1774; dundee@chatsubo.com; www.chatsubo.com/dundee. Golf with outstanding views of the Bras d'Or. Marina and boat rentals, indoor and outdoor pools. Hotel, cottage, or three-bedroom chalet. Open May to November. $$/$$$

- Haus Treuburg, Central Ave., Box 92, Port Hood, B0E 2W0; 787-2116; www.auracom.com./~treuburg. Guest house and cottages close to warm saltwater swimming. Complimentary German-style breakfast at guest house. Licensed restaurant. Open April 15 to December 31. $/$$

- Inverary Inn and Resort, Shore Rd., Box 190, Baddeck, B0E 1B0; 1-800-565-5660; inverary@atcon.com; www.InveraryResort.com. Two restaurants, indoor and outdoor pools, complimentary boat tours and other resort facilities. Open year-round. $$$

- Keltic Lodge, Middle Head Peninsula, Ingonish Beach, B0C 1L0; 1-800-565-0444; www.signatureresorts.com. Full-scale luxury resort with championship golf course (many say the best in Nova Scotia). Choose from the main lodge, White Birch Inn, or cottages. Outdoor pool, hiking trails. Open May to October (ski season: January to March). $$$

- Laurie's Motor Inn, Main St., Box 1, Cheticamp, B0E 1H0; 224-2400;

laurie@ns.sympatico.ca; www.lauries.com. Fifty-five motel units, bicycle rentals, whale cruises arranged. Open year-round. $$

- MacNeil House, Shore Rd., Box 399, Baddeck, B0E 1B0; 1-888-662-7484; www.MaritimeInns.com. Luxury suites with all the amenities. Swimming pool or saltwater swimming in the Bras d'Or. Eco-tourism and other packages available. Open May 15 to October 31. $$$

- Markland Coastal Resort, Dingwall, B0C 1G0; 1-800-872-6084; markland.resort@ns.sympatico.ca; www3.ns.sympatico.ca/markland.resort. Secluded coastal resort with log cabins, outdoor pool, beachfront, and gourmet dining. Open mid-May to October. $$/$$$

- Normaway Inn, Egypt Rd., Box 101, Margaree Valley, B0E 2C0; 1-800-565-9463; normaway.com. Relaxing old-style resort (four of the cabins have jacuzzis). Cottages with wood stoves. Excellent salmon and trout fishing nearby. Open mid-June to mid-October. $$$

- Telegraph House, Chebucto St., Box 8, Baddeck, B0E 1B0; 295-1100. On Baddeck's main street. Choose from motel-style units or rooms in the old-fashioned inn. Room No. 1 was Alexander Graham Bell's before he built Beinn Breagh. Open year-round. $/$$

MARCONI TRAIL

Sydney and Glace Bay

- Cambridge Suites Hotel, 380 Esplanade, Sydney, B1P 1B1; 1-800-565-9466; reservations@syd.cambridgesuites.ns.ca; www.centennialhotels.com/cambridge. On Sydney waterfront. Suite accommodation with housekeeping facilities. Rooftop spa pool and exercise facilities. Open year-round. $$$

- Cranberry Cove Inn, 17 Wolfe Street, Louisbourg, B0A 1M0; 1-800-929-0222; www.auracom.com/~crancove. Seven guest rooms (some with jacuzzi) in a fully renovated turn-of-the-century home. Licensed

dining. Open June 1 to October 15 (off-season by reservation) $$$
- Gowrie House Country Inn, 139 Shore Rd., Sydney Mines, B1V 1A6; 1-800-372-1115; www.gowriehouse.com. Beautifully furnished 1830 home with elegant antique-filled guest rooms. Garden House has four suites with all modern amenities. Exceptional dining. Open April 1 to December 30. $$$
- Louisbourg Harbour Inn, 9 Warren St., Louisbourg, B0A 1M0; 1-888-888-8466; louisbourg@sprint.ca. Eight well-appointed guest rooms in a century-old captain's house overlooking Louisbourg Harbour. Open June to October. $$$

DINING

Nova Scotia cuisine is a delight. Tastefully and imaginatively prepared seafood, fresh Annapolis Valley produce, and Pictou County lamb are among the many specialities of Nova Scotia restaurants. Local wines are inexpensive and surprisingly good.

Where to Eat in Canada (Oberon Press) is updated annually and includes many of the province's finer restaurants. *Maritime Flavours* (Formac Publishing, 2000) is an illustrated guide to the best and most distinctive dining establishments in the Maritime provinces, accompanied by a selection of their favourite recipes.

Approximate prices are indicated, based on the average cost, at time of publication, of dinner for two including wine (where available), taxes, and gratuity: $ = under $45; $$ = $45-$80; $$$ = over $80.

HALIFAX

- Cafe Chianti, 5165 South St., Halifax; 423-7471; www.cafechianti.com. A dark and intimate cave-like atmosphere, with all the inviting smells and sounds of Italian and Eastern European cooking. Open every day; dinner only Saturday and Sunday. $$$
- The Cellar, 5677 Brenton Pl., Halifax, 492-4412. Big helpings and first-class cooking features salads, pasta and pizza. Open Mon. - Thurs. 11:30 am-11:30 pm. Fri. and Sat. to 12:30 am. Closed Sunday. $$
- The Chickenburger, 1531 Bedford Highway, Bedford. A landmark since the 1940s. Still has a juke box (although now it plays compact discs). Chicken burgers and real, old-fashioned milkshakes are the staples. Open 9 am-1 am daily. $
- Da Maurizio, 1496 Lower Water St., Halifax; 423-0859. Elegant Italian dining in the restored Brewery Market complex. Open Monday-Friday for lunch and dinner to 10 pm, Saturday dinner only. Closed Sunday. $$$
- Halliburton House Hotel, 5184 Morris St., Halifax; 420-0658; www.haliburton.ns.ca. Specialties include fresh Atlantic seafood and wild game entrées. Try lunch in the outdoor garden café. Open daily 5:30-10 pm. $$
- Il Mercato, 5475 Spring Garden Road, Halifax; 422-2866. Casual northern Italian dining with great desserts. Busy and friendly. Open Monday to Saturday 11am to 11pm. $$
- Inn-on-the-Lake, Fall River, Box 29, Waverley; 861-3480; innonthelake.com. Located on beautiful Lake Thomas, meals are served in the dining room, on the terrace or by the gazebo bar in the park. Open daily from 7am. $$
- Kinh-Do, 1284 Barrington St., Halifax; 425-8555. Inexpensive, authentic Vietnamese cuisine. Open daily 11:30 am-10 pm. $
- La Maison, 5688 Spring Garden Road, Halifax; 492-4339. French bistro-style cooking. Open daily 11:30am-10pm; bar and grill until 11:30pm. $$
- La Perla, 71 Alderney Dr., Dartmouth; 469-3241. Distinctive northern Italian cuisine, a minute's walk from the Halifax-Dartmouth ferry terminal. Open daily for dinner to 9:45 pm, lunch on weekdays only. $$
- MacAskill's, 88 Alderney Dr., Dartmouth; 466-3100. Best view of Halifax Harbour and the cityscape. Located in the ferry terminal on the Dartmouth waterfront. Open daily for dinner, lunch Monday-Friday. $$$
- McKelvie's, 1680 Lower Water St.,

Halifax; 421-6161. Imaginative preparation of fresh seafood, also an on-site bakery — sample the homemade bannock before your meal. Open daily 11:30 am-10:30 pm (shorter hours and dinner only on Sunday in off-season). $$

• Maple, 1813 Granville St., Halifax; 425-9100; http://maplerestaurant.com. Canadian cuisine by Chef Michael Smith. Select from either the five course Taste of Canada menu or the seven course Celebration menu. Open Monday-Saturday for dinner only. $$$

• Nemo's Restaurant, 1865 Hollis St., Halifax; 425-6738. Intimate dining in the heart of downtown Halifax, featuring Provençal and northern Italian dishes. Open Monday-Saturday for lunch (to 2 pm), daily for dinner (to 10 pm). $$$

• Ryan Duffy's Steak and Seafood, 5640 Spring Garden Rd., Halifax; 421-1116. The city's best steaks, cut to the size you want, and Caesar salads made at your table. The bar and clubroom are less formal (and less expensive) alternatives to the dining room. Open daily 11:30 am-midnight. $$$

• Satisfaction Feast Vegetarian Restaurant, 1581 Grafton St., Halifax; 422-3540. Delicious and inexpensive vegetarian fare, especially the soups and breads. There is a bakery on-site; breads, muffins, and bagels can be purchased for take-out. Open weekdays and Saturday 8 am-9 pm Sunday 10 am-2 pm. No smoking, no liquor. $

• The Sweet Basil, 1866 Upper Water St., Halifax; 425-2133. Fine presentation and service. Great for lunch. Open daily 11:30 am-11:30 pm. Shorter hours during off-season. $$

• Unni's, 1569 Dresden Row, Halifax; 422-3733. Innovative cuisine. Open 11:30 am-3 pm; 5 pm-10 pm. Closed on Sunday. $$

• Upper Deck Waterfront Fishery and Grill, Privateers' Warehouse, Historic Properties, Halifax; 422-1289. Fine seafood dining in an historic waterfront building. Open daily for dinner to 10 pm. $$$

LIGHTHOUSE ROUTE

Peggys Cove

• Candleriggs, Indian Harbour; 823-2722. Traditional Scottish dishes and contemporary fare. Also a fine craft shop adjacent to the restaurant. Open daily 8 am-10 pm (weekends only, noon to sunset, January to mid-April). $$

• Sou'Wester, Peggys Cove; 823-2561. Excellent chowders, tasty lobster and traditional Nova Scotia desserts like gingerbread and blueberry cake.Open daily 8 am-10 pm (November-April until 6 pm or sunset). $$

Chester and Mahone Bay

• Campbell House, 321 Lacey Mines Rd., Chester Basin; 275-5655. Fine country dining and a panoramic view of Mahone Bay. Open daily noon-3 pm and 5 pm-9 pm. Open April-December. $$

• Captain's House, 129 Central St., Chester; 275-3501. In the 1822 home of New Englander Rev. John Secombe. Open May to October. $$$

• The Galley, Marriott's Cove, Chester; 275-4700. A relaxed setting with views of Mahone Bay and the yachts at South Shore Marine. Menu features chowders, summer salads, and seafood. Open daily 11:30 am-9 pm. Reservations recommended. Open March-October. $$

• Haddon Hall Inn, 67 Haddon Hill Road, Chester; 275-3577 or 275-3578. 1905 historic home on 90 acres. Open 5 pm-9 pm. April-Thanksgiving. $$

• Innlet Cafe, Keddy's Landing, Mahone Bay; 624-6363. Refreshing seafood-garnished salads or more substantial dishes for dinner. Try the front terrace on a warm evening, with a view of the water and Mahone Bay's three churches. Open daily 11:30 am-8:30 pm. $$

• Julien's, 43 Queen St., Chester; 275-2324. A French pâtissier featuring croissants, crêpes, soups and salads. Open daily 8 am-6 pm. Shorter hours and closed Monday during off-season. No liquor. $

• Mimi's Ocean Grill, 662 Main St., Mahone Bay; 624-1342. Fresh market and ocean cooking. Wide selection of homemade desserts. Unusually good children's menu. Open daily for lunch and dinner, April to December. $$

- Old Settler's Place Steakhouse & Restaurant, 16 Orchard St., Mahone Bay; 624-0046; www.abatrex.com/settlersplace. Swiss specialties and impressive desert menu. Open Tuesday-Sunday from 11:30 am, May-December. $$
- Seaside Shanty, Highway 3, Chester Basin; 275-2246. Big helpings of fresh seafood. Open daily 11:30 am-10 pm. Shorter hours during off-season. $

Lunenburg

- Arbor View Inn, 216 Dufferin St., Lunenburg; 634-3658; www.arborviewinn.ns.ca. Full breakfast for guests and candlelit dinner for guests and public. Open Tuesday-Sunday 5:30-10 pm. $$$
- Boscawen Inn, 150 Cumberland St., Lunenburg; 634-3325. A restored Victorian mansion specializing in fresh local seafood. Afternoon tea in the drawing rooms. Open for breakfast and dinner (5:30 pm-9:30 pm) daily, Easter–December 31. $$$
- LaHave Bakery, LaHave; 688-2908. Home baking using clear spring water and locally-grown, fresh-milled grains. Sandwiches made to order. Open Monday to Friday 9 am-5:30 pm, weekends 9 am-7 pm. Longer hours during season. No liquor. $
- Madelyn's Bistro at Prince's Inlet Retreat, Lunenburg; 634-3223; www.comsearch-can.com/pirmb.htm. Dine in upscale, 200-year-old Cape Cod or on patio deck. Open Monday to Saturday 11:30 am-9 pm, Sunday for brunch. $$$
- Magnolia's Grill, 128 Montague St., Lunenburg; 634-3287. Bustling atmosphere, tasty and innovative dishes, and lots to look at on the walls while you wait. Key lime pie for dessert. Open Monday to Saturday for lunch and dinner, April to late October. $$

Liverpool and Shelburne

- Charlotte Lane Café and Crafts, 13 Charlotte Lane, Shelburne; 875-3314; www.destination-ns.com/lighthouse/charlottelane. Relaxed dining, meals prepared by award-winning chef in a heritage property. Open May-December, Tuesday-Sunday, 11:30 am-8 pm. $$
- Cooper's Inn, 36 Dock St., Shelburne; 875-4656; www3.ns.sympatico.ca/coopers. Imaginative cooking, salmon smoked on the premises and an ever-changing array of fresh seasonal vegetables. A Registered Nova Scotia Heritage Property built in 1785. Open daily for dinner to 9 pm (in season). Closed on Monday in off-season. $$
- Quarterdeck Beachside Villas and Grill, Port Mouton; 683-2998; www.quarterdeck.ns.ca. Bright restaurant with view of white beaches serving good food. Open daily 10 am-9 pm July-August, 4 pm-9pm May, June, September and October. $$
- White Point Beach Lodge Resort, White Point; 354-2711; www.whitepoint.com. Informal dining room, suitable for children, serves steak and seafood. Open daily 6:30 am-9 pm. $$
- Whitman Inn, Caledonia; 682-2226; www.whitman.ns.ca. Tucked away, off the beaten track near the entrance to Kejimkujik National Park. A fixed menu, entrées delicately seasoned with fresh herbs from the garden. Everything down to the butter is homemade. Open for dinner by reservation only. Picnic lunches on request. Closed Sunday and Monday. $$

Yarmouth

- Harris's Quick and Tasty, 5 kilometres (3 miles) from Yarmouth ferry on Route 1; 742-3467. Seafood and delicious homemade desserts in a friendly diner atmosphere. Open daily 11 am-9 pm (10 pm in summer), mid-March to mid-December. $
- Little Lebanon, 100 Main St., Yarmouth; 742-1042. Offers Lebanese and vegetarian meals. Open Monday-Friday 11:30 am-8 pm; Saturday 2:30 pm-8 pm. Closed Sunday. License pending. $

EVANGELINE TRAIL

- Acton's Grill and Café, 268 Main St., Wolfville; 542-7525. Elegant summer lunches, chilled soups, an interesting buffet and open-air patio. One of Nova Scotia's very best restaurants. Open daily for lunch and dinner. $$
- Austria Dolfgasthaus, Granville Ferry; 532-7300. Right on the water. Delicious pumpkin soup and assorted schnitzels. Open daily 5 pm-10 pm. Closed Monday to Thursday in winter. $
- Blomidon Inn, 127 Main St., Wolfville; 542-2291. Dine in an elegant restored sea captain's mansion, built in 1877. Open daily for lunch and dinner (to 9:30 pm). $$$
- Brier Island Lodge, Westport, Brier Island; 839-2300. Acadian dishes and lots of seafood, from fish cakes to Solomon Gundy. Open 7 am-10:30 am, 5 pm-9:30 pm daily, April-December. $$
- The Cape View, Mavilette Beach. Acadian Rappie Pie a specialty. Open daily 7:30 am-10 pm, early March to late October. $$
- Chez La Vigne, 17 Front St., Wolfville; 542-5077. Daily pasta, fresh meats, seafood and vegetarian fare. Open daily 11 am-9:30 pm. $$
- Evangeline Snack Bar, Evangeline Motel, Highway 1, Grand Pré; 542-2703. Fabulous Valley fruit pies. Open daily to 7 pm, early May to late October. No liquor. $
- Fairy Tailor's Tea Garden, 67 McInnis Rd., Port George; 825-3726. Great salads, lamb and free-range chicken are among the delights offered at this beautiful location. Open Wed., Fri.-Sun, 5:30 pm-8:30 pm, June to October. $$
- Falcourt Inn, 8979 Hwy. 201, Nictaux; 825-3399. A restored fishing lodge with an exceptional view, specializing in seafood, and featuring creative beef and chicken dishes. Open 11:30 am-2 pm; 5 pm-9 pm; June 1-October 31, 11:30 am-2 pm. $$
- Garrison House Inn, 350 Saint George St., Annapolis Royal; 532-5750; www.come.to/garrison. Understated entrées with fresh and simple vegetable accompaniments. Save room for dessert – the strawberry rhubarb pie is wonderful! Open for breakfast 8 am-9:30 am, dinner 5:30 pm-9 pm, May-November. $$
- Leo's Cafe, Annapolis Royal, Saint George St., Annapolis Royal; 532-7424. Tasty soups and sandwiches. Don't expect a quick lunch in mid-summer; it's apt to be crowded. Open daily 11:30 am-6 pm, mid-March to late December. Licensed for beer and wine only. $
- The Lobster Pound, Halls Harbour; 679-5299. Only lobster, but some of the best to be had anywhere. Take it away to cook yourself, or take it to the boiling shack. Open noon-6 pm, mid-May to Labour Day. $
- Newman's Restaurant, 218 Saint George St., Annapolis Royal; 532-5502. A lively menu, ranging from calamari to lamb to black bear. Open Tuesday to Sunday, noon to 9 pm, early April to late October. Open Mondays in peak season. $$$
- Pines Resort Hotel, Shore Rd., Digby; 245-2511; www.signatureresorts.com. Specializing in local fish and seafood, in the luxurious surroundings of the Pines Resort Hotel. One of Nova Scotia's best restaurants. Open daily for breakfast 7 am-10 am, restaurant lunch 12 pm-2 pm, dinner 6 pm-9 pm, May to December. $$$
- Tattingstone Inn, 434 Main St., Wolfville; 542-7696; www.tattingstone.ns.ca. A beautifully appointed country inn, with all the touches that make a memorable gourmet dining experience. Open for breakfast and dinner (to 9:30pm). No smoking. Reservations recommended. $$$
- White Raven Inn; Highway 1, Granville Ferry; 532-5595. Fresh seafood is one of the specialties at this inn dating from the early 18th century. Open mid-June to Labour Day, noon-2:30 pm, 5:30 pm-7:30 pm. $$$

GLOOSCAP TRAIL

- The Bake Shop, Highway 209, Advocate Harbour; 392-2330. Splendid pies – fresh fruit in summer, apple and cream pies in the winter. Open Monday-Saturday 8 am-5 pm. $
- Cobequid Inn, Selma, near Maitland; 261-2841. Fresh seafood and meats served with seasonal vegetables from the inn's own garden. Open for dinner 5 pm-9 pm, May- October. $$
- Country Rose Tearoom, 125 Victoria St. E., Amherst; 667-6100. A wide variety of teas, hot soups, salads, and quiche. Great chocolate cake. Open Mon.-Thurs., Sat. 7:30 am-4:30 pm; Friday 7:30 am-7:30 pm. Closed Sunday. $
- Palliser Restaurant, Exit 14 off Highway 102, Truro; 893-8951. Traditional boiled lobster, poached salmon, or roast chicken dinners. The dining room, overlooking the Salmon River, offers twice-daily views of the tidal bore. Restaurant and motel have been operated by the same family for four generations. Open daily 7:30 am-8:30 pm, May-October. $$

SUNRISE TRAIL

- Amherst Shore Country Inn, Highway 366, Lorneville; 661-4800. A different four-course gourmet meal each night. Open daily 7:30 pm by appointment, May-mid-October. Reservations a must. $$$
- Braeside Inn, 126 Front St., Pictou; 485-5046. Fresh Nova Scotia seafood and prime rib of beef. Hillside view of Pictou Harbour. Open daily 6 pm-8:30 pm by reservation. $$
- Consulate Inn, 157 Water St., Pictou; 485-4554; www.pictou.nsis.com/consultaeinn. Specialties include fresh Atlantic seafood. Open for dinner, May-October. $$
- Des Barres Manor County Inn, 90 Church St., Guysborough; 533-2099; www.desbarresmanor.com.

Fresh local produce, seafood and lamb. Open daily at 7 pm by appointment only. $$
- Gabrieau's Bistro, 350 Main St., Antigonish; 863-1925. Innovative appetizers, light pasta and exceptional desserts. Open Monday to Saturday, 11 am-3 pm, 5 pm-9:30 pm. $$
- Jubilee Cottage Country Inn, Highway 6, Wallace; 257-2432; www.bbcanada.com/1602.html. Local grain-fed chicken, Pictou County lamb, Atlantic salmon, Digby scallops and home-grown herbs. Open daily at 7 pm by reservation only. No smoking. $$
- Mill Room, Balmoral Hotel, Highway 6, Tatamagouche; 657-2000. German specialties including sausages, sauerkraut, and pickled herring. Open daily 7:30 am-9 pm June-October. $$
- Pictou Lodge Resort, Braeshore Rd., Pictou; 485-4322. A spectacular oceanfront property, operating as a resort since the 1920s. Hours vary seasonally. $$$
- Piper's Landing, Highway 376, Lyons Brook; 485-1200. Fresh and tasty seafoods are complemented by salads and sweets for dessert. Open Mon.-Thurs. 11 am-2:30 pm, 4:30 pm-9 pm; Fri.-Sun. 11 am-9 pm. Open year-round. $$

MARINE DRIVE

- Liscombe Lodge, Highway 7, Liscomb Mills; 779-2307; www.signatureresorts.com. A relaxed resort setting and casual dining room with an accomplished kitchen. Planked salmon is a specialty–watch it being cooked on the outdoor open fire. Open daily for breakfast, lunch, and dinner, May-October. $$$
- Marquis of Dufferin, Highway 7, Port Dufferin; 654-2696. An 1859 heritage property. Seafood, including smoked salmon from Willie Krauch's smokehouse in nearby Tangier. Open daily 7:30 am-9:30 am, 5:45 pm-8 pm, May-October. Reservations required. $$
- Salmon River House, Highway 7, Head of Jeddore; 889-3353; www.highway7.com. Fresh boiled

lobster and steaks on the verandah overlooking the Salmon River. Open daily for breakfast and dinner (by reservation only from November to April). $$

- Sea Wind Landing Country Inn, 1 Wharf Rd., Charlos Cove; 525-2108; www.seawind.ns.ca. Picnic lunches available to guests. Open to the public for dinner by reservation only, May 1 to October 30. $$

- Tea & Treats, East Petpeswick Rd., Musquodoboit Harbour; 889-3288. Light Austrian-style lunches and delicious chocolate cake. Open 9 am-9 pm, year-round. $

CAPE BRETON AND THE CABOT TRAIL

- Acadien, 774 Main St., Cheticamp; 224-2170. Authentic Acadian specialties including tourtière, chowders, and fish cakes. Open daily, early May to late October. Hours vary depending on time of year. High season (late June to late September): 7 am-9 pm. $$

- Duncreigan Country Inn, Mabou; 945-2207; www.auracom.com/~mulldci. High-quality country dining in a tranquil setting. Open for dinner by reservation only, mid-June to mid-October. $$

- Haus Treuburg, Highway 19, Port Hood; 787-2166. German-style breakfast. Try the fish for dinner. Open daily 7:30 am-9 am; 7 pm-9 pm, mid-May to Hallowe'en. $$$

- Heart of Harts, Northeast Margaree; 248-2765. Soups, salads and entrées change daily. Roasted garlic soup, potato cake layered with gruyère cheese. Open daily from 7 pm by reservation only, May 1 to October 31. No liquor. $

- Herring Choker Deli, on the Trans-Canada between Baddeck and Whycocomagh; 295-2275. Specialty and natural food items. Treats from the Indian Bay Bakery. Open daily, year-round. $

- The Highwheeler Cafe, Chebucto St., Baddeck; 295-3006. The perfect place to stock up for a picnic–deli sandwiches, cookies, cakes, fruit, and pasta salads. Open daily 7:30 am–6 pm, longer hours in summer (closed Sunday in off-season). $

- Inverary Inn and Resort, Shore Rd., Baddeck; 295-3500, www.inveraryresort.com. The main dining room offers a full-scale menu, with Scottish touches like smoked salmon and bannock. The Fish House Restaurant on the waterfront is more casual, and features seafood appetizers and entrées. Open daily, May-November. Fish House open in summer months only. $$$

- Keltic Lodge, Middle Head Peninsula, Ingonish Beach; 285-2880; www.signatureresorts.com Fine formal dining. One of Nova Scotia's best restaurants. Five-course evening meal, menu changes daily. Open daily for breakfast, lunch, and dinner (to 9 pm), June to mid-October. $$$

- Markland Coastal Resort, Dingwall; 383-2246. Fresh Cape Breton lamb and local seafood, with a beautiful view of Aspy Bay from the oceanside deck. Enjoy a walk on the beach before dinner. Open 7:30 am-9 pm, mid-June to mid-October. $$

- The Mull Cafe, Mabou; 945-2244. Casual and quick, hearty deli sandwiches with take-out available. Open daily 11 am to 5 pm (lunch), 5 pm to 9 pm (dinner). $

- Normaway Inn, Egypt Rd., Margaree Valley; 248-2987. Beautifully situated in the Margaree Valley. Four-course country gourmet meals with attentive but unobtrusive service. Open for breakfast and dinner mid-June to mid-October. $$$

- Rita's Tea Room, Big Pond; 828-2667. Baked goods and Rita's Tea Room Blend Tea. Rita MacNeil's awards and photographs are on display. Open daily 9am-7pm, June to mid-October. $

- Telegraph House, Chebucto St., Baddeck; 295-9988. Traditional dinners and generous helpings — poached salmon with egg sauce, roast turkey, meat loaf. One of the best breakfasts in Nova Scotia; be sure to sample the oatcakes. Open daily for breakfast, lunch, and dinner. $$

- Tin Pan Galley, Salty Mariner's Motel, Pleasant Bay; 224-1400.

Cajun shrimp with tomatoes, red and green peppers and onions the favourite. Open daily 8 am to 10 am, 6 pm to 9 pm, Easter to October 31. $$

- Vollmer's Island Paradise, Janvrin Island; 226-1507. Make reservations a day ahead for fish or meat. No liquor. No smoking. Open 8 am to 9 pm by appointment only. $

MARCONI TRAIL

- Isle Royale Dining Room, Coastal Inn Louisbourg, 7464 Main St., Louisbourg; 733-2844. Reliable fresh seafood and roasts. Open daily for breakfast, lunch, and dinner. $$
- Gowrie House, 139 Shore Rd., Sydney Mines; 544-1050; www.gowriehouse.com. Antique-filled country inn, beautiful grounds and gardens. Fine meals are prepared from the freshest Nova Scotia ingredients. One of the province's best dining experiences. Open daily, one sitting at 7:30 pm, April-October. Reservations essential. Dinner for residents only rest of the year. Bring your own wine. $$$

ATTRACTIONS

The Nova Scotia Travel Guide (see Travel Essentials) provides exhaustive listings of the province's attractions. Guided walking tours or brochures for self-guided tours are available for many Nova Scotia communities (make inquiries at the closest Visitor Information Centre). Here we provide a selective listing of many of the points of interest.

HALIFAX

- Anna Leonowens Gallery, Granville St., Halifax; 422-8223; www.nscad.ns.ca/~gallery (Nova Scotia College of Art and Design).
- Art Gallery of Nova Scotia, 1741 Hollis St., Halifax; 424-7542.
- Bedford Institute of Oceanography, located near Dartmouth side of MacKay Bridge, Halifax; 426-4306.
- Black Cultural Centre for Nova Scotia, Route 7 at Cherrybrook Rd., near Dartmouth; 434-6223;

bccns@istar.ca; home.istar.ca/~bccns

- *Bluenose II*, at Privateers' Wharf, Historic Properties, Halifax (or the Fisheries Museum of the Atlantic, Lunenburg).
- Brewery Market, Hollis and Lower Water St., Halifax; 429-6843.
- Cathedral Church of All Saints, 1320 Tower Rd., Halifax; 423-6002.
- Discovery Centre, 1593 Barrington St., Halifax; 492-4422; handsonfun@discoverycentre.ns.ca; www.discoverycentre.ns.ca.
- Fort McNab National Historic Site, McNab's Island; information, 426-5080.
- Government House, 1451 Barrington St., Halifax. Lieutenant-governor's residence since early 1800s.
- Grand Parade, between Barrington and Argyle St., Halifax.
- Halifax Citadel National Historic Site, overlooking downtown Halifax (you can't miss it). Group reservations, 426-5080; denise_graham@pch.gc.ca; parkscanada.pch.gc.ca.
- Halifax Public Gardens, Spring Garden Rd., at South Park St., Halifax.
- Halifax Regional Library, 5381 Spring Garden Rd., Halifax; 421-6983.
- Historic Quaker Whalers' House, 57-59 Ochterloney St., Dartmouth; 464-2300; pricea@region.halifax.ns.ca; www.region.halifax.ns.ca
- Hemlock Ravine Park, Kent Ave. off Bedford Highway.
- Historic Properties, on the Halifax waterfront.
- HMCS *Sackville*: Canada's Naval Memorial, at the wharf of the Maritime Museum, Halifax; 429-5600; rascousie@iworks.net; www.hmcssackville-cnmt.ns.ca.
- Little Dutch Church, Brunswick St. at Gerrish, Halifax; 425-3658.
- Maritime Command Museum, Admiralty House, CFB Halifax; 427-0550; museum@marlant.halifax.dnd.ca; www.marlant.halifax.dnd.ca/museum.
- Maritime Museum of the Atlantic, 1675 Lower Water St., Halifax;

424-7490;
educmmat.lunnge@gov.ns.ca;
mma.ednet.ns.ca.
- Micmac Heritage Gallery, Barrington Place Shops, Halifax; 422-9509.
- Nova Scotia Centre for Craft and Design, 1683 Barrington St., Halifax; 424-4062; tyler@gov.ns.ca; crafts.ednet.ns.ca.
- Nova Scotia Museum of Natural History, 1747 Summer St., Halifax; 424-7353; www.nature.ednet.ns.ca.
- Old Town Clock, at the base of the Citadel. Halifax's most famous landmark.
- Old Burying Ground and Welsford-Parker Monument, Barrington St. (across from Government House), Halifax.
- Pier 21, 1055 Marginal Rd., Halifax; 425-7770; pier21@pier21.ns.ca.
- Prince of Wales Tower National Historic Site, Point Pleasant Park, Halifax; 426-5080; parkscanada.pch.gc.ca.
- Province House, 1726 Hollis St., Halifax; 424-4661.
- Regional Museum of Cultural History, 100 Wyse Rd., Dartmouth; 464-2300.
- Royal Artillery Park, Sackville Street (at the base of Citadel Hill), Halifax.
- St. George's Round Church, Brunswick St. at Cornwallis, Halifax; 425-3658; awest@ns.sympatico.ca; www3.ns.sympatico.ca/stgeorge (damaged by fire June 1994; restoration underway).
- St. Paul's Anglican Church, at the Grand Parade, Halifax; 429-2240; stpauls@chebucto.ns.ca; www.chebucto.ns.ca/Religion/StPauls.
- Sir Sanford Fleming Park (the Dingle), Dingle Rd., off Purcell's Cove Rd. on North West Arm.
- Shearwater Aviation Museum, at CFB Shearwater; 460-1083.
- Shubenacadie Canal Interpretive Centre, 140 Alderney Dr., Dartmouth; 462-1826; shubie.canal@ns.sympatico.ca
- Uniacke Estate Museum Park, Mount Uniacke; 866-2560.
- York Redoubt National Historic Site, off Purcells Cove Rd.,

Halifax; 426-5080; parkscanada.pch.gc.ca

LIGHTHOUSE ROUTE

Peggys Cove
- Swiss Air Memorial, Peggys Cove.
- William E. deGarthe Memorial Provincial Park (sculpture), Peggys Cove.

Chester and Mahone Bay
- Amos Pewter Economuseum, 589 Main St., Mahone Bay; 1-800-565-3369; www.amospewter.com.
- Mahone Bay Settlers Museum, Main St., Mahone Bay; 624-6263
- Oak Island, near the village of Western Shore.
- Ross Farm Museum, New Ross (on Route 12, inland from Chester Basin); 689-2210.
- St. James Anglican Church, Edgewater St. (Route 3), Mahone Bay.

Lunenburg
- DesBrisay Museum, Jubilee Rd., Bridgewater; 543-4033; desbrisaymuseum@town.-bridgewater.ns.ca
- Fisheries Museum of the Atlantic, Montague St. (on the water), Lunenburg; 634-4794; tupperja@gov.ns.ca; www.ednet.ns.ca.
- Houston North Gallery, 110 Montague St., Lunenburg; 634-8869.
- Lunenburg Art Gallery, 19 Pelham St., Lunenburg.
- Lunenburg Academy, atop Gallows Hill, Lunenburg.
- Morash Gallery, 55 Montague St., Lunenburg; 634-8904.
- Scotia Trawler Company (formerly the site of Smith and Rhuland Boatbuilders), Montague St., Lunenburg.
- St. John's Anglican Church, between Townsend and Cumberland St., Lunenburg; 634-4994; stjohns.lun@ns.sympatico.ca
- Wile Carding Mill, at Pearl St. and Victoria Rd., Bridgewater; 543-8233.

Liverpool and Shelburne
- Archelaus Smith Museum, Route 330, Centreville (across the causeway).
- Argyle Township Court House &

Gaol, 8168 Route 3, Tusket; 648-2493; atch@fox.nstn.ca; ycn.library.ns.ca/~ipatcha.
- The Dory Shop Museum, Dock St., Shelburne; 875-3219; beureegm@gov.ns.ca; museum.ednet.ns.ca
- Hank Snow Country Music Centre, off Bristol Avenue en route to Liverpool; 354-4675; into@hanksnow.com; www.hanksnow.com.
- Perkins House, 105 Main St., Liverpool; 354-4058; rafusela@gov.ns.ca; museum.ednet.ns.ca
- Queens County Museum, Main St., Liverpool; 354-4058; rafusela@gov.ns.ca; www.geocities.com/Paris/2669.
- Ross-Thompson House and Store Museum, Charlotte Lane, Shelburne; 875-3141.
- Shelburne County Museum, Dock St., Shelburne; 875-3219.
- Sherman Hines Museum of Photography & Galleries, 219 Main St., Liverpool; 354-2667.

Barrington
- Barrington Woollen Mill, 2368 Route 3, Barrington; 637-2185; cshsbarr@ednet.ns.ca; museum.ednet.ns.ca.
- The Old Meeting House Museum, Route 3, Barrington; 637-2185; cshsbarr@ednet.ns.ca; museum.ednet.ns.ca.
- Seal Island Lighthouse Museum, Route 3, Barrington; 637-2185; cshsbarr@ednet.ns.ca.

Yarmouth
- Firefighters Museum of Nova Scotia, 451 Main St., Yarmouth; 742-5525; Firemuse@sympatico.ca; museum.ednet.ns.ca.
- Killam Brothers Building, at the foot of Central St. on the waterfront; 742-5539; ycn0056@ycn.library.ns.ca; www.ycn.library.ns.ca/museum.yarcomus.htm.
- Yarmouth Light, Cape Fourchu; 742-1433.
- Yarmouth County Museum, 22 Collins St., Yarmouth; 742-5539; ycn0056@ycn.library.ns.ca; www.ycn.library.ns.ca/museum/yarcomus.htm.

EVANGELINE TRAIL

- Admiral Digby Museum, 95 Montague Row, Digby; 245-6322.
- Annapolis Royal Historic Gardens, Upper Saint George St., Annapolis Royal; 532-7018 www.HistoricGardens.com.
- Annapolis Royal Tidal Power Project, at the Annapolis River Causeway; 532-5454.
- Annapolis Valley Macdonald Museum, 21 School St., Middleton; 825-6116; macdonald.museum@ns.sympatico.ca.
- Centre Acadien, Université Sainte Anne, Pointe de l'Eglise; 769-2114; cacadien@ustanne.ednet.ns.ca.
- Fort Anne National Historic Site, Saint George St., Annapolis Royal; 532-2397; parkscanada/pch.gc.ca/parks/Nova_Scotia/fort_anne/fort_annee.htm.
- Fort Edward National Historic Site, near Exit 6 on Highway 101, Windsor; 542-3631.
- Gallery at Saratoga, Carleton Corner on Highway 201 West, Bridgetown; 665-4508.
- Grand Pré National Historic Site, 542-3631; donna_doucet@pch.gc.ca; parkscanada/pch.gc.ca.
- Haliburton House, Clifton Ave., Windsor; 798-2915; dauphiar@gov.ns.ca; museum.ednet.ns.ca.
- Hantsport Marine Memorial Museum (Churchill House), Hantsport; 684-3365.
- L'Église Saint-Bernard (Church of Saint Bernard), St. Bernard; 837-5687; tourism@municipality.clare.ns.ca.
- L'Église Sainte-Marie (Church of Saint Mary), Pointe de l'Église; 769-2808 or 769-2832.
- La Vieille Maison, Meteghan; 645-2389; tourism@municipality.clare.ns.ca; www.munisource.org/clare.
- Kentville Agricultural Centre and Blair House, Route 1, Kentville; 679-5333.
- North Hills Museum, Granville Ferry; 532-2168; 532-7754; kirbywr@gov.ns.ca; museum.ednet.ca.
- Oaklawn Farm Zoo, Highway 101,

Exit 16, Aylesford; 847-9790.
- O'Dell Inn Museum, Lower Saint George St., Annapolis Royal; 532-7754; kirbywr@gov.ns.ca.
- Old Kings Courthouse Museum, 37 Cornwallis St., Kentville; 678-6237.
- Old St. Edward's Loyalist Church Museum, 34 Old Post Rd. (off Route 1), Clementsport; 532-0917 or 245-2762.
- Port Royal National Historic Site ("the Habitation"), 12 kilometres (8 mi.) southwest of Granville Ferry at Port Royal; 532-2898; parkscanada.pch.gc.ca/parks/Nova_Scotia/port_royal/portroyale.htm.
- Prescott House, 1633 Starr's Pt. Rd. (off Route 358) Starr's Point (near Wolfville); 542-3984; mortonnl@gov.ns.ca; museum.ednet.ns.ca.
- Randall House Historical Museum, 171 Main St., Wolfville; 542-9775, 684-3876 (off season); norangel@cnet.windsor.ns.ca; cnet.windsor.ns.ca/Museum/Randall.
- Shand House, Avon St., Windsor; 798-8213; dauphiar@gov.ns.ca; museum.ednet.ns.ca.
- Upper Clements Park, 6 kilometres (3.5 mi.) west of Annapolis Royal on Route 1; 532-7557; fun@upperclementspark.com; www.upperclementspark.com.
- Upper Clements Wildlife Park, 8 kilometres (5 mi.) west of Annapolis Royal on Route 1; 532-5924.

GLOOSCAP TRAIL

- Anne Murray Centre, Main St., Springhill; 597-8614; amcentre@auracom.com.
- Cumberland County Museum, 150 Church St., Amherst; 667-2561; business.auracom.com/madhouse/ccm.
- Fundy Geological Museum, Parrsboro; 254-3814; fundyg@ns.sympatico.ca; www.fundygeomuseum.com.
- Joggins Fossil Centre, Joggins; 251-2727, 251-2618 (off-season).
- Lawrence House, Route 215, Maitland; 261-2628; levyje@gov.ns.ca; museum.ednet.ns.ca.
- Ottawa House Museum by-the-Sea, Partridge Island (near Parrsboro).

- Parrsboro Rock and Mineral Shop and Museum, 39 Whitehall Rd., Parrsboro; 254-2981.
- Shubenacadie Provincial Wildlife Park, near Exit 11 on Highway 102, Shubenacadie; 758-2040 or 424-5937; wildpark@nova.net; www.gov.ns.ca/natr.wildpark.
- Springhill Miners Museum, 145 Black River Rd., Springhill; 597-3449.

SUNRISE TRAIL

- Balmoral Grist Mill, off Route 311, Balmoral Mills; 657-3016; taylorje@gov.ns.ca; museum.ednet.ns.ca.
- Fraser Cultural Centre, Main St., Tatamagouche; 657-3285, 657-3231 (off-season).
- Hector Heritage Quay, 33 Calah Ave., Pictou; 1-888-485-4844; picrec@nsis.com; www.pictou.nsis.com.
- Hector National Exhibit Centre, Old Haliburton Rd., Pictou; 485-4563.
- Jost Vineyards, Route 6, Malagash; 1-800-565-4567; info@jost.ns.ca; www.jost.ns.ca.
- McCulloch House, Old Haliburton Rd., Pictou; 485-4563; pcghs@ednet.ns.ca; www.rootsweb.com/~nspcghs
- Northumberland Fisheries Museum, 71 Front St., Pictou; 485-4972.
- Sunrise Trail Museum, Main St., Tatamagouche; 657-3007.
- Sutherland Steam Mill, Route 326, Denmark; 657-3365; taylorje@gov.ns.ca; museum.ednet.ns.ca.

MARINE DRIVE

- Canso Museum, Whitman House, Canso; 366-2170 or 366-2525; canconn@atcon.com.
- Fisherman's Life Museum, 58 Navy Pool Loop, Jeddore Oyster Pond; 889-2053; monkma@gov.ns.ca; museum.ednet.ns.ca.
- Grassy Island National Historic Site, off the coast of Canso; for information, 295-2069; agbellhs@auracom.com.
- Moose River & Area Museum, Moose River Rd., Route 224;

Moose River Gold Mines; 384-2006.
- Musquodoboit Railway Museum, Route 7, Musquodoboit Harbour; 889-2689.
- Sherbrooke Village, off Route 7, near the modern village of Sherbrooke; 1-888-743-7845; andersje@gov.ns.ca; museum.ednet.ns.ca

CAPE BRETON AND THE CABOT TRAIL

- Acadian Museum, 744 Main St. (at Cooperative Artisanale de Cheticamp Lté.), Cheticamp; 224-2170.
- Alexander Graham Bell National Historic Site, Baddeck; 295-2069; agbellhs@auracom.com.
- *An Drochaid* (The Bridge), Route 19, Mabou; 945-2311.
- Dr. Elizabeth LeFort Gallery and Museum, Les Trois Pignons, Cheticamp; 224-2612 or 224-2612; pignons@auracom.com; www.lestroispignons.com.
- Gaelic College of Celtic Arts and Crafts, South Gut St. Anns; 295-3441 or 295-2912; gaelcoll@atcon.com; www.gaeliccottage.edu.
- Giant MacAskill Museum, Route 312, Englishtown; 929-2925.
- Inverness Miners Museum, in the old CNR station, Inverness.
- L'Église Saint-Pierre (Church of Saint Peter), Cheticamp; 224-2062.
- Lone Shieling, at the base of North Mountain, Cape Breton Highlands National Park.
- Margaree Salmon Museum, North East Margaree; 248-2848/2765/2623.
- Nova Scotia Highland Village Museum, Route 223, Iona; 725-2272; hvillage@highlandvillage.ns.ca; www.highlandvillage.ns.ca
- Reed Timmons' Studio, Pleasant Bay; local artists' folk art creations of seabirds and whales.
- Scarecrow Theatre, Cap Lemoine (near Cheticamp); 235-2108.

MARCONI TRAIL

- Cossit House, 75 Charlotte St., Sydney; 539-7973 or 539-1572; maltby.janet@ns.sympatico.ca;

museum.ednet.ca.
- Fortress of Louisbourg National Historic Site, Louisbourg; 733-2280, 733-3546 (off-season); louisbourg_info@pch.gc/ca;/parkscanada.pch.gc.ca.
- Marconi National Historic Site, Timmerman St., Glace Bay; 295-2069; agbellhs@auracom.com.
- Miners' Museum, Quarry Point, Glace Bay; 849-4522; cbminers@highlander.cbnet.ns.ca; www.cbnet.ns.ca/cbnet/comucntr/miners/museum.html.
- Sydney and Louisbourg Railway Museum, Louisbourg; 733-2157; fortress.uccb.ns.ca/historic/s_l.html.

FESTIVALS AND EVENTS

What follows is a listing by area of some of the best and most popular festivals and events in the province. For a complete listing, consult the *Nova Scotia Travel Guide* (see Travel Essentials). The scheduling of many of these events is subject to change; the Check In Reservation and Information Service will provide updated information (Tel. 1-800-565-0000).

HALIFAX

Year-round
- Brewery Farmers' Market (Halifax). Saturday morning farmers' market where local crafts, baked goods and produce are available.

May/June
- Scotia Festival of Music. Internationally renowned festival of chamber music.

June
- Greek Festival. Three-day feast put on by the Halifax Greek community.
- Nova Scotia Multicultural Festival (Dartmouth). Food, music and dancing offered by Nova Scotia's different ethnic communities.

July
- Nova Scotia International Tattoo. A musical extravaganza with a military flavour.

- Halifax Highland Games. A Scottish festival with pipes and drums, heavy events, and more.
- Maritime Fiddle Festival (Dartmouth). Top-notch competitors from Canada and the United States.
- Atlantic Jazz Festival. Outdoor concerts and late-night sessions in city bars.
- Africville Reunion. The spirit of the Black community of Africville is revived at a picnic, church service, and dance.

August
- Halifax International Busker Festival. Street performers including jugglers and clowns provide 10 days of fun along the waterfront.
- Nova Scotia Designer Crafts Council Summer Festival. A juried market draws many of the province's best craftspeople.

September
- Atlantic Film Festival. Independent films and parties celebrating the industry.
- Atlantic Fringe Festival. Alternative plays performed around the city.
- Nova Scotia International Airshow. Atlantic Canada's largest demonstration of aerial acrobatics.

Sept./Oct.
- Studio Rally Weekend. Craft studios across the province open to the public.
- Word on the Street. Book sales, displays, author readings and entertainment along Spring Garden Road.

LIGHTHOUSE ROUTE

June
- Loyalist Descendants Week (Shelburne). Nova Scotia's Loyalist town celebrates its heritage.

June/July
- Privateer Days (Liverpool). Festival recalling the town's tumultuous early years.

July
- Lunenburg Craft Festival. Quality crafts from the province's top

artisans.
- South Shore Exhibition (Bridgewater). Century-old agricultural exhibition featuring ox-pulls among the many events.
- Shelburne Founders' Days. Commemorates the arrival of thousands of United Empire Loyalists in the 1780s.

August
- Chester Race Week. Atlantic Canada's largest regatta. The Front and Back harbours are crowded with sleek yachts.
- Fishermen's Picnic and Reunion. A festival for the fisheries that features unusual and entertaining competitions like net mending, scallop shucking, and dory racing.
- Lunenburg Folk Harbour Festival. The Lunenburg waterfront provides an idyllic setting for a series of performances by folk musicians.
- Mahone Bay Wooden Boat Festival. Boatbuilding competitions and demonstrations, and many other events recalling the town's shipbuilding era.
- Nova Scotia Folk Art Festival. Celebrates the work of Nova Scotia's best folk artists.

EVANGELINE TRAIL

May
- Annapolis Valley Apple Blossom Festival (Windsor to Digby). Community-based celebrations herald the arrival of another growing season.

July
- Bear River Cherry Carnival. Parade, auction, woodsmen's show and more in one of Nova Scotia's prettiest communities.
- Festival Acadien de Clare. Colourful Acadian celebration that runs the length of the French Shore.
- Heart of the Valley Days, Middleton. Parade, concert and fireworks.

August
- Annapolis Valley Exhibition, Lawrencetown. Showcase of Valley agriculture, with top-name entertainment.
- Digby Scallop Days. A feast of

Digby scallops, scallop-shucking competition.

- Natal Day Craft and Antique Show (Annapolis Royal). Fast-growing community of craftspeople displays its wares.

Sept./Oct.

- Annapolis Royal Arts Festival. Best-selling Canadian authors are among the participants at this annual gathering.
- Berwick Gala Days, Berwick. Traditional end-of-summer celebrations with parades, family entertainment.
- Hants County Exhibition (Windsor). North America's oldest agricultural fair.
- Pumpkin Festival, Hants County Exhibition Grounds, Windsor. Growers of giant pumpkins vie for World's Biggest Pumpkin title.

GLOOSCAP TRAIL

August

- Irish Festival, Springhill. Celebration of Irish culture through food and music.
- Nova Scotia's Gem and Mineral Show (Parrsboro). An agate and amethyst hunt along Parrsboro-area beaches.

SUNRISE TRAIL

July

- Antigonish Highland Games. Highland competitions from dancing to caber tossing make this Nova Scotia's best Scottish festival.
- Festival of the Tartans (New Glasgow). Includes piping, dancing, drumming, and Scottish heavy events.
- Gathering of the Clans and Fishermen's Regatta (Pugwash). A Scottish festival capped off by a lobster dinner.
- Pictou Lobster Carnival. Fishermen's competitions and Northumberland Strait lobsters are the highlights at this community festival.

August

- Hector Festival (Pictou). Celebrates the coming of the Scots to Nova

Scotia aboard the *Hector*.

September

- Oktoberfest (Tatamagouche). Post-war immigration to the North Shore gave rise to this traditional German celebration.

MARINE DRIVE

July

- Stan Rogers Folk Festival, Canso. A celebration of the music of one of Canada's most celebrated folk musicians.

August

- Clam Harbour Beach Sand Castle and Sculpture Contest. The fine, white sand along one of Nova Scotia's best beaches is an ideal building material.

CAPE BRETON AND THE CABOT TRAIL

June/July

- Mabou Ceilidh. See for yourself why this village of 400 is home to several of Nova Scotia's best musicians. There are also Wednesday night ceilidhs throughout July and August.

July

- Big Pond Festival. Cape Breton music highlighting Big Pond's most famous resident, Rita MacNeil.
- Broad Cove Scottish Concert (near Inverness). A highlight of the summer ceilidh season.
- Judique-on-the-Floor Days. More of Cape Breton's best music.

July/August

- Festival de l'Escaouette (Cheticamp). An Acadian celebration featuring a special mass in Cheticamp's exquisite church.

August

- Baddeck Regatta. Highlight of Baddeck's summer sailing season since 1904.
- Gaelic Mod (South Gut St. Anns). Music and other Gaelic arts at the home of the Gaelic College.
- Feast of St. Louis. An 18th-century feast at the Fortress of Louisbourg.

Sept./Oct.
- Celtic Colours. An island-wide celebration of Celtic music featuring Cape Breton and international performers.

THEATRE

Halifax is home to Neptune Theatre, Nova Scotia's only professional live repertory theatre group, and Symphony Nova Scotia. Also, a surprising number of communities throughout the province, including Halifax, are summertime venues for live theatre. Many productions are distinctly Nova Scotian — revealing much about the province and its people.

- Astor Theatre, Gorham St., Liverpool; 354-5250. Featuring the Liverpool International Theatre Festival in May.
- Atlantic Theatre Festival, Wolfville; 1-800-337-6661.(June-September).
- Bicentennial Theatre, 12390 Route 224, Middle Musquodoboit; 384-2819.
- Centrestage Theatre, 363-R Main St., Kentville; 678-8040.
- The Chester Playhouse, Pleasant St., Chester; 275-3933. Site of the Chester Theatre Festival during July and August.
- Dartmouth Players, 5 Crichton Ave., Dartmouth; 465-7529.
- deCoste Entertainment Centre, Water St., Pictou; 485-8848.
- Eastern Front Theatre, Alderney Landing, Dartmouth; 466-2769.
- Evangéline, Université Ste.-Anne; 769-2114. Musical based on Longfellow's poem in Acadian French. (June-Sept.).
- Festival Antigonish, St. Francis Xavier University, Antigonish; 1-800-563-7529 (July-August).
- Grafton Street Dinner Theatre, 1741 Grafton St., Halifax; 425-1961.
- Halifax Feast Dinner Theatre, Maritime Centre, Barrington St., Halifax; 420-1840.
- Irondale Ensemble, 2182 Gottingen St., Halifax; 429-1370. Critical and thoughtful alternative theatre.
- Jest In Time Theatre, 1541 Barrington St., Halifax; 423-4647.

- King's Theatre, Lower Saint George St., Annapolis Royal; 532-5466. Site of the Annapolis Royal Summer Theatre Festival in July and August.
- Lunenburg Opera House, 290 Lincoln St., Lunenburg; 634-4010.
- Louisbourg Playhouse, 11 Aberdeen St., Louisbourg; 733-2996; 1-888-733-2787. (June-Oct.).
- Mermaid Theatre, 132 Gerrish St., Windsor; 798-5841. Touring puppet theatre for children.
- Mulgrave Road Co-op Theatre, Guysborough; 533-2092.
- Neptune Theatre, 1593 Argyle St., Halifax; 429-7070; 1-800-565-7345.
- The Rebecca Cohn, Dalhousie University, Halifax; 494-2646. A variety of live performances including the Symphony Nova Scotia concert series.
- Savoy Theatre, 19 Union St., Glace Bay; 842-1577. Highlights include the Cape Breton Summertime Revue, a lively blend of Celtic music and satire.
- Ship's Company Theatre, 38 Main St., Parrsboro; 1-800-565-7469. Innovative theatre aboard the MV *Kipawo*, a restored car ferry (July-September).
- Theatre Arts Guild, 6 Parkhill Rd., Halifax; 477-2663.
- Th'Yarc, 76 Parade St., Yarmouth; 742-1103, 1-800-561-1103. Yarmouth Summer Stage is held in July and August.

SHOPPING

CRAFT SHOPS

- Jennifer's of Nova Scotia, 5635 Spring Garden Rd., Halifax. Easy to find on Halifax's main downtown shopping street, Jennifer's features exclusively Nova Scotian crafts, especially pottery, pewter, and knitted items. Also located on Route 333 between Halifax and Peggys Cove. Halifax store open 9 am-5:30 pm daily (Thursday and Friday to 9 pm). Store on Route 333 open 8 am-7 pm daily in summer, off-season 9 am-5 pm daily.
- Suttles and Seawinds, 466 Main

St., Mahone Bay and Historic Properties, Halifax. Brilliant colours and fine design in clothing that borrows from quilting methods to create high fashion. Also patchwork accessories including tote bags and jewellery rolls. Both shops open year-round.

- Black Duck, 8 Pelham St., Lunenburg. A long-standing craft co-operative with adjoining art gallery and a fine selection of books on Nova Scotia and the Maritimes. Open year-round.
- The Weave Shed, Main Street, Wolfville. Everything for the hooked rug enthusiast and quality craft by local artisans. Open year-round.
- Flight of Fancy, Main St., Bear River. Selling the work of over 100 craftspeople, this is a beautifully appointed shop in the picturesque village of Bear River—worth a trip just for the drive. Open Monday-Saturday 9 am-5 pm, Sunday 11 am-5 pm, late May to mid-October.
- Glooscap Trading Post, Highway 102, Truro. Traditional Mi'kmaq crafts, featuring woven baskets and twig furniture. The wonderful smell of sweet grass will make you want to browse just a little longer. Open daily, 9 am-7 pm (summer),10 am-5 pm (fall to Christmas).
- Canadian Sterling Silver and Goldsmiths, Durham St., Pugwash. Hand-crafted silver jewellery made on the premises and a wide selection of other local crafts. Open Monday-Friday 8 am-8 pm, Saturday 9 am-6 pm, Sunday 10 am-7 pm. Summer hours.
- Arts North, just west of Cape North on the Cabot Trail. Fine craft, featuring the pottery of Linda and Dennis Doyon and the jewellery of Johanna Padelt. Open daily from mid-June to mid-October.
- Co-operative Artisanale de Cheticamp Ltée., 774 Main St., Cheticamp. This is the place for hooked rugs in all shapes and sizes (as well as mats, coasters, and wall-hangings). Watch how the hooking is done during one of the frequent daily demonstrations here or at any one of the numerous craft shops in Cheticamp. Open daily 8 am-9 pm, June 15-September 15, variable hours in off-season.

- Flora's, Point Cross (near Cheticamp) on the Cabot Trail. Large craft shop with a wide selection of hooked rugs. Open daily during tourist season.
- Leather Works, at Indian Brook (between Baddeck and Ingonish) on the Cabot Trail. Historic reproductions and a variety of contemporary leather goods by John Roberts. Open daily mid-May to October.
- Negemow Basket Shop, Highway 105, Whycocomagh. Beautiful handmade baskets from native artisans throughout the Maritimes. Open daily.
- School on the Hill, overlooking the North River on the St. Ann's Bay Loop. Wide selection of fine Atlantic Canadian crafts. Open daily June to mid-October.
- Wild Things, near Tarbotvale on the St. Anns Bay Loop. Fallen trees become creative wood turnings and carvings in the studio behind this shop. Open daily mid-June to mid-October.

FINE JEWELLERY AND CRAFTS

- Fire Works Gallery, 1569 Barrington St., Halifax. An eclectic mix of silver and gold jewellery, some made by the shop's resident jewellers, and funky pottery by well-known local artist Jane Donovan and others. Open daily except Sunday.

PEWTER

- Amos Pewterers, 589 Main St., Mahone Bay. Economuseum and studio. Contemporary designs including picture frames, goblets, and jewellery. Tours Monday-Friday, 9 am-5 pm. Open Monday-Saturday 9 am-5:30 pm, Sunday afternoons. Second location Historic Properties, Halifax.
- Seagull Pewter, Route 6, Pugwash. Full line of pewter products. Family operation now international in scope. Open daily. Second location Barrington Place Shops, Halifax.

POTTERY

- Nova Scotia Folk Pottery, Front Harbour, Chester. Colourful platters, plates, bowls, and serving dishes by Jim Smith. Open daily 10 am-6 pm, mid-May to mid-October; off-season by appointment, 275-3272.
- Birdsall-Worthington Pottery Ltd., 590 Main St., Mahone Bay. Slip-decorated earthenware pottery, including commemorative plates and handmade earrings. Open Monday-Saturday 10 am-5 pm, Sunday 1 pm-5 pm, July to September; limited hours in off-season.
- K.R. Thompson, 492 Main St., Mahone Bay. Sea-inspired functional soda-fired porcelain in greens and blues. Open daily 11 am-5 pm in summer; closed Sunday and Monday in off-season.
- Goose Cove Pottery, at St. Anns on the Cabot Trail. Carol MacDonald's stoneware and porcelain; studio on site. Open daily 9 am- 5 pm, June to September.

FOLK ART

- Gallery Shop, Art Gallery of Nova Scotia, 1741 Hollis St. at Cheapside, Halifax. Good selection of folk art, among the featured works of a wide variety of Nova Scotia artists and craftspeople. Open daily except Monday. Evening hours on Thursday.
- Wood Studio, Highway 1, Meteghan. New and restored quilts and local folk art. Open daily 10 am-6 pm, May 1-October 31.
- Folk Art by Reed Timmons, Pleasant Bay on the Cabot Trail. Specializing in hand-carved whales, gulls, roosters, and fishermen. Open daily June to October.
- Rose Cottage Gallery, Water St., Baddeck. A whimsical collection of Cape Breton carving (including exceptional pieces by William Roach, one of Canada's best folk artists), wind machines, pottery, weaving, hooked mats, and quilts. Also paintings and specialty children's items. Open 10 am-8 pm daily in July and August, variable hours in June, September, and October.
- Sunset Art Gallery, Cheticamp. Bright, whimsical wood carvings (lots of people and birds) by William Roach.. Open daily May 24 to October 15 or by appointment.
- Le Motif, Main Street, Cheticamp. Specializing in rag rugs, carving, twig baskets, and other local folk art. Open daily, June to mid-October.

GIFT SHOPS

- Sou'wester Gift Shop, Peggy's Cove. Large selection of Nova Scotia crafts including hand-knitted sweaters. Open year-round.
- Warp and Woof, Water St., Chester. China, quilts, and linens; good selection of cookbooks; fine gift items. Open daily, late May to October.
- The Teazer, Edgewater Dr. (Route 3), Mahone Bay. Upscale local crafts and imported gift items, kitchen ware, and fine clothing. Open daily (Sunday in afternoon only), April to Christmas.
- Treasures, Elm Avenue, Wolfville. A quirky gift shop featuring unusual gardening supplies and Victorian housewares. Open year-round.
- Kidston Landing, Chebucto St., Baddeck. Extensive selection of Nova Scotia crafts, Scottish woollens, men's and women's clothing including wool and cotton sweaters. Open daily.
- Sea Shanty Crafts and Antiques, Beach Point at the Englishtown Ferry. Interesting collectables including vintage china and glassware, and a good selection of new and antique quilts. Open daily June to September.
- Seawinds Chandlery, on the Government Wharf, Baddeck. Fine hand-made sweaters, gift items, and marine supplies. Open daily during tourist season.

SPECIALTY SHOPS

- The Book Room, 1546 Barrington Street, Halifax. Enjoy browsing in the city's largest bookstore. Large selection of regional books. Open

Mon-Sat.

- Halifax Folklore Centre, 1528 Brunswick Street, Halifax. Large selection of traditional musical instruments and Nova Scotian recordings. Open Mon-Wed, noon - 5:30 pm, Thurs-Fri noon-9 pm, Sat 10 am-5 pm.
- Nova Scotia Government Bookstore, 1700 Granville Street, Halifax. Maps and publications to assist in planning outdoor activities. Open year round.
- Montague Woolens, Montague and King streets, Lunenburg. Featuring beautiful Icelandic wool and angora sweaters.
- Box of Delights, Main Street, Wolfville. Good general bookstore with the Valley's best selection of local titles. Open year-round.
- Magasin Campus (Campus Bookstore), Université Sainte-Anne, Pointe de l'Église. Books dealing with the history and culture of the Acadians. Open Monday-Saturday 9 am-5 pm.
- Grohmann Knives, 116 Water St., Pictou. Fine knives for every use made on-site. Plant tours Monday-Friday 9 am-3 pm. Open Monday-Saturday 9 am-8 pm, Sunday afternoons.
- The Outdoor Store, Chebucto Street, Baddeck. Quality outdoor clothing, equipment, and gifts. All inclusive packages available.
- Sew Inclined, near Tarbot on the St. Ann's Loop. Specializing in designer vests, hats, and pants. Custom orders and sewing services available. Open daily June to October.

TREATS

- Clearwater Lobster Shops, 757 Bedford Highway, Bedford, Halifax International Airport, and other locations in metro Halifax. Live lobster packed for travel. Open daily.
- Spring Garden Place Market, Spring Garden Road, Halifax. Specialty foods available from a variety of shops. Open daily
- LaHave Bakery, Route 331, LaHave. Whole grain and herb breads, and sweets. From Lunenburg, a short drive and cable ferry ride across the LaHave River.
- Sainte Famille Wines, corner Dyke Rd. and Dudley Park Lane, Falmouth. Vineyard at site of early Acadian settlement. Daily tours 11am and 2 pm. Wine, gift baskets, and crafts at gift shop. Open daily to 6pm (Sunday noon-5 pm).
- The Tangled Garden, Route 1, Grand Pré. Herb jellies and vinegars; also finely crafted natural dried flower wreaths and other arrangements. Open daily, 10 am-6 pm.
- Jost Vineyards, Route 6, Malagash. Family-run winery on 10 hectares (24 acres). Retail store, daily tours at 3 pm in summer. Open daily, to 6 pm (closed Sunday mornings) shorter hours in off-season.
- J. Willie Krauch and Sons Smoked Fish, Tangier. Danish-smoked Atlantic salmon, mackerel, and eel; orders filled worldwide. Open daily from 8 am.

OUTDOOR RECREATION

PARKS AND NATURAL ATTRACTIONS

Included among the province's outstanding natural attractions are two national parks, Kejimkujik and Cape Breton Highlands. Nova Scotia also has 127 provincial parks. These range from sites of natural or historical significance to pleasant spots for a picnic or swim. Some have campgrounds. For more information on provincial parks, consult the detailed listings in the *Nova Scotia Travel Guide* (see Travel Essentials) or write to the Nova Scotia Department of Natural Resources, RR1, Belmont, NS, B0M 1C0.

Halifax
- Point Pleasant Park, in the South End of Halifax. Shaded walking paths and views of Halifax Harbour and the Northwest Arm.
- Sir Sandford Fleming Park (The Dingle), off Purcells Cove Rd., overlooking the Northwest Arm. Beautiful view of the Arm along walking trails. Dedicated in 1912, the Dingle Tower was built to

commemorate 150 years of representative government for Nova Scotia.

Peggys Cove
• The waves, the rocks, and the lighthouse at Nova Scotia's most famous fishing village.

Lunenburg
• Ovens Natural Park, Route 332 southeast of Lunenburg, near Riverport. Coastal caves and cliffside hiking trails highlight this privately owned park.
• Blue Rocks, east of Lunenburg on Lunenburg Bay. This tiny, rockbound fishing village is a favourite haunt of local artists.

Liverpool and Shelburne
• Kejimkujik Seaside Adjunct National Park, off Route 3 between Port Joli and Port Mouton. This beautiful stretch of isolated coastline is accessible by hiking trails. This is a nesting area for the endangered piping plover and sections of the beach are closed mid-April to mid-August.

Annapolis Valley
• The Lookoff, Route 358 north of Wolfville, on Cape Blomidon. Panoramic view of the Minas Basin and six river valleys.

Annapolis Royal
• Kejimkujik National Park, off Route 8 between Annapolis Royal and Liverpool (park headquarters at Maitland Bridge). Situated in the interior of southwestern Nova Scotia, this 381-square-kilometre (147-sq.-mi.) wilderness area is a favourite of campers and canoeists. For more information contact Kejimkujik National Park, Box 236, Maitland Bridge, NS, B0T 1B0; 682-2772.

Glooscap Trail
• Victoria Park, Brunswick St. and Park Rd., Truro. Recreational facilities, hiking trails, and two waterfalls make this 400-hectare (1000-acre) park ideal for family outings.
• Joggins Fossil Cliffs, Joggins. Sandstone cliffs with 300 million-year-old fossil material. The cliffs

themselves are off-limits but erosion ensures a steady supply of fossils on the beach. Tours available (see listing under Attractions).
• Cape d'Or Lighthouse Lookoff, off Route 209, Advocate Harbour. Breathtaking view of the Bay of Fundy and Minas Channel.
• Five Islands Provincial Park, Route 2 east of Parrsboro, at Five Islands. Camp, hike, or picnic in this beautiful park overlooking five islands in the Minas Basin.

Marine Drive
• Taylor Head Provincial Park, Route 7 east of Spry Bay. Hiking trails, wildlife habitat, and coastal views along Taylor Head Peninsula.
• Tor Bay Provincial Park, Tor Bay (south of Larry's River). Contemplate the vastness of the Atlantic while picnicking on this rocky point.

Cape Breton and the Cabot Trail
• Cape Breton Highlands National Park, northern Cape Breton. Nova Scotia's most spectacular scenery. The 950-square-kilometre (365-sq.-mi.) park affords abundant opportunities for camping and hiking. For more information contact Cape Breton Highlands National Park, Ingonish Beach, NS. B0C 1L0; 285-2691.
• Cabot's Landing Provincial Park, Cape North. Reputed to be the site where John Cabot landed in 1497. Picnic and enjoy the pleasant views of Aspy Bay.
• Marble Mountain, on the shores of the Bras d'Or, overlooking the village of the same name. After a steep hike, beautiful views of Cape Breton's inland sea. Swimming at the crushed marble beach.
• Uisge Ban Falls Park, near Baddeck Bridge. A network of hiking trails leads through hardwood forest to a dramatic gorge and waterfalls.

GOLF

For more information on golf courses in Nova Scotia, visit the Nova Scotia Golf Association website at www3.ns.sympatico.ca/nsga.

- Grandview Golf & Country Club (18-hole), Dartmouth; 435-3767.
- Granite Springs Golf Club (18-hole), Prospect Road (near Halifax); 852-4653.
- Oakfield Country Club (18-hole), Grand Lake (near Halifax International Airport); 861-2658.
- River Oaks Golf Club (18-hole), Meaghers Grant (Route 357 through the Musquodoboit River valley); 384-2033.
- Chester Golf & Country Club (18-hole), Chester; 275-4543.
- Bluenose Golf & Country Club (9-hole), Lunenburg; 634-4260.
- Osprey Ridge (18 hole) Bridgewater; 543-3273; tom@ospreyridge.ns.ca.
- Liverpool Golf & Country Club (9-hole), White Point Beach; 1-800-565-5068; resort@atcon.com; www.whiteppoint.com.
- The Pines Golf Club (18-hole), Digby; 245-4104; pines@gov.ns.ca; www.signatureresorts.com.
- Amherst Golf & Country Club (18 hole), Amherst; 667-8730.
- Paragon Golf & Country Club (18-hole), Kingston; 765-2554.
- Ken-Wo Golf & Country Club (18-hole), New Minas; 678-5388.
- Northumberland Sea Shore Golf Links (18-hole), Gulf Shore (near Pugwash); 243-2808; norlinks@istar.ca; norlinks.pugwash.ns.ca.
- Sunrise Beach Golf & Country Club (9-hole), Brule Point (near Tatamagouche); 657-2666.
- Pictou Golf Club (9-hole), Pictou; 485-4435.
- Abercrombie Country Club (18 holes), New Glasgow; 752-6249.
- Antigonish Golf Club (18-hole), Antigonish; 863-4797.
- Dundee Resort and Golf Course (18-hole), Dundee (on the south shore of the Bras d'Or); 1-800-565-1774; proshop@auracom.com; www.chatsubo.com/dundee.
- LePortage Golf Club (9-hole), Cheticamp; 224-3338; LePortage@capebretonGolf.com; www.capebretongolf.com.
- Highlands Links (18-hole), Ingonish Beach (at Keltic Lodge); 285-2600;1-800-441-1118; gordie_callan@pch.gc.ca.
- Bell Bay Golf club (18 hole), Baddeck; 1-800-565-3077; bellbaypro@auracom.com; bellbaygolfclub.com.

SEASONAL BOAT TOURS

(See also Whale-Watching and Fishing)
- Murphy's on the Water, Cable Wharf, 1751 Lower Water St., Halifax; 420-1015; www.murphysonthewater.com. Harbour tours, some with commentary, aboard a variety of vessels.
- Four Winds Charters, Cable Wharf, Unit 4, Halifax and St. Margarets Bay; 492-0022; www3.ns.sympatico.ca/fourwinds. Whale-watching, history tours, ferries to George's and McNab's Islands
- Fundy Voyager, Hall's Harbour; 538-8199. Cruises of the Bay of Fundy and Minas Basin. Picnics and rockhounding.
- New Glasgow Marina Water Taxi, Highway 104, Exit 27 to Route 245, Merigomish; 926-2305. Deep-sea fighing, sightseeing and entertainment cruises.
- Cape Breton Lobster Adventure Tours, Baddeck waterfront; 295-2564; beasty@auracom.com. Catch and learn about lobsters and tour the Bras d'Or Lakes.
- Star Charters, 2 Bluenose Drive, Lunenburg; 634-3535. Harbour and bay tours on a variety of boats.

WHALE-WATCHING

- Peggys Cove Whale and Puffin Tours, Route 333 Peggys Cove; 823-1060; www.peggys-cove.com. Two cruises daily. Whales, dolphins, seals, puffins and other seabirds.
- Brier Island Whale and Seabird Cruises, Westport; 1-800-656-3660; www.municipalities.com/briwsc. 2-5 times daily, 3-5 hour cruises on the Fundy. Greatest variety of whales in Nova Scotian waters. Rainchecks are given on the rare occasions when no sightings are made.
- Atlantic Whale Watch, Ingonish beach; 285-2320. Three trips daily. Sightings of whales, seals and

seabirds.
- Whale and Seal Cruise, Pleasant Bay; 1-888-754-5112; www.cabottrail.com/whalewatch. Three trips daily (off-season trips.)Hear and see whales, cruise past sea caves, waterfalls and pioneer settlements.
- Seaside Whale & Nature Cruises, Cheticamp; 1-800-959-4253; lauries@ns.sympatico.ca; www.lauries.com. Three tours daily. Accommodation and cruise packages available through Laurie's Motor Inn (see Lodging).
- Whale Cruisers (Cheticamp), Cheticamp; 224-3376; 1-800-813-3376; www.whalecruises.com. Frequent sightings of pilot, minke, and finback whales. Landward view of the coastline of Cape Breton Highlands National Park. Three cruises daily (less frequent in May, June, and late September).
- Sea Visions Whale Watch, Ingonish Ferry, 285-2628; seavisions@nscn.ns.ca; www.capebreton.com/Ingonish/Sea Visions. Three trips daily. See whales and seabirds from the 35-foot sailing vessel *Resplendent*.
- Coastal Whale Watching Boat Tours, Ingonish Harbour; 285-2714; www.angelfire.com/biz/whalecomet ocoastal. Three cruises daily. Sightings of minke and pilot whales.
- Whale Watch Bay, St. Lawrence, N.S., B0C 1E0; 383-2981. Seabirds and whales abound in the waters off Cape Breton's northernmost tip. Three tours daily.

HIKING

Hikers will find plenty to choose from in Nova Scotia — spectacular ocean views, desolate highland plateaus, thick boreal forest, and more. There are trails suitable for family outings and trails to challenge the most serious hikers.

Useful information for hikers is available from a number of sources. Loose topographic maps (1:50,000) and *A Map of the Province of Nova Scotia* (a series of 46 topographic maps that cover the whole of Nova Scotia at a scale of 1:250,000) can be

purchased from the Nova Scotia Government Bookstore, Box 637, Halifax, NS, B3J 2T3; 424-7580. *Hiking Trails of Nova Scotia*, a publication of the Canadian Hostelling Association, is also available in bookstores. These publications can also be purchased at outfitters throughout the province.

For information on hiking trails in Nova Scotia's two national parks, Kejimkujik and Cape Breton Highlands, write Parks Canada, Atlantic Region, Historic Properties, Upper Water Street, Halifax, NS, B3J 1S9; 426-3436. *Walking in the Highlands* is a guide to the 28 marked and serviced trails in the Cape Breton park.

WHITE-WATER RAFTING

The tidal bore on the Shubenacadie River provides a unique upriver rafting experience. Check ahead to find out when the bore is at its peak.
- Shubenacadie River Adventure Tours, 40 Kearney Lake Rd., Halifax. NS, B3M 2S4; 1-888-878-8687. Open May 15-Nov. 15. Reservations recomended.
- Shubenacadie River Runners, 8681 Rte 215, Maitland, NS, B0N 1T0; 261-2770, 1-800-856-5061; river.runners@ns.sympatico.ca; www3.ns.sympatico.ca/river.runners. Open seasonally. Reservations recommended.
- Tidal Bore Rafting Limited, RR 4 Shubenacadie, NS, B0N 2H0; 1-800-565-7238; raftcamp@fox.nstn.ca; fox.nstn.ca/~raftcamp. Open seasonally. Reservations recommended.

BIRDING

Nova Scotia is an important stopover on the Atlantic flyway for many species of migratory birds. Late summer sees thousands congregate on Fundy shores. Whale-watching tours (see listings above) also provide an excellent opportunity to observe seabirds, guillemots, kittiwakes, gannets, cormorants, and more. Atlantic puffins and bald eagles are special attractions. Serious birders can purchase Robie Tufts' beautiful guidebook, *Birds of Nova Scotia*, from local bookstores.

CANOEING AND KAYAKING

Opportunities for freshwater paddling and sea kayaking in Nova Scotia are practically unlimited. Much of the interior of the province is a wilderness area studded with lakes and creased by rivers and streams. There are also long stretches of sheltered coastline on both the Atlantic and the Fundy shores. The *Nova Scotia Travel Guide* lists a number of outfitters, as well as suppliers of equipment, maps and useful information.

BICYCLING

An extensive series of secondary roads has helped to make cycling one of the fastest growing sports in Nova Scotia. Serious cyclists can challenge the world-famous Cabot Trail while others may choose a gentler route like the Sunrise Trail along the shores of the Northumberland Strait. *Bicycle Tours in Nova Scotia,* which describes 20 of the province's best routes, can be purchased from the Touring Chairman, Bicycle Nova Scotia, Box 3010 South, Halifax, NS, B3J 3G6.

The Nova Scotia Bicycle Book, with extensive route information, is available from Atlantic Canada Cycling, Box 1555, Station M, Halifax, NS, B3J 2Y3; 423-2453.

CAMPING

Nova Scotia's two national parks, Kejimkujik and Cape Breton Highlands, and many of the province's 127 provincial parks have campground facilities (see Parks and Natural Attractions for addresses and information). There are also close to 130 privately owned campgrounds in Nova Scotia. Exhaustive listings and information on camping facilities are provided in the *Nova Scotia Travel Guide* (see Travel Essentials).

FISHING

Deep-Sea Fishing
Options for saltwater fishing range from relaxing outings, often in combination with some cultural or historical commentary, where sedentary groundfish are the catch, to serious searches for large gamefish — bluefin tuna, shark, and bluefish. Murphy's on the Water (see Seasonal Boat Tours) is one of several charter companies that operate out of Halifax Harbour. For complete listings consult the *Nova Scotia Travel Guide* (see Travel Essentials).

Freshwater Fishing
Many species are caught in Nova Scotia lakes and rivers, but the province owes its lofty reputation among anglers to the speckled trout and the Atlantic salmon. The Margaree River in western Cape Breton and the St. Marys on the Eastern Shore have attracted anglers from around the world. These rivers and several others in the province are posted for fly-fishing only. Information on scheduled rivers, licenses, seasons, and bag limits is available from outfitters and tackle shops or from all district offices of the Department of Natural Resources (Halifax 424-5419). For information on the salmon fishery, write the federal Department of Fisheries and Oceans, Box 550, Halifax, NS, B3J 2S7; 426-5952.

SAILING

Nova Scotia is a popular destination for sailors. The island-studded bays and sheltered harbours of the South Shore and the unique sailing experience afforded by Cape Breton's inland sea, the Bras d'Or, have created yachting havens like Chester and Baddeck. Yacht clubs at these communities and several others, including Halifax, host colourful regattas during the summer months.

Operators of pleasure craft are required to report to Canada Customs by calling 1-888-226-7277 on arrival in the first Canadian port of call. Customs information concerning pleasure craft, and a list of Customs offices providing marine services, are available from Revenue Canada, Customs border services, PO Box 520, Halifax, NS B3J 2R7; 426-2911, 1-800-461-9999; fax 426-6522.

For general information on

boating safety write to the Rescue Coordination Centre, HMC Dockyard, Department of National Defence, Halifax, NS, B3K 2X0; 427-8200, 1-800-565-1582. The best source for charts and other nautical information is the Canadian Hydrographic Service, Bedford Institute of Oceanography, Box 1006, Dartmouth, NS, B2Y 4A2; 426-2373.

USEFUL ADDRESSES

It is possible to make detailed plans for your Nova Scotia vacation before leaving home by contacting Nova Scotia's Check In Reservation and Information Service. Travel Counsellors will provide invaluable advice, reservation services, and a wealth of written material to make travel planning easier. In North America, call 1-800-565-0000 or write to Nova Scotia Information and Reservations, Box 130, Halifax, NS, B3J 2M7.

Once in Nova Scotia, the same services are available at any of the province's Visitor Information Centres. These are indicated by a "?" on the official highway map of Nova Scotia and can be found at key locations throughout the province, including the New Brunswick – Nova Scotia border and the Halifax International Airport.

In Halifax, the International Visitor Centre on Barrington Street offers many services including currency exchange, tour packages, and reservations. The centre can provide you with a wealth of information about the province.

Visitors from the United States who need to contact home in case of an emergency may do so through the Consulate General of the United States of America, Suite 901, Cogswell Tower, Halifax, NS, B3J 3K1; 429-2480.

SPECIAL TRAVEL SERVICES

Visitors with Disabilities
Contact the Nova Scotia League for Equal Opportunities, 2786 Agricola St., Suite 208, Halifax, NS, B3K 4E1; 455-6942 for general information on the services available in the province. The *Nova Scotia Travel Guide* indicates which lodgings and attractions offer wheelchair access. To find out what additional services may be available, visitors are urged to make specific inquiries. Where possible, it is advisable to book in advance; the Nova Scotia Check In Reservation and Information Service will assist (in North America, 1-800-565-0000).

Students
Student discounts are available for a variety of travel services. In order to qualify, students are advised to buy an International Student Identity Card. In Canada, cards may be purchased at Travel Cuts, a travel agency for students found on many Canadian university campuses. Halifax branches are located at St. Mary's University (494-7027) and Dalhousie University (494-2054). Students from the US, can obtain cards from Council Travel, Council on International Educational Exchange, 205 E. 42nd Street, New York, NY, 10017; 212-661-1450, or from a local branch office.

To find out about hostelling in the province, contact Hostelling International–Nova Scotia, 5516 Spring Garden Rd., Box 3010 South, Halifax, NS, B3J 3G6; 425-5450.

Seniors
There are discounts for seniors on many travel services including transportation and accommodation. Make inquiries before making reservations and have your senior citizen identification card at the ready.

Many of the private tour operators in the province offer coach tours at reduced rates for seniors (several companies are listed in the Getting Around section).

GENEALOGICAL SOURCES

- Nova Scotia Archives and Records Management, 6016 University

Avenue, Halifax, B3H 1W4; 424-6060. Hours are 8:30 a.m.-4:30 p.m., Monday to Friday; 9 a.m.-5 p.m. Saturday. Closed Sundays, holidays and Saturdays on holiday weekends.

- Acadia University, Vaughan Library, Wolfville, B0P 1X0.
- Argyle Township Courthouse and Goal, Box 10, Tusket, B0W 3M0.
- Cape Breton Genealogical Society, Box 53, Sydney, B1P 6G4.
- Centre d'Études Acadiennes, Université de Moncton, Moncton, NB, E1A 3E9
- Colchester Historical Society, 29 Young Street, Truro, B2N 5C5.
- Deputy Registrar-General, Box 157, Halifax, B3J 2M9.
- Genealogical Association of Nova Scotia, Box 641, Station Central, Halifax, B3J 2T3.
- Kings Courthouse Heritage Museum, 37 Cornwallis Street, Kentville, B4N 2E2.
- Pictou County Genealogical Society, Box 1210, Pictou, B0K 1H0.
- Shelburne County Genealogical Society, 24 Dock Street, Shelburne, B0T 1W0.
- Yarmouth County Historical Society, 22 Collins Street, Yarmouth, B5A 3CB.

INDEX

to Credits

Legend: Top - T; Centre- C; Bottom - B

Photographs by Keith Vaughan, except as listed below:
Bay Ferries Limited: p.7T; p.113C; Julien Beveridge: p.21B; p.69C; p.88C; Steven Isleifson: p.105B; Jocelyne Lloyd: p.120B; Micmac-Maliseet Nations News: p.17T; p.18T; Peggy McCalla: maps, p.4-5; p.76; p.77; p.95; p.114; p.129; p.134; p.140; p.145; p.161; Nova Scotia Archives and Records Management, W.G. MacLaughlan, HRC Collection, 1976-166, #63: p.54; Nova Scotia Tourism: p.2T; p.3C; p.7; p.9T; p.19T; p.22T; p.31T,B; p.38B; p.39C; p.45T; p.61T,B; p.62T,C,B; p.71B; p.72B; p.85T; p.108B; p.121C,B; p.128T; p.138B; p.139C; p.144T,B; p.158C; Parks Canada: p.109T; Port Bickerton and Area Planning Association: p.143B; Gil Reynold: p.57B; Shakespeare By the Sea: p.57T; Jamie Steeves Slide Show: p.88CB; United States National Archives, Washington, C.D., Photo #165-WW-158A-15AU: p.52; University of Lethbridge Art Gallery, gift of Mr. G. Pencer: p.53

Canadian Cataloguing in Publication Data
Poole, Stephen, 1963–
Nova Scotia
4th. ed.
(Colourguide series)
Includes index.
ISBN 0-88780-516-7
1. Nova Scotia — Guidebooks. I Kingsbury, Al II. Title. III. Series: Colour guide (Halifax, N.S.)
FC2307.P66 2000   917.1604'4   C00-950074-X   F1037.P66 2000

Formac Publishing Company Limited
5502 Atlantic Street
Halifax, Nova Scotia B3H 1G4

Printed and bound in Canada

Distributed in the United States by: Distributed in the United Kingdom by:
Seven Hills Book Distributors   World Leisure Marketing
1531 Tremont Street   9 Downing Road
Cinncinnati, Ohio 45214   West Meadows Industrial Estate
                                         Derby, England DE21 6HA